"Zimbalist is a consummate and impeccably credentialed outsider, and this splendid book is the real deal. . . . Rational baseball fans will rejoice in this tough but fair view of a decent man in a thankless job."—John Thorn, editor of *Total Baseball*

"A book certain to stir debate among sports business experts and fans alike." —*Boston Herald*

"Andrew Zimbalist has written an insightful and thought-provoking book that peels the cover off the ball of the position of the commissioner to see the threads inside."—Maury Brown, *Hardball Times*

"Andrew Zimbalist, a man who has become a go-to guy on matters of sports economics, uses an academic approach to explain—and, perhaps surprisingly, defend—Bud Selig's 13-year tenure as commissioner of baseball."—*New York Daily News*

"I read *In the Best Interests of Baseball?* start to finish in one evening. Zimbalist has provided a tour de force. It's an incredibly interesting read that ends with a vision for the sport that is squarely on target and a clarion call to our industry."—John Henry, principal owner of the Boston Red Sox and member of the MLB Executive Committee

"For those who follow the often-depressing business of baseball, this makes thought-provoking reading."—Alan Moores, *Booklist*

"By looking at baseball from the perspective of the commissioner's office and its many challenges, Professor Zimbalist has been able to use his scholar's eye and his fan's heart to see the game as an ongoing enterprise that needs refreshment. The fair but unsparing portrait of Bud Selig he paints is of a man who is nobody's fool, and nobody's tool—now, those of us who love the game need him to start the rally that will restore baseball in America's esteem."— Scott Simon, host of NPR's *Weekend Edition Saturday* and author of *Jackie Robinson and the Integration of Baseball*

"Andy Zimbalist's book is a thoughtful and objective analysis of baseball's labor and economic policy evolution. The book is interesting, relevant, and a good read."—Randy Levine, president of the New York Yankees

In the Best Interests
of Baseball?

In the Best Interests of Baseball?

Governing the National Pastime

Andrew Zimbalist

With a new preface and epilogue by the author

University of Nebraska Press
Lincoln and London

Photo credits: Chicago History Museum, 33; courtesy of Fay Vincent, 102; courtesy of Major League Baseball, 99, 113, 127, 137, 185; courtesy of the Milwaukee Brewers, 122, 179; National Baseball Hall of Fame, 16, 21, 23, 35, 53, 64, 73, 80, 93; courtesy of the San Diego Padres, 172; courtesy of Wendy Selig, 124.

Library of Congress Cataloging-in-Publication Data
Zimbalist, Andrew S.
In the best interests of baseball?: governing the national pastime / Andrew Zimbalist, with a new preface and epilogue by the author.
p. cm.
Originally published: Hoboken, NJ: Wiley, 2006.
Includes bibliographical references and index.
ISBN 978-0-8032-4535-8 (pbk.: alk. paper) 1. Baseball—Management. 2. Baseball commissioners.
3. Selig, Bud, 1934– I. Title.
GV875.7.Z56 2013
796.357068—dc23   2012035500

Preface to the Nebraska Paperback Edition

Major League Baseball's constitution gives the commissioner broad powers to act "in the best interests of baseball." Most would agree that the "best interests of baseball" are defined by maximizing the game's popularity, and many believe that this is congruent with maximizing the game's revenues. Problems arise because baseball's commissioner is hired by the thirty team owners, who have very different ideas about how to operate and grow the game.

Some large-market teams generate several hundred million dollars more a year than some small-market teams. Some teams own their own regional sports channel. Some play in stadiums that cost over $1 billion to build and others in venues costing less than $200 million. Yet all the teams must go to the same players' market to fill their rosters.

Team owners, by their nature, are hypercompetitive. They also want their investments to be successful. And like the rest of us, team owners have different personalities and political preferences, and they seek out others who share their perspectives and needs.

The players too are organized, into a union. The union president has a desirable job—high paying, high profile, lots of perks. To get elected (and re-elected), the union president must please the players, which more often than not means pleasing the players' agents, particularly the agents who represent a lot of players. It is reasonable to assume that these agents have considerable power over the union and that their primary goal is to maximize their own income.

Into this imbroglio steps baseball's commissioner. He must attend to all these constituents, plus the fans, the media, and the politicians. Good luck!

This book is about how baseball's nine commissioners have confronted this challenge—a challenge that has morphed and grown more complex over time. Each commissioner has had his failings, some more glaring than others. Bud Selig has been commissioner since 1992, and his current term goes through 2014; by then he will have served for twenty-three years—as long as baseball's first commissioner, Kenesaw Mountain Landis—and will have reached over eighty years of age.

Selig has presided over a particularly contentious, yet successful, period of baseball history. The owners have repeatedly voted to extend his term, suggesting that they can't imagine the game without his leadership. What has Selig's leadership meant to baseball and what will happen to the game after he steps down? The pages that follow attempt to answer these and other questions.

In the Best Interests of Baseball? was originally published in 2006. The current edition includes an epilogue that discusses developments in the baseball industry since 2005, including two new collective bargaining agreements (on which I worked as a consultant to Rob Manfred, baseball's vice president for labor relations) extending the sport's labor peace that has held since 1995, the redesign of revenue sharing, tumultuous franchise sales and ownership turnover, new stadium construction, the development and maturation of mlb.com and the MLB Network, the explosion of television contracts and structural shifts in the delivery of video programming, and the new format for the postseason, among other transformations. The epilogue also anticipates what lies ahead for our national pastime.

To my wife,
Shelley Abend Zimbalist,
with abounding love and admiration

CONTENTS

PREFACE

I first met Bud Selig in December 1992 in the chambers of the United States Senate. He had been named chair of the executive council (aka acting commissioner) three months earlier. We were both seated, listening to former commissioner Fay Vincent testify on baseball's antitrust exemption before Senator Howard Metzenbaum's Committee on the Judiciary. Bud and I were waiting to testify. At one point, I turned around and asked him a question. He answered briefly, and then, moments later, he tapped me on the shoulder and said that he would love to talk to me about the baseball business and that he would do it anytime, anywhere, even in Northampton, Massachusetts. It sounded like a good offer. George W. Bush, then an owner and managing partner of the Texas Rangers, showed up a little later and sat behind Bud. Bush's father, of course, was president of the United States at the time.

I next met Bud the following summer at the evening gala before the All-Star Game at Camden Yards in Baltimore. *USA Today* held a forum on labor relations in baseball the day before the game. *USA*'s executives had invited me, along with Don Fehr, Dick Ravitch (the owners' chief negotiator at the time), Ken Burns, Bob Watson, and Bob Costas, to participate on the panel. I brought my two sons, Jeffrey and Michael, along to experience all the hype of the events. That night we went to the gala—a massive outdoor party with dozens of tents, each filled with baseball-themed activities, full-service bars in each tent, and cocktail waitresses serving soft-shelled crabs, among other delicacies. Bud was at the gate greeting all the guests. I introduced him to my sons; he was as engaging and gracious as anyone could ask.

Twelve years elapsed before I talked with Bud Selig again. I had developed something of a reputation for being one of Selig's and baseball's harshest critics. Most people in Major League Baseball's central office had no interest in talking with me. A few times I called and reminded them that Bud had offered to talk to me "anytime, anywhere," but no one seemed particularly impressed. Over the years, as I did more writing about and consulting in the sports industry, I came to know, and even consult for, many owners and executives. Several of them commented to me that I ought to get to know Bud. Eventually I e-mailed Bob DuPuy, baseball's chief operating officer and a longtime associate of Bud Selig's, and suggested that it might be interesting for him and me to get together. He agreed. Bob DuPuy and I met in early October 2004 at the Yale Club in New York City over a drink. I told him that I was thinking about writing this book and wondered whether baseball would cooperate with me. He assured me that he would be disposed to do all he could to help me. He lived up to his word.

DuPuy helped me arrange my initial interview with Bud Selig. He told me that I'd be getting a call from the commissioner. Selig phoned me at my office on January 5, 2005, to set a date for the interview. He was immediately, disarmingly charming. "Andy, it's Bud Selig," he began. "I want to tell you right at the outset that I am not nearly as villainous as you think I am." I think of myself as pretty quick witted, but this time I could think of nothing to say.

I flew to Milwaukee to meet with Bud at his suite of offices on February 1, 2005. I was there to interview Bud, but he began our exchange by announcing that he had a few things he wanted to discuss with me first. Again, he was taking control of the conversation and flattering me at the same time. We spent the next thirty minutes talking about a study the Brewers had just commissioned on the economic impact of the team and their new stadium on Milwaukee. We didn't agree, but Bud was showing me that we could disagree and still respect each other. Of course, I already knew that, but Bud, I assumed, was making sure that the atmosphere was as propitious as possible for our interview. We then continued talking for the next several hours.

The point of all this is to show that Bud Selig has uncommonly effective interpersonal skills. They are skills that he has needed and put to good effect in his job as commissioner. In a sense, the commissioner has to please not one but thirty people, thirty people who have a history of disagreeing with one another and who have reason to sit constantly in judgment of him. They are, after all, his employers.

Most of what I have written about sports has involved analyzing the economic structures and incentives of the industry, including the functioning of labor markets, team profitability, and the antitrust status of the leagues. These structures are acted upon by real people, and the ways that the people and the structures interact have important implications for how a league functions.

Over the years I have worked with players' unions, cities, owners, and leagues. Once I worked in direct opposition to the interests of Bud Selig and Major League Baseball. In early 1994, I was approached by two members of the U.S. Congress and a leading investment banker in New York City to consult in an attempt to establish a rival league to MLB. The would-be rival league was called the United Baseball League. The league was moving forward until we hit a brick wall with our bid for a national television contract. We had signed a long-term, national broadcasting deal with Liberty Media and called a national press conference to announce the agreement. However, a week after the deal was consummated, Rupert Murdoch's News Corp bought Liberty Media, and a week or two after that, Fox reached an agreement with Major League Baseball to be its national broadcaster for the next four years. Peter Barton at Liberty Media told us that they would be reneging on our deal. We called in some of the country's leading antitrust lawyers to discuss our options. We concluded that we had viable claims of breach of contract and antitrust injury, but these would cost millions of dollars and many years to prosecute. We had launched our project as idealists who wanted to bring competition to the baseball industry. After the intervention by Fox, our

goal seemed out of reach. Even though the lawyers were willing to
go forward on a contingency basis, none of us wanted to spend the
next several years embroiled in a contentious lawsuit. We closed
our doors.

I also worked as a consultant with the Major League Baseball
Players Association during the period of the 1994–1995 strike. I
was in the back room, cranking out analyses of team financial
statements and models of revenue sharing. Here, too, I was operating out of a different bunker than Selig.

Two years later, I was asked to join the bargaining team at
the NBA Players Association (NBPA) for the 1997–1998 negotiations. In this matter, I sat at the bargaining table. I got to see first-
hand David Stern's incisive brilliance, sharp sense of humor, and
Caligula-like need to manipulate and control. I also got glimpses of
an insecure man who could be cowed in the presence of Michael
Jordan or in the face of Billy Hunter's anger. Stern and his associate Russ Granik played a good cop, bad cop game during the bargaining sessions. They also would single out individual members
of our bargaining team to denigrate at each session, hoping to turn
us against one another. Sometimes they threw childish fits. To us,
it all seemed choreographed to throw us off guard and divide us.
As far as I could tell, none of the executives for the NBPA and
none of the player reps were anything but annoyed that Stern and
company played these games and wasted our time. I also joined
the NBPA's bargaining team for the 2004–2005 negotiations. I participated in several rounds of talks until I came to feel that the
process had become too political to be open to my intellectual
input. I thanked Billy Hunter for the ride, bid him good luck, and
resigned. In truth, games are played on each side of the bargaining
table, and, in the end, something other than an efficiently designed
system of pay and incentives results.

These and many other experiences in the sports business led
me to reflect on the role of personalities and the nature of governance in sports leagues. Baseball's governance experience is both
richer and more complex than is the experience of the other sports.
Organized baseball dates back to the 1850s and the first professional league to 1871. Baseball has had the peculiar and special

institution of the commissionership since 1921 and an antitrust exemption since 1922. These characteristics, along with the fact that baseball had no effective competition from other team sports at least until the late 1950s, bred an attitude of insouciance and arrogance in the management of our national pastime. Baseball was cheating its fans, and, as its popularity began first to stagnate and then to wane, it was cheating itself. Poor governance contributed to its tumultuous labor relations, which fed back on the game's economic travails.

It is the story of this governance that I seek to uncover and evaluate in this book. The story begins in the 1870s, follows the National Commission from 1903 to 1920, and explores the work of each of the eight commissioners who preceded Bud Selig. The story concentrates, however, on the period since 1992 under Bud Selig. The decision to focus most carefully on Selig flows from the facts that (1) I have known and followed him for nearly fifteen years; (2) unlike other leaders in baseball, football, basketball, and hockey, he has been a team owner and a commissioner at the same time; (3) he has transformed the nature of the commissioner's office and changed the course of the industry's governance; and (4) he is the man who is guiding baseball into the twenty-first century. Ultimately, we study history to understand our present and our future, and that's what I've tried to do in this book.

In writing this book, I have benefited from the invaluable support of Bob DuPuy and his team at Major League Baseball. Not only have I interviewed Bud Selig several times, but I interviewed Bob DuPuy and Rob Manfred, MLB's executive vice president for labor relations, and exchanged dozens of e-mails with all of them. They have also provided me with numerous historical baseball documents. In addition, I have interviewed Fay Vincent, Richard Ravitch, Don Fehr, Paul Beeston, Wendy Selig, Randy Levine, Steve Greenberg, Tom Werner, Larry Lucchino, John Moores, Larry Baer, Len Coleman, Bob Bowman, and many others who have been involved with the baseball industry. Among those who have talked with me and/or given me comments on parts of my manuscript are Paul Weiler, Fred Claire, Brad Humphreys, John Yee, Stan Kasten, Gene Budig, David Wolff, Peter Magowan, Jim Gallagher, Ralph

Andreano, Mike Bauman, Bill Francis, Chris Hayward, Paul Mif-
sud, John Henry, Dick Moss, Murray Chass, Steve Fehr, John Gen-
zale, Jim Duquette, Rick White, Tim Brosnan, Marvin Goldklang,
Peter Kanter, Peter Carfagna, Clark Griffith, Janet Marie Smith,
Bob Costas, Jerome Holtzman, David Pietrusza, Beverly Stengel,
Lisa Steinman, John Hanson, John Helyar, Mike Weiner, Peter
Gammons, Lee Lowenfish, Sandy Alderson, Eleanor Abend, Steve
Ross, Stefan Szymanski, Marvin Miller, Gary Gillette, Bill Kir-
win, Chuck Korr, Jonathan Kraft, Tom Reich, Lee Lowenfish,
Leonard Koppett, Evan Weiner, Jim Wetzler, John Abbamondi,
Maury Brown, Michael Haupert, Don Walker, and Tom Reich.
Henry Miller, a reference archivist at the Wisconsin Historical
Society, and the archive staff at the Golda Meier Library at the
University of Wisconsin, Milwaukee, as well as Tim Wiles and his
superb staff at the National Baseball Hall of Fame library in Cooperstown, New York, were all extremely helpful. Kate Oakley provided valuable assistance in transcribing several interviews. Thanks
also to my agent, Andrew Blauner, for his unflagging enthusiasm,
encouragement, and insightful suggestions, as well as to my editor
Stephen Power for shepherding the book through its final stages of
production.

My largest debt of gratitude, along with big love, goes to my
family (Shelley, Alex, Ella, Jeffrey, and Michael), who put up with
a distracted husband or father more often than they should have
and did so with scarcely a whimper of complaint.

In the Best Interests
of Baseball?

1

Introduction
Running a League

It was November 2, 2004. The day that George W. Bush was elected to his second term as U.S. president, and just six days after John Henry's Boston Red Sox had shattered the curse of the Bambino by defeating the St. Louis Cardinals in four straight games of the World Series. With the busy and mostly successful season behind him, Commissioner Bud Selig took a breather for his annual medical checkup. For a seventy-year old, Selig was remarkably fit. He told one reporter, "I've never been sick in my life."[1] And, sure enough, his physician, Ian Gilson, finished up Selig's exam and proclaimed the commissioner to be in superb health.

Selig had just completed one year out of six in his extended contract as commissioner. Gilson joked, "I've got to keep you going great for another five years."

Then Selig got up to leave the office. As he approached the door, the doctor intoned, "Come back here. What's that on your face?" The doctor had noticed a blotch over Selig's right eye. The next day, as the Bush family celebrated, Selig visited a dermatologist. Two days later the commissioner learned that he had stage four melanoma. How dire the consequences would be depended on whether the cancer had spread.

Selig's surgery was scheduled for December 6. The month's wait was not easy. On top of his medical anxiety, the latest BALCO (Bay Area Laboratory Cooperative) scandal erupted when the *San Francisco Chronicle* released the supposedly confidential grand jury testimonies of sluggers Jason Giambi and Barry Bonds, each admitting to steroid use. Negotiations with Orioles owner Peter Angelos and the Washington, D.C., city council over terms for the move of the Expos to the nation's capital were heating up.

Selig recounted that one day he took his three granddaughters shopping. He sent them into one store by themselves because, he said, "I was so distraught that I sat in my car and cried."

The surgery lasted three hours. Two lymph nodes were removed. Then Selig had to wait seven days for the final results. On December 13, the surgeon passed along the good news: "You're clear and clean as hell."

Selig's first confrontation with serious illness left him reflective. "We need reminders of what is important. Take some vacation. Calm down." There are few jobs to which this advice better applies than the commissioner of baseball.

Governing a Sports League

The major sports leagues in the United States today each have thirty to thirty-two teams at the top level. Each team has separate ownership. Depending on the league, revenues from the top to the bottom teams can diverge by $100 million or by $300 million. These revenue disparities give the franchise owners very different perspectives on the economics of their leagues and on the strategies for team success. Some owners want more revenue sharing across the teams; some want less. Some want stiff luxury taxes on high team payrolls; some want none. Most owners want a salary cap, but salary caps come in different sizes and shapes.

Some owners are feisty; others are diffident. Some are political; others are not. Some are Republicans; fewer are Democrats. Some own team-related media, real estate, concessions, or other businesses; others do not. Managing and molding thirty different perspectives and thirty different personalities take more than a little skill and patience.

But orchestrating the owners is only step one. There's also the players' union. Although the NFL has had peaceful labor relations since the settlement of the Freeman McNeil lawsuit over free agency in 1993, matters were not always so placid. Nor is there any guarantee that labor peace will continue to prevail in football. Recent collective-bargaining experience in the NBA and the NHL has been turbulent. The basketball owners locked out the players in 1997, before the 1998–2005 labor agreement was signed. The hockey owners locked out the players in 1994 and again in 2004–2005. The entire 2004–2005 NHL season was lost. In baseball, until 2002, when a last-minute settlement averted a work stoppage, the sport had a work stoppage before every labor agreement since 1972. The commissioner must conduct relations with the players' association in a way to minimize disruption in the playing seasons, to project a positive public image of the sport, and to ensure the financial stability of the league.

The commissioner must also deal with corporate sponsors, host cities, congressional inquiries and legislative initiatives, banks, broadcasters, and the fans.[2] Like any business, for a sports league to be successful, it needs a strategy to guide its choices and plan for the future. Having dissension within and between ownership groups, not to mention all the other constituencies that demand attention, sports leagues often seem to operate with a problem-solving or crisis mentality, rather than with a long-term strategic-planning perspective.

Today it is commonplace to hear the NFL extolled as the ideal league, with its extensive revenue sharing, peaceful labor relations, and massive media contracts. Pete Rozelle, the NFL's commissioner from 1960 to 1989, is often heralded as a forward-looking model executive who pioneered the establishment of the league's revenue-sharing policies and forging owner unity.

Rozelle was a good leader in many ways, but he did not invent NFL revenue sharing. In fact, the NFL shared net gate revenues on a 60/40 basis since the league's inception in 1920. At the time, ticket sales were pretty much the whole revenue story. During the 1940s and the 1950s, the league was more than ably managed by Commissioner Bert Bell. Bell, too, deserves considerable credit. Nor were the NFL's emerging glory years of the late 1950s through the 1980s characterized by great harmony among the owners or by deep respect from all owners for the commissioner. The story of Carroll Rosenbloom, the former owner of the Baltimore Colts and the Los Angeles Rams, amply illustrates this point.

Under the urging of his friend Bert Bell, Carroll Rosenbloom bought the Baltimore Colts in 1953 for $250,000. In July 1972, he did what had never been done before and has never been done since in the NFL, MLB, or the NBA: he swapped his Colts team to Bob Irsay for the Los Angeles Rams. That is, he traded the franchise, not the players in it. It was a nice deal for Rosenbloom. His only problem was that the Rams were performing abysmally on the field, and Rosenbloom was itching for another championship. He did what few NFL owners were willing to do in those days. He signed free agent wide receiver Ron Jesse from the Detroit Lions. Owners were reluctant to sign other teams' free agents because they would be subjected to the so-called Rozelle Rule. This rule allowed for Pete Rozelle to determine the compensation for any free agent signing. Rozelle, if he wanted, could take away two top players from the signing team and award them to the team losing a free agent. Thus, it was a considerable risk and potentially a very costly move to sign a free agent. Rosenbloom did it anyway, and he did it at a time that the Rozelle Rule was being challenged in court (*Mackey v. NFL*) as a restraint of trade—which it indubitably was.

Thinking that the court challenge might induce Rozelle to behave more timidly in awarding any compensation, Rosenbloom took the chance. Rozelle did not respond timidly. He awarded to the Lions the Rams' very promising fullback, Cullen Bryant, and suggested that there would also be future draft picks in the compensation package. Rosenbloom went ballistic and arranged for a new litigation against Rozelle. But luckily for Rosenbloom, the NFL was losing the *Mackey* case, and the judge in that case enjoined the award of Bryant to the Lions. Rozelle relented and lowered the award to one first- and one second-round draft choice.

Rosenbloom still wasn't happy and sought revenge. He hired a private detective to dig up all the dirt he could on Rozelle prior to the next owners' meeting in November. Armed with his detective's report (which apparently had flimsy evidence at best), Rosenbloom launched into a one-hour-plus screaming, threatening diatribe against Rozelle. When he finished, the room was stone silent. After a break, the meeting resumed without Rosenbloom, but the tensions between the two men were to last for some time.

Rosenbloom was not the only owner with whom Rozelle had trouble. Others included Al Davis, Edward Bennett Williams, Robert Irsay, Chuck Sullivan, and Leonard Tose. The NFL also had more than its share of disputes between owners and sometimes between ownership partners in the same franchise. In 2005, the NFL owners were feuding again over the extension of revenue sharing. Like all businesses, sports leagues experience cycles. Smart leaders will never take their success for granted.

The foregoing is not to suggest that Rozelle was an ineffective commissioner. On the contrary, his reputation is basically well deserved. Indeed, amid all the turmoil of the 1970s, including the *Mackey* antitrust case for free agency that the league lost, competition from the upstart rival World Football League, the financial difficulties of Eagles owner Leonard Tose, the real estate struggles of Art Modell, and his conflicts with his co-owner Bob Gries, the owners stood by Rozelle, giving him a ten-year extension in 1977.

Rather, it is to indicate the inherent complexity of a commissioner's job: the need to juggle dozens of balls at once, yet still be able to anticipate and plan for the future. The job only becomes more difficult, as in the case of baseball, when there is less revenue sharing in the league, the union is more militant and cagey, and there is an expectation that the commissioner will be an omnipotent savior.

Sports Leagues as Monopolies

United States sports leagues have been insulated from some normal pressures of doing business because each league essentially functions as a monopoly. There is only one top-level producer of baseball, football, basketball, hockey, and soccer in the United States. Each of these leagues is closed; that is, entry is strictly controlled by existing owners. Like all good monopolists, U.S. leagues artificially restrict output in order to raise the price of their product and the value of their enterprise.

To enter a league, by purchasing either an existing or an expansion team, a prospective owner must be vetted and must receive permission. Once approved, he or she must pay a healthy "ransom," usually between $200 million and close to a billion dollars, depending on the league and the team, to join the elite club.

But there is no divine rule that sports leagues must be closed monopolies. Indeed, outside the United States, soccer leagues are organized as open promotion/relegation structures. Each country has a hierarchy of soccer leagues. The bottom two to four teams in each league get relegated, or demoted, after each season to the next league down, while the top two to four teams are promoted to the next league up. A new team cannot buy its way into the top league; rather, a team is formed and competes at the bottom level. Only through perennial success does the team rise up within the hierarchy, eventually arriving at the highest level. No expansion fee "ransom" is paid to the team owners in the top league.

Furthermore, this system allows teams to be rationally apportioned across all markets. If a large city has only one team and it can support more, an enterprising owner can act on his or her own accord and establish a new team in the city. By this process, it is unlikely in the extreme that any team would develop an inherent advantage, such as the Yankees in New York, that would endure in an open league. London, for instance, hosted six teams in the top-level English Premier League in 2004.

In open promotion/relegation leagues, all teams have an incentive to be as competitive as possible. In U.S. leagues, owners of teams in the bottom half of the standings may take a lackadaisical attitude, believing that since they can't win, they might as well minimize payroll. They will even be rewarded for poor performance with earlier draft picks and, in baseball, with more revenue-sharing transfers from the rich teams. Not so in open leagues. If a team is in the bottom half, it must exert itself to avoid relegation to a lower league, which also entails a sharp drop in revenues. Fans stay interested in the competition to win, as well as in the competition to avoid relegation.

Another feature of open leagues is that since there is no artificial scarcity of teams and no team is guaranteed a permanent berth in the top league, it is not possible for teams to extort public stadium subsidies by threatening to relocate. Sometimes there are public subsidies for stadiums in open leagues, but the process, the proportions, and the purpose differ.[3]

However, owners of teams in closed leagues have no reason to embrace the open league structure, no matter how fan friendly or theoretically appealing it might be. By doing so, the owners would be giving away their market power and surrendering significant franchise value.

Moreover, U.S. leagues do not accept the proposition that they are monopolies. They maintain that they are a single product in the larger entertainment industry and they compete with the industry's other products for the leisure dollar. As the argument goes, when a consumer decides to go to a basketball game, he is simultaneously deciding not to go to a hockey game, a bowling alley, or the opera house. Thus, in this reckoning, basketball competes with these and other entertainment products. At some level of abstraction, this claim is correct, but it is also correct to say that when a fan spends $100 at a basketball game, it is $100 that he or she cannot spend on clothing or food. Yet nobody claims that the NBA competes with Stop & Shop or Filene's.

For an economist, the key to understanding monopoly, or more generally, market power, is to identify how closely products are related to one another. The test is to see how a small change in the price of one product affects the consumption of another product. When this relationship is tight, then the products would be considered to be in the same market. Statistical tests indicate that the sports leagues are not in close competition with one another or with other products in the entertainment industry.

The profitability of sports teams is often not what it appears to be. Franchise owners can take their financial returns in a plethora of ways. First, if the team owner also owns a local media outlet (such as a regional sports channel, as is the case with the Yankees and YES [Yankee Entertainment and Sports Network] and the Red Sox and NESN [New England Sports Network]), the stadium, a concessions company, a real estate firm, a jet or a car rental company, or another enterprise that does business with the team, then he or she can readily shift profits toward the other entity. There are many reasons why an owner may want to do this. In baseball there's an additional reason—to reduce a team's revenue-sharing obligation to the other teams. This technique, known as related party transactions, can diminish a team's reported revenues by as much as tens of millions of dollars annually (though baseball has recently developed an auditing process to curtail this practice).[4]

Second, a sports team can enable an owner to develop new assets. George Steinbrenner developed the YES network from his ownership of the Yankees. When YES was launched in March 2002, it was implicitly valued (based on Goldman Sachs's investment in it) at $850 million—more than the Yankees' franchise was worth at the time.

Third, a sports team gives the owner prominence in the community, which can be used to establish new business connections and political sway. These relationships may open up new investment opportunities, as well as enhance existing ventures.

Fourth, sports team ownership can be an excellent tax shelter. New legislation from 2004 extends the preexisting shelter by allowing owners to amortize all intangible assets of the franchise over a fifteen-year period. While team owners argue that nonsports companies have been allowed to amortize most intangible assets for some time and the new law simply puts them on equal footing with the rest of corporate America, sports teams are different because the overwhelming share of their value is intangible. Their value rests on the fact that each owner has a scarce berth in a popular monopoly league. In reality, this scarcity value does not naturally diminish over time.

Fifth, owners can hide profits by loaning money to the team partnership. The owner then takes part of his or her return by receiving interest on the loaned capital.[5] The same interest payments appear as costs to the team and lower book profits. Owners can also take consulting fees or salaries for themselves or relatives.

Sixth, team owners receive part of their investment return from the perquisites, enjoyment, ego gratification, power, and exposure that come with ownership. The best indication that these indirect returns are present in owning a sports team is the fact that franchise values rise consistently over time. Moreover, the rate of return on franchise ownership has been above the growth rate of the S&P 500 over the last four decades.[6] If the reported financial losses of franchises (excepting the NFL, where all franchises acknowledge profitability) were the whole story, it would defy all the laws of economics for team values to be rising over the years.

That said, it must also be recognized that sports leagues do compete indirectly with one another in some ways. An NBA and an NHL team in the same city, for example, compete to attract a given number of corporations to buy luxury suites, to purchase arena signage, or to establish sponsorships. They also compete indirectly with the growing number of niche sports, video games, and the Internet.

As new entertainment options proliferate, sports leagues do experience competitive pressure. The languid approach that may have worked for sports leagues, particularly baseball, in the past no longer suffices. If an owner assumes that all he or she has to do is field a team and the fans will come to the ballpark, his or her team will fall into obscurity.

Economic theory generally predicts that monopolists will earn higher profits—called monopoly rent—than competitors do. The monopoly rent in sports leagues, however, has been dissipated by two factors. First, the advent of free agency and the strength of the player unions have pushed salaries to a level that enables players to share monopoly rents with the owners. Second, monopoly rents have tended to be capitalized in the inflated value of the franchises. As new owners buy into a league, they pay a higher price for the team than they would if there were no artificial scarcity of franchises. The higher price of the investment generally lowers the rate of return to more normal levels.[7]

The upshot of the foregoing is that the financial lifeline in sports leagues at the beginning of the twenty-first century is considerably tighter than it was in the 1950s or the 1960s. This observation is especially true of baseball, which pretty much sat alone on the U.S. sports pedestal until the 1960s. Furthermore, baseball was granted an exemption from the country's antitrust laws by the U.S. Supreme Court in 1922. This exemption meant that many of baseball's restrictive practices (such as the reserve clause, the minor leagues, control over franchise movements, national television contracts, and prohibitions on municipal ownership, among others) were never challenged or were challenged unsuccessfully.

Thus, baseball had an even greater degree of insulation from competitive pressure. This insulation led to lax and inefficient practices. The baseball commissioner from the 1920s through the mid-1970s at least had to worry little about good management and business practices. The emergence of free agency and a more competitive environment, however, began to alter the picture since the late 1970s. As we shall see, the commissioner's role eventually was expanded. As the commissioner's job grew to include economic management, revenue disparities across the teams exploded, creating even greater friction and still less unity of vision among the owners. The commissioner's functions, then, were increasingly complex as his objectives were intractable. Few commissioners were up to the task.

Antitrust and the Commissioner's Powers

In baseball, the commissioner's role has been intricately tied up with the sports antitrust exemption from the start. When the commissioner's post was first created on January 12, 1921 (thirty-seven days after the District of Columbia Court of Appeals ruled that baseball was exempt from the nation's antitrust laws, though sixteen months before this decision was sanctioned by the U.S. Supreme Court), the commissioner was given plenary powers to govern the game. Yet it was understood at the time that his main function would be to clean up the game's image by ridding it of gambling. The commissioner also became the arbiter of disputes around the player reserve clause and disputes between teams. In this capacity, the commissioner made decisions—such as deciding whether a player would play for one team or another—that could be construed to be abridging the free labor market rights of both players and owners. Still more suspect of antitrust violation would be the commissioner's decisions to ban a player from baseball even when the player had been found innocent of a gambling accusation in a court of law. To be sure, as the following testimony suggests, the commissioner made a host of judgments that might invite antitrust scrutiny.

Thus, for a commissioner to be able to carry out his mandate to "act in the best interests" of baseball in any circumstance, the antitrust exemption was seen as fundamental. Until 1957, the other, and still emerging, team sports believed that they benefited from the same treatment under the law as baseball. In February of that year, however, the Supreme Court, in *Radovich v. NFL*, declared football to be subject to antitrust statutes and asserted that baseball's exemption was "unreasonable, illogical and inconsistent."[8]

Once the *Radovich* decision indicated that they were operating under a misapprehension, the NFL, the NBA, and the NHL hastily dispatched their commissioners to the U.S. Congress in search of legislative protection. At hearings before both the House and the Senate Judiciary Committees during the summers of 1957 and 1958, the commissioners of all four major sports argued that the exemption was necessary for them to be able to act in the best interests of their sports.

This is how then NFL commissioner Bert Bell made the case to the Senate hearing as he laid out the various functions of his office:

> I should like to say a few words about my authority as commissioner of the National Football League. Long ago, when the league was first created, it was recognized that if professional football was to deserve public support and if each of our players was to be an example for young people to follow, then football would have to be above reproach. To achieve this we require that

our players, owners, coaches, officials, and even those who do the broadcasts live up to a high standard of ethics and honesty.

Someone must see that this program is followed, so the commissioner enforces this code.

The league will not permit a person to own an interest in more than one football team. Nor will it permit an owner, a player, [a] coach, or an official to own stock in or to lend money to another team. Because there are situations of doubtful ethics which cannot be spelled out ahead of time, the commissioner is also empowered to punish for "conduct detrimental to professional football." This means that the commissioner must take action for similar breaches of ethical standards.

Likewise, to assure maintenance of high ethical standards the league requires the commissioner to pass upon those who sponsor the broadcasts and telecasts of our games and to select, from among a panel of names submitted to him, the persons who broadcast the games.

In addition, the commissioner may also be called upon to act as an arbitrator. For example, where there is a dispute which involves a player, coach, or employee, the services of the commissioner are available in the role of umpire or arbitrator if the parties desire to avail themselves of his services. He also is designated as the arbitrator where the dispute involves questions of policy.[9]

Soon thereafter, baseball stood this argument (the antitrust exemption was necessary to support the commissioner) on its head, telling Congress that the commissioner, with his plenary powers, looked out for the best interests of fans and assured that monopoly abuses would not occur. Thus, the commissioner became an argument to support baseball's exemption.[10]

This claim regarding the commissioner's role is, of course, subject to empirical inquiry. Has the commissioner, in fact, defended the consumers' best interests over the years? As we shall see, many questioned whether this claim was ever valid. Whatever thin plausibility this assertion may have had in the past, when Bud Selig, the long-standing owner of the Milwaukee Brewers, was made acting commissioner in 1992, the contention lost its last shreds of credibility.

2

The History of the Commissioner's Role

When the first professional baseball league was formed in 1871, it had no commissioner. In fact, it scarcely had anything. It is hard to assert that the league had a problem with governance, because it virtually had no governance.

Nor did it have much of a marketing sense. Both its name and its acronym, the National Association of Professional Base Ball Players (NAPBBP), seemed to be purposely chosen to ensure that they would never be mentioned.

In conception, the association was an open players' league. Teams were organized either as joint stock companies that paid players fixed salaries or as cooperatives that shared gate receipts with the players. The association's one enduring contribution is that it established the notion of a national championship. Prior to the association, teams competed in ad hoc contests or local championships. The association had not quite invented a league, though, because its teams were free to fix their own schedules.

The absence of a unified schedule seemed minor compared to the association's other problems, such as rampant corruption:

> Corruption was rife and the chief ingredients of life were bribery, contract breaking, and the desertion of players. . . . Discovering

that their salaries represented only a fraction of what they could make by dealing with the gamblers, the players traveled from city to city like princes, sporting diamonds, drinking champagne at dinner every night, and ostentatiously paying the tab by peeling off folding money from the wads of the stuff that mysteriously reproduced itself.[1]

The baseball historian George Moreland writes of the association:

Bribery, contract-breaking, dishonest playing, pool-room manipulations and desertion of players became so shameful that the highly respectable element of patrons began to drop out of attendance, until the crowds that came to the games were composed exclusively of men who went to the grounds to bet money on the results. The money was bet openly during the progress of the game.[2]

One section of the crowd at Brooklyn Atlantics games was reserved for bettors. The section came to be known as the "Gold Board," where action resembled that on the floor of today's stock exchange.

Some of the team owners were mixed up with the sordid corruption of city politics. The New York Mutuals, for instance, were owned by William Marcy "Boss" Tweed. Tweed had effective control over New York City politics. Among other things, he had the city sign contracts with and purchase objects (chairs, desks, cuspidors, and cabinets) from his companies. Sometimes the city paid Tweed for phantom goods or services.

Tweed had taken over the Mutuals in 1857. He might be credited with originating the idea of public subsidies for sports teams. By the late 1860s, Tweed had the city underwriting the growth of baseball. His aldermen voted for one appropriation of $1,500 from the city treasury to fund a prize for a local baseball tournament.

The Mutuals players were originally firemen but were transferred to the city's street-cleaning department by Tweed. As city employees, the Mutuals had no problems skipping work for practice or games, so the team played a more extensive schedule than others did. The Mutuals became charter members of the association in 1871. Tweed's control of the Mutuals faded after his first jail term during 1873–1874. He was found to have pilfered over

$30 million from the city's coffers—a tidy sum back in the depression years of the 1870s.[3]

The Philadelphia Athletics were another team with propitious connections to city government. One baseball historian wrote of the association's Philadelphia team that "an inordinate number of baseball club officials held office as city or county treasurer, tax collector, comptroller, assessor . . . or clerks and deputies working with city finances."[4]

The association's last season was 1875. It began with thirteen teams and ended with seven. Over the league's five years, twenty-five different clubs participated, and eleven of these did not survive a single year.

The baseball historian Lee Allen writes that "Drunkenness among the players in 1875 became so prevalent that it presented a problem almost as serious as the throwing of games."[5] The only team not plagued by the drinking problem was the Boston Red Stockings, and they dominated the league, winning all but the first of the five championships. The teams that were organized as joint stock companies with the wealthiest backers were able to hire the best players. The average yearly salary of joint stock teams was $1,200, while that for teams organized as cooperatives (where players shared in gate receipts but received no base salary) was only $300. The Boston team, organized as a joint stock company, paid an average salary of $1,450 in 1871 and $2,050 in 1875. In 1875, the Red Stockings won seventy-one games and lost only eight—an .899 winning percentage! Baseball's competitive imbalance was not invented by Bud Selig's Blue Ribbon Panel in its 2000 report.

Given these problems, it is hardly surprising that the association's attendance fell each year of its existence. The combination of falling attendance, corruption, inebriation, and competitive imbalance also meant that ownership squabbles were endemic, but they were particularly acute between Eastern and Western clubs, the latter feeling repeatedly disadvantaged by association policies.

William Hulbert was made president of the association's Chicago White Stockings in 1875. Hulbert and other owners of the league's "Western" teams felt that the "Eastern" teams kept stealing the better players. Hulbert decided to take matters into his own hands.

William Hulbert, the founder of the National League. Distressed by the problems of the loosely structured and corrupt NAPBBP, Hulbert created the concept of a closed monopoly sports league.

Hulbert was resentful over the association's decision in 1875 to resolve a dispute over a player contract between his White Stockings and the Philadelphia club in favor of Philadelphia. The player was Davy Force, the winner of the batting title in 1872 with a .406 average. One baseball historian wrote that in reaction to the loss of Davy Force, "Hulbert . . . was so infuriated that he resolved to bring the Association to its knees. In another year, the Association was dead and Hulbert had fathered the National League."[6]

Hulbert's first step was to hire Boston's star pitcher A. G. Spalding for the 1876 season. He then went after three other stars of the Boston team by offering healthy pay increases.[7] Hulbert clearly violated the association's rules by signing these players and Cap Anson from the Philadelphia Athletics for the 1876 season prior to the completion of the 1875 season. Although the players agreed not to disclose their new contracts, the news eventually leaked out.

Faced with the likelihood that he and his five new stars might be expelled from the association, Hulbert hit upon the idea of starting his own league. With the assistance of Spalding and Harry Wright, Hulbert drafted a constitution for his new league and then contacted the backers of the St. Louis, Cincinnati, and Louisville clubs in the association. These Western club owners, all resentful of the greater power of the Eastern teams in the association anyway, met with Hulbert on December 16 and 17, 1875, in Louisville and endorsed Hulbert's plan.

Hulbert then persuaded Morgan Bulkeley (a prominent politician/financier from Connecticut, the owner of the association's Hartford franchise, and a future governor and U.S. senator) to chair the meeting of the new league and eventually to serve as its first president. Hulbert's next step was to hold individual meetings with the backers of the four Eastern clubs in the association to pre-sell his plan.[8] The decisive meeting took place on February 2, 1876, at the Grand Central Hotel in New York City, where the resolution to launch the National League (NL) was adopted unanimously.

It is not without irony that William Hulbert was born in 1832 in Otsego County, New York, just twenty miles down the road from Cooperstown. His family moved to Chicago shortly after he turned two years old. In his early adult years, Hulbert developed a lucrative wholesale grocery business and became a successful coal merchant and a member of the Chicago Board of Trade.[9] Hulbert was a great booster of Chicago and became actively involved in its civic affairs. His Chicago chauvinism is well represented in his brash assertion: "I would rather be a lamp post in Chicago than a millionaire in any other city."[10]

Hulbert bought three shares of stock in the White Stockings in 1870 and was elected president of the team's board of directors in 1875. A. G. Spalding, Hulbert's partner in building the NL, described Hulbert as "strong, forceful and self-reliant . . . and a man of tremendous energy and courage, [who did things] in a businesslike way."[11]

Hulbert's National League appears to be the first example of a closed professional team sports league anywhere in the world. At least, there are no known models from which Hulbert borrowed and no known preexisting leagues.[12] Rather than borrowing from someone else's model, Hulbert, as a successful capitalist with a good knowledge of commodity and financial markets, as well as the emerging aggressive, predatory practices of the robber baron era, appears to have used the association as an anti-model. He then added elements of what Alfred Chandler describes as the evolving rational business paradigm in the United States during the last quarter of the nineteenth century.

A basic characteristic of the new paradigm was owner control over the production process. Worker or player control was unacceptable. A. G. Spalding portrayed Hulbert's vision as "reducing the game to a business system such as had never heretofore obtained. . . . It was, in fact, the irrepressible conflict between labor and capital asserting itself under a new guise."[13] The rudiments of Hulbert's NL organization included the establishment of a league bureaucracy with team owners and a president, a secretary-treasurer, and a board of directors with undisputed authority to enforce rules and implement disciplinary measures. Again, the players were excluded from these management organs. The new rules tightly bound players to their contracts; limited franchises to cities with at least seventy-five thousand inhabitants; granted teams territorial monopolies; mandated the completion of team playing schedules under threat of expulsion for missing contests; imposed uniform ticket prices at all ballparks; proscribed Sunday play, alcohol, and betting; and hired paid umpires.

Member clubs were to pay annual dues of $100, ten times those of the association. Each team was to play ten games (five home, five away) against each other team between March 15 and November 15. The team with the most victories at season's end would be declared the champion and awarded a pennant worth not less than $100.

Hulbert's White Stockings finished their first NL season with an .800 winning percentage and, apparently, were the only team to turn a profit that year. The New York Mutuals and the Philadelphia Athletics did not even finish their schedules and were summarily booted out of the league by the uncompromising Hulbert, leaving only six NL clubs for the league's second season.

Hulbert's strong and principled leadership was also evident after the Louisville scandal in 1877. The Lousiville Grays began the 1877 campaign in convincing fashion, winning fifteen of their first twenty games. Their dominant play continued into early August, when they inexplicably went into a prolonged slump that lasted until September 30, when Boston clinched the championship. Then the team suddenly came alive again, playing winning ball until season's end in mid-October. The involved players foolishly flamed suspicions by sporting new diamond jewelry. Hulbert ordered an investigation, wherein it was discovered that four leading players on the team had taken bribes to throw games. The players confessed, and Hulbert immediately expelled them, then turned a deaf ear to their repeated emotional appeals for readmission.[14]

If Hulbert ever compromised his principled leadership, it was on behalf of improving the already dominant strength of his Chicago White Stockings. With their five new players for 1876, the White Stockings easily won the first NL championship with a 56 and 14 record.

Hulbert was the George Steinbrenner of his day—always on the lookout to acquire new star players. During the 1877 season, Si Keck, the owner of the Cincinnati NL team, failed to pay his dues. He also refused to pay his team's expenses for an Eastern road trip. In June, when Keck declared that he was disbanding his team, Hulbert opportunistically seized the chance to sign two of Cincinnati's stars. A few weeks later, a group of Cincinnatians bought the team and sought the return of their stars from Chicago. Hulbert at first refused, but after considerable public uproar, he compromised and returned one of the two players.

Some objected to a different compromise—that Hulbert continued to be both president of the White Stockings and president of the National League. Although Hulbert was the leading figure in the NL in 1876, the nominal president of the league in that year was Morgan Bulkeley. Bulkeley, however, did little more than fulfill the minimal statutory functions of his office, which amounted to chairing the annual meeting of the league's board of directors. When Bulkeley's Eastern political connections were no longer useful to launch the new league, he was dispatched after just one year, and the real leader of the NL, William Hulbert, was properly installed. Hulbert was to remain president until his death in 1882.

In the 1876 constitution, the NL's ultimate decision-making authority rested with the board of directors, which consisted of five randomly selected owners. The board, in turn, selected a president from among its ranks. Each board member and the president would serve for only one year at a time. The board was to meet once a year (at a site equidistant from the league's franchises, so as not to favor either the Eastern or the Western clubs), although allowance was made for additional meetings on an emergency basis. Neither the board members nor the president functioned as operating officers, and none received a salary.

The only executive operating officer was the secretary-treasurer. The constitution stipulated that this executive (1) could not be affiliated with any of the league's franchises, (2) would be paid an annual salary of between $300 and $500, and (3) would be reimbursed for necessary expenses. Thus, while not allowing the league's top operating officer to be a team owner, the constitution did allow for its president to be an owner. When Hulbert became the president in 1877, the *Chicago Tribune* roared its approval: "Who should boss the League if not Chicago?" and then added, reminiscent of Charles Wilson's famous defense of General Motors, "What is good for base-ball in Chicago is good for the League as a whole."[15]

But a potentially more serious conflict was brewing. Back in the last quarter of the nineteenth century, there were few barriers to entry into the baseball business. Playing grounds were inexpensive, players were cheap, and there were no media contracts that favored the existing leagues. Easy entry, together with the fact that the NL was designed as a closed league with careful control over the number of its teams, was a recipe for emergent competition from rival leagues. Thus, after the installation of the player reserve clause in 1879, most of the business of running the NL for the next two and a half decades consisted of fending off challenges from new leagues and making arrangements with subordinate leagues to provide a steady supply of new players.[16]

The next major change in the internal governance structure of baseball occurred with the 1903 peace agreement between the National League and its upstart rival the American League (AL).

Ban Johnson, the founder of the American League and the dominating member of the National Commission, which governed baseball from 1903 to 1920.

The latter was formed as a minor league in the 1890s and, under the aggressive leadership of Ban Johnson, declared its intentions to become a major league in September 1900.

Johnson himself was a law school dropout who became a sports-writer at the *Cincinnati Commercial-Gazette*. He later became the sports editor and frequently used his pages to criticize the parsimony of John T. Brush, the owner of the NL's Cincinnati Reds. One of Johnson's closest friends was Reds manager Charles Comiskey (the noted penny-pincher of the infamous 1919 Black Sox scandal). Comiskey, in turn, persuaded his boss, John Brush, to hire Johnson to be president of the new minor circuit, the Western League. Brush, who owned a team in the league, liked the idea of removing Johnson from the *Commercial-Gazette* and thereby silencing his sharpest critic. Johnson later expanded the Western League, renamed it the American League, and went on to challenge the NL. In the meantime, Comiskey bought the St. Paul franchise in the Western League. When the AL was established, Johnson arranged for Comiskey to move his team to Chicago and become the owner of the AL's Chicago team.

The AL's initial pledge to repudiate salary caps, along with its lucrative offers, lured some one hundred players to desert the NL. Among those enticed to sign with AL teams were Honus Wagner, Cy Young, and Napoleon Lajoie. Despite the defection of these stars, the NL still outdrew the AL at the gate by a small margin in 1901. In 1902, however, the AL attracted a reported 2.21 million fans to the NL's 1.68 million. The postseason salary wars between the AL and the NL picked up full force following the conclusion of the competition in 1902. The leagues decided it was in their best interest to call a truce and work together, which they did in January 1903—creating the modern monopoly of baseball, as we know it today.

The new dual-league structure of organized baseball required a new constitution (known as "The National Agreement"). The leagues were to be governed by a National Commission, consisting of the president of the AL (Ban Johnson), the president of the NL (Harry Pulliam), and a third commissioner (Garry Herrmann), selected by the first two. The third member was designated as chairman of the National Commission. His term was renewed on a yearly basis. The commission was endowed with the "power to construe and carry out the terms and provisions" of the National Agreement, which in practice included passing on player options, draft policies, trades, and sales. The commission also had the authority to levy fines or suspensions on violators of the agreement. Interestingly, the "best interests" clause—which would become so prominent in the 1921 constitution and thereafter—did not appear in the 1903 agreement, even though a close cousin of it, allowing fines and penalties to be levied by the board of directors on those found "guilty of conduct detrimental to the general welfare of the game," had appeared in the National Agreement of 1896.[17] (The "best interests" clause, however, was preserved in the description of the powers of the league presidents, suggesting that the leagues and their presidents were still perceived to be important loci of authority.) The chairman of the National Commission was given the additional authority to adjudicate disputes between teams over rights to individual players and to call meetings of the commission.

Harry Pulliam, the president of the National League and a member of the National Commission from 1903 to 1909. He was criticized by the NL owners for allowing Ban Johnson to control the commission, and he committed suicide in July 1909.

It was not so much the structure of the National Commission as it was the commissioners who eventually created a problem and, indeed, by 1919 rendered the body dysfunctional. Ban Johnson, for all his intelligence, creativity, and leadership ability, was too power hungry and capricious to give baseball the steady hand it needed. Although Garry Herrmann was the chair of the commission and as the owner of the Cincinnati Reds was a National Leaguer, he and NL president Pulliam did not rule the commission. Rather, Herrmann was a close friend of Johnson's and generally sided with the AL president. It was not without reason that Johnson was dubbed the "Czar of Baseball."

Herrmann himself was a dubious character. He was described by one historian as a "loyal lieutenant" of George B. Cox.[18] Cox was the undisputed boss of Cincinnati politics from 1884 until his death in 1916. He was often referred to as "owning" Hamilton County. The corrupt Republican government he ran—not out of City Hall but from an Over-the-Rhine beer hall on Vine Street—led to a clean government campaign whose remnants still affect how Cincinnati governs itself. More dubious still, in 1906, Herr-mann admitted that he bet $6,000 that the Pittsburgh Pirates would not win the pennant. Though he claimed that he later backed out of the wager, some still wondered whether Herrmann had traded his star outfielder Cy Seymour (who had a batting average of .377 and a slugging percentage of .559 in 1905) to the front-running Giants as insurance against a Pirates' pennant.

Rectitude and effective leadership would not get much help from the third commissioner, NL president Harry Pulliam. Pulliam was a sportswriter from Kentucky who was first recruited into the Pirates' organization and then selected as NL president in 1903. He was very knowledgeable about baseball but was temperamen-tally unfit to be league president. Pulliam was overwhelmed by his responsibilities and was content to let Johnson and Herrmann have their way on the National Commission. Pulliam came under criti-cism for his passivity from NL owners and apparently fell deeper and deeper into a depression. On July 28, 1909, after a long day at the office, Pulliam returned to his room at the New York Athletic Club and fatally shot himself in the head.

The sport itself, however, flourished. With the reserve clause in place and the absorption of the only rival league with the 1903 agreement, the baseball monopoly had relatively clear sailing through its first decade. As the urban share of the U.S. population grew from 40 to 46 percent between 1900 and 1910, major league attendance increased from 4.75 million fans in 1903 to 7.25 mil-lion in 1909. Team revenues soared, but player salaries languished, and as late as 1914 the average player salary was only $1,200.[19]

It would have been hard for any governance body to have messed up this party. Most of the business of the National Com-mission until 1914 concerned the movement of players between major and minor league teams and player fines or suspensions. The 1903 agreement contained a ban on "farming." Farming was the binding transfer of on-loan players between major and minor league teams. The farming ban was intended, on the one hand, to limit the ability of rich teams to hoard player talent and, on the other, to enable minor league teams to fully benefit from the sale of their reserved players.

With the National Commission providing a wink, major league clubs increasingly found ways around the farming ban. One circumvention was the use of "optional assignments" or "options." Options allowed a major league team to sell a player to a minor league team and then repurchase the player at a later time. The optional assignment was controlled by waiver rules, which allowed a player to be claimed by another major league club before he was optioned to the minors. Responding to the protests of several teams, the National Commission began to put some constraints on this practice. In 1907, the National Commission allowed a particular player to be optioned only once per year and limited a team to eight optioned players per year. In 1908, the commission set a minimum repurchase price of an optioned player at $300.

In 1905, the New York Giants pioneered another loophole in the farming ban: the so-called working agreement. The working agreement usually provided a minor league club with financial assistance and help assembling its roster. In exchange, the major league club gained the right to exercise fixed price options at season's end. The National Commission judged the "working agreement" relationship to be compatible with the no-farming rule.

Another way around the no-farming rule was for the major league club to draft and put on reserve increasing numbers of players. By 1909, most teams had more than forty players on reserve, and eight teams had more than fifty. In 1912, a new National Agreement limited the number of reserved players to thirty-five per team and to only twenty-five in midseason between May 15 and August 20.

The stronger challenges to the commission were still to come. The first came from the formation in September 1912 of the Fraternity of the Professional Baseball Players of America. This incipient union embodied the growing disgruntlement of players who saw a booming industry with little growth in their salaries. Within a few months, the fraternity signed up 288 players, each paying $18 annual dues. The fraternity's momentum accelerated during a spring 1913 salary confrontation between some star players and their teams. Most visible was the holdout of Ty Cobb. Cobb had won five consecutive batting titles, the last three with averages of

.385 in 1910, .420 in 1911, and .410 in 1912. Meanwhile, Cobb's salary was stuck at $9,000 throughout this period. Cobb asked for $15,000, which still would not have been the highest in baseball. The Tigers' owner, Frank Navin, refused to budge on his offer to Cobb. When Cobb refused to report, Navin suspended him. The National Commission did Navin one better, putting Cobb on the ineligible list. Following threats from two members of Congress from Georgia, Cobb's home state, to look into baseball's possible violation of the country's antitrust statutes, and Cobb's coming to terms with Navin at $11,332, the National Commission reinstated Cobb after levying a token fine of $50.

The fraternity continued to bring grievances before the commission for the next four years. The commission refused to give formal standing to the fraternity and generally would not allow the fraternity's president, David Fultz, to appear before it. In 1914, the challenge from the fraternity took a back seat to the Federal League (FL).

The Federal League was founded in 1913 as a minor league but in August of that year announced that it would seek status as a major league. Desiring to take advantage of the players' disgruntlement, the FL repudiated the reserve clause and in its stead offered players long-term contracts. While only 18 players jumped to the FL in 1913, their salaries doubled on average. Despite Ban Johnson's threat to permanently banish those who jumped to the FL, higher salaries lured an additional 221 players (including 81 major leaguers) to the FL during 1914 and 1915.[20] The AL and the NL responded by raising salaries. Cobb's salary, for instance, rose to $20,000 in 1915. According to one account, the average pay of twenty major league regulars practically doubled, from $3,800 in 1913 to $7,300 in 1915.[21] The National Commission also permitted covert collusion between the major and the minor leagues to hide talent from the FL.[22]

These salary wars led to losses for both leagues. Attendance at NL and AL games dropped from 6 million in 1913 to 4.1 million in 1914. By one estimate, together the two leagues lost some $10 million.[23] The larger losses were suffered by the FL, which began with smaller cash reserves.

With the National Commission doing all it could to block FL access to both major and minor league talent, the FL's only real hope appeared to be to pursue litigation. In January 1915, the FL's lawyers filed an antitrust suit against the AL and the NL club presidents and the National Commission in the U.S. District Court of Northern Illinois for denying the FL access to baseball's labor markets. This was the circuit of Judge Kenesaw Mountain Landis, who eight years earlier had earned a reputation as a vigorous enforcer of the 1890 Sherman Antitrust Act. On that occasion, not only did Landis require the sixty-eight-year-old John D. Rockefeller to leave his vacation in upstate New York and travel to Landis's courtroom in Chicago to give a brief (and basically irrelevant) testimony, but he issued a verdict of $29 million against Standard Oil—a verdict that was subsequently overturned on appeal. But, it turned out, Landis, ever quixotic and capricious, had more loyalty to baseball than he did to the fight against monopoly power. Landis tipped his hand early on in the trial when he asked one of the FL attorneys: "Do you realize that a decision in this case may tear down the very foundation of the game?"[24] When FL lawyers attempted to present evidence about exploitation in baseball's labor market, Landis asserted, "As a result of thirty years of observation, I am shocked because you call playing baseball labor."[25] Landis told the parties that he would take the case under advisement, knowing full well that the FL's financial situation was too precarious for it to hang on long. Sure enough, after waiting almost a year, in November 1915, the FL and organized baseball reached a settlement. It included $600,000 total compensation divided unequally among several FL owners, while two FL owners were allowed to buy into NL or AL clubs.

The disappearance of one-third of major league jobs and the absence of competition meant, of course, that the clubs again had the upper hand over their players. Salaries dipped in 1916. The players' fraternity president, David Fultz, called upon players to refuse to sign contracts for 1917 and to prepare to strike. In January 1917, Fultz held talks with the American Federation of Labor's Samuel Gompers about joining ranks. Talk was easier than action. As January drew to a close, some players began to sign contracts, and the union ranks withered. Fultz had overplayed his hand. The players' fraternity faded, and the National Commission had yet another victory.

The commission's ascendance, however, was not to last. After President Wilson declared war on Germany in April 1917, hundreds of players were drafted for the war effort. The major league clubs proceeded to raid the minors in order to restock their rosters. Minor league operators found their players being siphoned away both to the armed forces and to the major leagues. Despite the increased demand for minor leaguers, draft prices were fixed in the National Agreement. To make matters worse, the U.S. economy entered a period of war-driven inflation, with the consumer price index increasing some 59 percent between 1916 and 1919.

With the troops returning home before the 1919 season, the minor league operators felt it was time to recover their standing. They appealed to the majors for higher prices for their drafted players. When the majors refused, the minors broke ranks and suspended the majors' draft and optional-assignment rights. The National Commission tried to restore the status quo ex ante but failed.

Matters grew more ominous for the National Commission. One key dispute was over minor league pitcher Scott Perry. In August 1918, the NL Boston Braves arranged with Atlanta of the International League (a minor league) to purchase Perry for $2,800 on a thirty-day trial basis, with a down payment of $500. Perry, however, did not report to the Braves but instead jumped to an outlaw league (a nonsignatory to the major-minor league agreement). The National Commission ordered Perry to return to the Boston Braves, but the Atlanta team made a new deal, this time with the AL's Philadelphia Athletics. The Athletics' Connie Mack, with the blessing of AL president Ban Johnson, then refused to send Perry to the Braves. The NL president, John Tener, resigned in protest, and the National Commission seemed to be losing its authority.[26]

Next, it was Ban Johnson's turn to have his authority undermined. In July 1919, Boston Red Sox pitcher Carl Mays walked off the field in the middle of a game. Then, instead of reporting to the ballpark the next day, Mays went fishing. For these acts of indiscipline, Johnson suspended Mays. Under the suspension's terms, Mays could not be sold or traded to another team while the penalty was in effect. Red Sox owner Harry Frazee, as a warm-up for his sale of Babe Ruth to the Yankees in January 1920, sold Carl Mays to the Yankees. When Johnson ordered the sale to be voided, the Yankees sued, claiming that Johnson was compromised because he reportedly owned a share of the AL's Indians. The Yankees first obtained an injunction, preventing Johnson from enforcing his suspension of Mays, and then got another injunction that prevented Johnson from using AL funds to fight the lawsuit.

The case was heard in New York District Court and was presided over by Judge Robert Wagner, who, as a U.S. senator, authored the National Labor Relations Act in 1935. Ban Johnson asserted that Article XX of the National Agreement gave him the authority for his action:[27]

> The president . . . shall have the power to impose fines or penalties, in the way of suspension or otherwise, upon any manager or player who, in his opinion, has been guilty of conduct detrimental to the general welfare of the game.

The Yankees' rebuttal, which persuaded Judge Wagner, was that Article XXIV assigned the responsibility of player discipline to the team:

> Each club belonging to this league shall have the right to regulate its own affairs, to establish its own rules, and to discipline, punish, suspend or expel its manager, players or other employees, and these powers shall not be limited to cases of dishonest play or open insubordination, but shall include all questions of carelessness, indifference, or other conduct of the player that may be regarded by the club as prejudicial to its interest.

In his decision granting a permanent injunction against the suspension of Mays, Wagner wrote,

> Under these rules it is the right and duty of the president to regulate the actual playing of the game on the field and to enforce the rules instituted for the governing of the game. Doubtless his powers would extend to the discipline of players for any

infringement of these rules upon the field, or for an overt act committed by a player on the field in violation of the rules.

What Wagner might have viewed as a rule violation on the field worthy of suspension or why Carl Mays's walking off the field in the middle of the game was not such a violation was left unexplained. Ban Johnson was widely considered to be the most powerful man in baseball. Wagner reduced Johnson's authority and, with it, further diminished the authority of the National Commission.

That wasn't enough for Yankees owners Jacob Ruppert and Cap Huston, who brought another suit against Johnson in February 1920. This one charged Johnson with attempting to manipulate the Yankees' lease at the Polo Grounds (the New York Giants' field) and drive the Yankees out of the major leagues. Johnson had indeed tried to convince the Giants to cancel the Yankees' lease. While the Yankees were not awarded any damages, the remaining teams in the AL that were loyal to Johnson joined the Yankees' bloc. The AL owners created a two-man board to review and possibly overturn any fines that were more than $100 or suspensions longer than ten days imposed by Johnson.

The final blow to the National Commission came in the George Sisler controversy. The Pittsburgh Pirates had purchased the rights to Sisler from a minor league team that had signed Sisler out of high school. Sisler appealed to the National Commission to invalidate the purchase so that he could attend the University of Michigan. The commission granted Sisler his petition and led the Pirates to believe that they would retain rights to Sisler when he turned pro. But Sisler signed with the St. Louis Browns when his college coach, Branch Rickey, joined the Browns' front office. Naturally, Pirates owner Barney Dreyfuss protested to the National Commission, but the commission allowed Sisler to go to the Browns. Dreyfuss rallied several other NL owners against the commission's Garry Herrmann, who was already disliked in the NL for his kowtowing to Ban Johnson, among other things. A vote of confidence went against Herrmann, who, in turn, resigned his commission post in February 1920, stating his strong conviction that no owner should serve on the national governing board. (Herrmann did not explain why it took him seventeen years to have this epiphany.) Johnson was upset to lose his ally and effectively blocked the appointment of a replacement for Herrmann. Thus, the National Commission faded into disuse during the 1920 season, and team owners began to talk about a single-man commission.

3

The First Commissioner
Kenesaw Mountain Landis

As the exercise of effective authority by the National Commission diminished, betting at the ballpark proliferated. Gamblers were making overtures to the players to fix games. With salaries deflated by the reserve clause and the absence of competition from a rival league, several players found the prospect of gamblers' pay-offs to be irresistibly alluring. To be sure, it was not only their stagnating salaries, but also their sense of mistreatment that led these players to rebel. Players had no job security and paid for their own travel when they were demoted to the minors. Their incipient union, the Players' Fraternity, had been defeated by the owners in 1917.

The worst-treated players, it seems, were the Chicago White Sox. Their owner, Charles Comiskey, was a notorious tightwad. White Sox player salaries were below those on other teams. Joe Jackson, one of the best hitters in baseball history, was purchased by the White Sox from Cleveland for $65,000, yet Jackson was never paid more than $6,000 a year.[1] Comiskey even made the players wash their own uniforms. Eliot Asinof, in *Eight Men Out*, tells the story of pitcher Eddie Cicotte being promised a $10,000 bonus if he won thirty games in 1917. When Cicotte reached twenty-nine wins, according to Asinof, Comiskey had him benched.[2]

An early 1921 portrait of Judge Kenesaw Mountain Landis (seated), the commissioner of baseball from January 1921 to 1944, in a Chicago courtroom, surrounded by team owners. Standing in the background (left to right): Connie Mack (Philadelphia Athletics, AL), Phil Ball (St. Louis Browns, AL), Barney Dreyfuss (Pittsburgh Pirates, NL), Clark Griffith (Washington Senators, AL), Frank Navin (Detroit Tigers, AL), Jacob Ruppert (New York Yankees, AL), Sam Breadon (St. Louis Cardinals, NL), Charles Ebbets (Brooklyn Dodgers, NL), James Dunn (Cleveland Indians, AL), Charles Stoneham (New York Giants, NL), Garry Herrmann (Cincinnati Reds, NL), Harry Frazee (Boston Red Sox, AL), William Veeck (Chicago Cubs, NL), and Robert Quinn (St. Louis Browns, AL).

The White Sox players were primed for a bribe when they reached the World Series in 1919. Players were offered between $10,000 and $20,000 to lose key games. Although the players were acquitted in a jury trial, baseball's new commissioner, Judge Kenesaw Mountain Landis, was determined to clean up the game and enforce a level of discipline that the National Commission never was able to attain. The following quote is indicative of Landis's messianic visions:

> It is a great game this baseball—a great game. . . . It is remarkable for the hold it has on people, and equally remarkable for its cleanness. . . . It is a compliment to the nation to love such a clean and thoroughly wholesome sport . . . We've got to keep baseball on a high standard for kids. That's why I took the job.[3]

Landis banned the eight accused White Sox players, including Joe Jackson and Eddie Cicotte, from the game. Landis then went on to ban fourteen others before 1927.

Landis had been chosen by the baseball magnates in November 1920 after a protracted internal political struggle between Ban

Johnson and the five owners loyal to him, on one side, and the remaining eleven teams, on the other. Along the way, many notables were considered for the new job of baseball commissioner, including former president William Howard Taft, General John Pershing, Republican senator from California Hiram Johnson, former secretary of the treasury (and Woodrow Wilson's son-in-law) William Gibbs McAdoo, and presidential contender General Leonard Wood. Landis had been considered for the commissionership or a similar job since early 1919 at least. The growing ineffectiveness of the National Commission and the resistance to Ban Johnson had inspired the search for a new governance system and a new leader well before news of the Black Sox scandal broke. When Johnson blocked the appointment of a replacement for Garry Herrmann after his resignation in February 1920 and the National Commission fell into disuse, the search for a new system went to the forefront on the owners' agenda.

When the owners told Landis of their decision to offer him the commissioner's job in November, Landis expressed gratitude but demurred, stating, "I love my work here as judge and I am doing important work in the community and in the nation," and explaining that such a big step required considerable contemplation.[4] Thus, Landis bought himself bargaining leverage. Scott Boras would not have done it any better.

Landis used this leverage not only to improve his compensation package but also to extract absolute authority to govern the game and to retain his federal judgeship. The owners acceded immediately to Landis continuing as district court judge. Federal courts, after all, were shut down from June to mid-September, a felicitous recess to accommodate most of the baseball season. Landis was earning $7,500 as a federal judge. Baseball offered him $50,000 to be its commissioner. Appearing scrupulous, Landis imposed another condition: "If I am to remain on the bench I desire to deduct my federal salary from the original amount you offered me."[5] Then Landis added that he wanted the $7,500 to be his expense account, a sum on which he paid no income tax. Since the steep wartime tax rates were still in effect, this arrangement was hardly a matter of trivial benefit to Landis.

Commissioner Landis
throwing out the first ball
at a game in Chicago in
1926.

Landis's bargaining over the precise powers of his new office continued into January 1921. At a meeting in the Congress Hotel in Chicago on January 12, Landis made a bold statement to the owners, parts of which follow:[6]

It is my duty to be very frank with you. When you came to me two months ago I got the impression from what you said, and made me believe . . . that you had calmly and thoroughly gone into your troubles and had a structure outlined which provided for authority to discharge a responsibility and that part of that authority would be control over whatever and whoever had to do with baseball.

Another impression was that there had grown up in baseball certain evils not limited to bad baseball players; that men who controlled ball clubs in the past had been guilty of various offenses and the time had come where somebody would be given authority, if I may put it brutally, to save you from yourselves. . . .

Now we meet again here today and this draft [of the National Agreement] comes in and there has been a change. You will readily understand the embarrassment with which I discuss this matter because it relates to the powers of the Commissioner to deal with the offender in baseball whoever he might be. The amendment in this document today limits the authority of the Commissioner to deal only with a crooked ballplayer. . . .

It is fundamental that the Commissioner upon whom you devolve this authority and whom you trust and hold out to the millions of fans in this country with your plea, "Gentlemen trust this man he is our Commissioner." But he must have the power. . . .

You can't hire me—there is not enough money in America . . . [unless you change your position] . . . whereas two months ago you were of the opinion there should be a Commissioner with power to deal with evil wherever he found evil, that you have now made up your minds that you went too far and that you propose now to sign an agreement that the Commissioner can deal with evil, provided the evil is found in a ballplayer.

Landis then told the owners the choice was theirs. Either they restored full powers to the office, or they would have to find another commissioner. Before finishing, however, Landis made it clear that he wanted an expanded expense account:

It is conceivable to me that the gentleman you are going to have as Commissioner may some day have occasion to hire somebody to go some place and do something. I would add something to that list of possible expenses in order that the Commissioner may feel at liberty—something may break loose in New York, Boston, St. Louis or some other place and the Commissioner might not want to ask Mr. Heydler or Mr. Johnson, in advance, to agree with what he is going to do.

Landis left the room. The owners had already told the world that Landis would be baseball's savior. It would not have been an easy spin if Landis walked away from the job. The owners knew this and promptly voted 15 to 1 to grant plenary powers to the new commissioner. Indeed, they went one step further by vow-

ing to never publicly criticize the commissioner in signing the following loyalty oath:[7]

> We, the undersigned, earnestly desirous of insuring to the public
> wholesome and high class baseball, and believing that we our-
> selves should set for the players an example of sportsmanship
> which accepts the umpire's decision without complaint, hereby
> pledge ourselves loyally to support the Commissioner in his
> important and difficult task, and we assure him that each of us
> will acquiesce in his decisions even when we believe them mis-
> taken and that we will not discredit the sport by public criticism
> of him and of one another.

When the owners wrote the new National Agreement on January 12, 1921, the high esteem and power of the commissioner's
office was enshrined in Article I, Section 6, on succession:

> The first Commissioner under this agreement shall be Kenesaw
> M. Landis. Upon the expiration of his term, or upon his resigna-
> tion or death during his term, his successor shall be chosen by a
> vote of the majority of the clubs composing the two Major
> Leagues. In the event of failure to elect a successor within three
> months after the vacancy has arisen, either Major League may
> request the President of the United States to designate a Com-
> missioner, and the person when thus designated shall thereupon
> become Commissioner, with the same effect as if named herein.

This succession provision, which remained throughout Landis's term, not only declared baseball's sense of self-importance, it
also reflected the owners' concern that the owners or the leagues
may have sharp disagreements, rendering it impossible to reach
agreement on a new commissioner. After all, it was just one year
earlier when the post of chair of the National Commission lay
vacant for a year due to such discord. As we shall see, discord
among the owners has been a steady theme in baseball and a central challenge for every commissioner to confront.[8]

Who, then, was this man to whom baseball's barons had sur-
rendered ultimate control over their business? Never reaching a
height above five feet six inches, or a weight above 130 pounds,

Kenesaw Mountain Landis was clearly not a mountain of a man. He was, however, named after one.

Abraham Landis was an assistant surgeon in the Union Army. He was one of a hundred thousand soldiers who marched with General Sherman's army from Tennessee into Georgia. In June 1864, some twenty miles northwest of Atlanta, Sherman deployed sixteen thousand troops to attack General Joseph Johnston's forces at Kennesaw Mountain. The result was one of the worst Union defeats during the Civil War. In the 1860s and 1870s, it was not uncommon for fathers to name their children after battles in which they fought during the war. Baseball's future commissioner had the misfortune of being named after a battle that was not only a defeat for the Union Army but was also a tragedy for his father, Abraham, whose leg was mangled by a cannonball. Abraham Landis's commanding officer and friend, Walter Quinton Gresham, also suffered a severe leg injury in the battle.

Some have claimed that not only did Landis bear this unfortunate name, but the name was misspelled at that. To wit, the child's first name contained but one *n*, while the mountain in Georgia was then spelled with two *n*'s. For this apparent oversight, however, we can forgive Dr. Abraham Landis, because in the nineteenth century the mountain in question had two common spellings.

Young Kenesaw, born in 1866, was the sixth of seven children to Abraham and Mary Landis. Two of Kenesaw's brothers ended up as U.S. congressmen. Kenesaw, however, had an inauspicious beginning to his career. At the age of fifteen he was introduced to algebra in school, and he did not like what he saw. He dropped out of high school, never to return.

Kenesaw took a job as a junior clerk at a local grocery store in Logansport, Indiana, at $3 a week. Over the next several years, Kenesaw jumped from one menial job to another. Although ambitious and enterprising, young Landis seemed to be spinning his wheels until 1886, when he helped his friend campaign for the post of Indiana's secretary of state. His friend won, and patronage landed Kenesaw a job as his assistant. After two years, Kenesaw took advantage of the Indiana law at the time to procure entry into the state's bar. As Landis later admitted, it didn't take much to enter the bar: "All a man needed was to prove that he was twenty-one and had a good moral character."[9] As we shall see, some later wondered whether Landis embodied both attributes.

His credentials, such as they were, were not strong enough to attract many clients, so after a frustrating year Kenesaw decided to enroll in Cincinnati's YMCA Law School in 1890. He did so without either a high school or a college degree. The following year Landis transferred to Chicago's Union Law School where he received his degree in June 1891.

Landis's next step was significant. Walter Quinton Gresham, his father's commanding officer during the war, had become a family friend and a prominent national political figure. Gresham had counseled Landis to go to law school in 1889. In 1893, Gresham was named U.S. secretary of state by President Grover Cleveland. Gresham had been a Republican, so he had to jump parties to serve under the Democrat Cleveland. Gresham asked Landis to come to Washington with him to serve as his personal secretary. Landis had to make the same conversion away from the Republican Party that Gresham had—one of many political switches Landis was to make. Gresham and Landis were inseparable, and when Gresham took ill, he became more and more dependent on Landis. President Cleveland was leery of Landis and on more than one occasion asked Gresham to find another secretary. Gresham refused.

In any event, Landis spent 1893 to 1895 making himself known to the Washington political elite. In 1905, the Republican trustbuster Teddy Roosevelt appointed Landis as federal judge in the Northern District of Illinois. Landis's service in this post was checkered, to say the least. There is little need here to detail his record in interpreting jurisprudence. We have already noted his extraordinary fine of Standard Oil of Indiana in a 1907 price discrimination, antitrust case and that his decision in this case was reversed on appeal.

Landis's chief characteristic on the bench was caprice, blended with a strong antipathy to any views to the left of Teddy Roosevelt, an abiding emotionalism, a flair for the media and the dramatic, and a foul tongue. Big Bill Haywood led the IWW or Wobblies, a left-wing, working-class organization that opposed the United States' entry into World War I. The radical Wobblies were only 10,000 strong in 1912, but they began to grow rapidly in popularity to 30,000 members in 1915 and more than 100,000 in 1917. Because the Wobblies were viewed as a threat to the country's economic system, on September 5, 1917, federal authorities raided forty-nine IWW halls around the country, including the national headquarters in Chicago. Five tons of IWW documents were seized, and 113 Wobbly leaders faced criminal charges for hindering the war effort. The trial took place in Judge Landis's courtroom.

Among the journalists covering the trial was John Reed, who had just returned from covering the Russian Revolution. Reed described Landis's presence in the courtroom in graphic detail: "Small on the bench sits a wasted man with untidy white hair, an emaciated face in which two burning eyes are set like jewels, parchment-like skin split by a crack for a mouth; the face of Andrew Jackson three years dead." The trial began on April 1, 1918, and lasted for seventeen days. After just one hour and ten minutes of deliberation, the jury delivered its verdict of guilty as charged. Landis curiously explained why the jury had no choice but to come to such a decision: "When the country is at peace it is a legal right of free speech to oppose going to war and to oppose preparation for war. But once war is declared that right ceases."[10] Haywood and his colleagues were guilty of saying the wrong things. Landis was equally harsh in his sentencing: Haywood and fifteen others received the maximum twenty years in Leavenworth and $30,000 in fines; other leaders received shorter sentences.

Next on Landis's political docket was the growing Socialist Party. In 1912, the Socialist candidate for president, Eugene V. Debs, received 3.5 percent of the votes. Two years earlier, Socialist Victor Berger was elected to the U.S. Congress from Milwaukee. That city had a Socialist mayor, and the party had a hundred thousand members. Much of the Socialist Party spoke out against U.S. involvement in the war, and the raids on the Wobblies in September 1917 had produced documents to affirm this opposition.

Five of the party's leaders, including Victor Berger, were charged with sedition and appeared before Judge Landis in October 1918.

The Socialists' lawyer asked for a change of venue because, he claimed, that Judge Landis had evinced a strong prejudice against Germans and his clients were all of German descent. Landis had allegedly commented on November 1, 1918: "If anybody has said anything about the Germans that is worse than I have said, I would like to hear it so I could use it myself." In refusing the change of venue plea, Landis elaborated, "You are of the same mind that practically all German-Americans are in this country, and you call yourself German-Americans. Your hearts are reeking with disloyalty."[11]

After the jury found the Socialists to be guilty, Landis sentenced each to the maximum twenty years in Leavenworth. In issuing the sentence, Landis stated, "So far as I can recall, no single word or act of any one of the defendants was apparently intended by any of the defendants to help this country win the war."[12] Then, at a speech to an American Legion post in Chicago, Landis intoned, "It was my great disappointment to give Berger only 20 years in Leavenworth. I believe the law should have enabled me to have him lined up against the wall and shot."[13]

The Socialists appealed. The Appeals Court sent the matter to the Supreme Court, which reversed the judgment. Among other things, the High Court ruled that when the defendants asked for a change of venue due to Landis's prejudice, Landis should have granted it.[14]

Landis's patriotism also found expression when, administering the citizenship oath to eighteen Chicago soldiers, he volunteered that he hoped they would kill one or more of the kaiser's sons. When the war ended, Landis told the soldiers, he wanted to try the kaiser in his court for the death of a Chicagoan in the sinking of the *Lusitania* in 1915.

Outside the political realm, Landis often betrayed a sentimentalism that subordinated the law. He acquitted an eighteen-year-old bank clerk who made off with $750,000 in Liberty Bonds and argued that the bank officials who had entrusted the lad with the bonds were guilty. In another case, a young man was charged with stealing valuable jewelry. In freeing the man, Landis proclaimed, "Here's a boy who admits to the crime, stealing jewelry out of the parcel post. And beside him is his little wife, recently a mother, heartsick over her husband's troubles. A hard case for me to decide. . . . Son, take your little wife and your baby and go home. I won't have that infant the child of a convict."[15]

Landis was a vocal advocate of prohibition before it took effect in January 1920 and became a strident enforcer of it in his courtroom. Throughout, he purchased bourbon by the caseload.[16]

Landis also had a reputation for having a foul mouth. Ford Frick, the NL president during much of Landis's term as commissioner, said in a 1972 interview,

> [Landis] was one of the most profane men I ever met. . . . [his] profanity was so sublime that I can't remember all the terms. Once he was talking about his golf game—he wasn't too good a golfer. Somebody asked him how he had done. He said, "I bitched my drive, boogered my mashie, fucked up my approach shot." I don't remember the entire sequence. But he just kept using words, every one of them worse than the one before.[17]

The journalist A. L. Sloan reflected in the *Chicago Herald American*, "The judge was always headline news. He was a great showman. He always had a crowd. There were no dull moments." In an obituary for Landis, the journalist Jack Lait had more poignant words, describing the judge as "an irascible, short-tempered, tyrannical despot. His manner of handling witnesses, lawyers—and reporters—was more arbitrary than the behavior of any jurist I have ever seen before or since. . . . He regarded his courtroom as his private preserve and even extended his autocracy to the corridors."[18] Leonard Koppett, the former *New York Times* sportswriter extraordinaire, had still harsher words for the judge: "His rulings from the bench were regularly overturned by higher courts and oscillated wildly from excessively harsh to unaccountably lenient. . . . His view of the world was shallow, bigoted, and ill informed, based on a poor education and thoroughly selfish impulses. He could be devious and vengeful."[19]

It would seem that Landis's fellow jurists also had less than an outstanding opinion of him or his actions. Following Landis's decision to remain on the bench after he accepted the post of baseball commissioner, the judge came under sharp criticism from several state bar associations. He responded to the Missouri Bar Association: "If there's an impropriety here I haven't seen it. . . . There is a method by which a federal judge may be removed from office if he is unsatisfactory, and that is by impeachment. But they will never impeach me."

Or so he thought. On February 14, 1921, U.S. congressman from Ohio Benjamin Welty spoke the following words on the House floor:

> On March 3, 1917, the Sixty-Fifth Congress passed an act which, in part, provides that:
> "No government official or employee shall receive any salary in connection with his services as such official or employee from any source other than the government of the United States. . . ."
> I therefore impeach said Kenesaw M. Landis for high crimes and misdemeanors as follows.[20]

Welty's charges were sufficiently plausible so that the House Judiciary Committee voted 24 to 1 to endorse a full investigation. Then, while the U.S. Congress was moving toward impeachment, on September 1, 1921, the American Bar Association formally censured Landis, asserting its "unqualified condemnation" of the judge and castigating him for holding the two jobs simultaneously as "derogatory to the dignity of the bench."[21]

Landis had had enough. On February 18, 1922, he resigned from his federal judgeship. His $7,500 judge's salary was restored to his compensation as commissioner.

This, then, was the man whom the baseball barons chose to cleanse and lead their game. Oddly enough, Landis's bold early measures, expelling gamblers from the game, seem to have been just the medicine the patient required. Landis's hand was heavy, even if it was not always consistent. After banning for life the players presumed to be connected to the Black Sox scandal, Landis went on to inflict lifetime bans on a dozen other players between 1921 and 1925. One of Landis's victims was thirty-one-year-old New York Giants solid-hitting outfielder Benny Kauff. Kauff was under indictment for alleged improprieties in his automobile agency. He was acquitted, but Landis didn't agree with the verdict and sent Kauff packing.

In the case of pitcher Rube Benton, who was on record as knowing about the 1919 series fix and was declared to be undesirable by NL president John Heydler, Landis absolved him. In doing this, Landis seemed to suggest that Heydler's position on the matter was irrelevant and to send a signal that league presidents were now secondary administrators relative to the commissioner.

Landis went to even greater lengths to put baseball's previous strongman, AL president Ban Johnson, in his place. In 1926, Johnson received documents accusing Ty Cobb, Tris Speaker, and Joe Wood of conspiring to fix a game in 1919. Johnson forwarded the documents to Landis. Cobb and Speaker then each resigned as player-managers of their respective teams. Two weeks after Speaker's resignation, baseball gave Landis another seven-year contract, this time with a $65,000 annual salary. The same day, December 21, 1926, Landis made the Cobb and Speaker documents public. Three weeks later, Ban Johnson gave an interview wherein he criticized Landis for releasing the documents but went on to state that neither Cobb nor Speaker would play again in the AL. That was all the incentive Landis needed. Two weeks after Johnson's interview, Landis issued a statement that completely exonerated both Cobb and Speaker. AL owners put Johnson on a leave of absence.

Despite some caprice and inconsistency along the way, Landis did succeed in cleaning up baseball's image in the 1920s. This is what the owners wanted him to do. Notwithstanding the open-ended language of the "best interests" clause, baseball's barons did not want the commissioner interfering with the underlying economics of the industry. When Landis trod on this ground, he had little success. For instance, he proved ineffective in implementing his vision for the minor leagues. Following the minor leagues' suspension of the draft in 1919, prices for minor league players increased rapidly. The NL and the AL owners responded by suspending the no-farming rules, which, among other things, allowed major league team owners to once again acquire minor league clubs. Then, in 1921, the owners reinstated the minor league draft. The new draft raised the top price for players to $5,000 and permitted individual minor league clubs to opt out of the draft system. That is, they could protect their own reserved players from the draft if they agreed not to select players from lower classification levels. Three minor league circuits chose to opt out of the draft on this basis, and the sale prices for their players skyrocketed, with the top prospects commanding prices in the $70,000–$100,000 range for the rest of the 1920s.

With the escalation of prices for drafting or purchasing minor league talent and the abolition of no-farming rules, the St. Louis Cardinals' Branch Rickey went to work developing baseball's first extensive farm system. Rickey's idea was to extend the working arrangements and cross ownership that existed between the majors and the top classification minors down to the lowest classification levels. By establishing a vast scouting and player development system, Rickey implemented a strategy to allow a relatively poor club like the Cardinals to procure top talent more cheaply, as well as to develop strong prospects to sell or trade to other teams. By 1928, Rickey's Cards owned five minor league teams and had working agreements with many more. By 1937, the Cards' farm system peaked at thirty-three clubs, controlling almost seven hundred players.

The Cards' increasing success at the major league level led other clubs to attempt to emulate Rickey's system. By 1929, major league franchises owned twenty-seven minor league teams. During the 1930s, both the Dodgers and the Yankees built extensive farm systems, though they never became as large as the Cardinals'.

Commissioner Landis was not a fan of large farm systems.[22] As an old trustbuster, Landis believed that farming had inherent monopolistic tendencies because it imposed severe restrictions on the labor-market mobility of young prospects.

The only time Landis's authority as commissioner was legally challenged was in the case of minor leaguer Fred Bennett. Bennett had been transferred several times by St. Louis Browns owner Phil Ball between minor league clubs owned by Ball. Major league rules restricted such transfers within an organization to two before the player was placed on waivers and made available to other clubs. Ball was clearly violating the rules, and Ball's challenge to Landis's authority was rejected by the federal judge who heard the case. In rejecting Ball's plea for the return of Bennett, Judge Lindley used his decision to reaffirm the powers of the commissioner:

> Apparently it was the intent of the parties to make the commissioner an arbiter, whose decisions made in good faith, upon evidence, upon all questions relating to the purpose of the organization and all conduct detrimental thereto, should be absolutely binding. So great was the parties' confidence in the man selected for the position and so great the trust placed in him that certain of the agreements were to continue only so long as he should remain commissioner.[23]

Just two years after this 1931 ruling, however, the majority "farm bloc" owners voted to push through new rules that facilitated the stockpiling of minor league players.

Landis proposed a universal draft that would allow any team to pick an attractive minor league player, preventing him from getting trapped in one team's system because of the presence of a star player at his position on the major league team.[24] Landis's protestations and recommendations, however, got nowhere with the owners. Happy Chandler, baseball's second commissioner, testified to Congress in 1951, "My predecessor [Landis] fought the farm system tooth and nail, but it prospered just the same as if he had been for it."[25]

In the end, Landis learned to accept his lack of influence over restructuring baseball's minor league system. After the initial morality purge of the 1920s, the game's image was pretty much restored. Also important was that Landis's authority and his proclivity to action successfully suppressed many of the battles among owners over player trades, options, and signings that were rife during the 1910s.

Throughout the 1920s, the 1930s, and the 1940s, there were really no pressing internal economic issues for baseball. Baseball was not only construed to be a legal monopoly, thanks to the 1922 Supreme Court decision, but it was alone on the spectator sports' stage. Labor was docile and under the thumb of the player reserve clause. With few exceptions, teams were making money, and, though far from ideal, competitive balance among teams had improved steadily from the late nineteenth century onward and had settled at a level that seemed to be acceptable to the fans.[26] Even if Landis had wanted to intervene in the sport's economy, other than in the minor leagues there was little to do. Landis had provided the illusion of a supreme being who protected the sport from the greedy, wanton, and miscreant behavior of the players and the owners. If the absence of competition in the product and labor markets did not lull baseball's barons into a deep state of lassitude, then the illusion of a commissioner safeguarding the game's best interests did. This condition left baseball unprepared to be challenged, first, over its antitrust exemption and, second, by the emerging popularity of football and basketball in the second half of the twentieth century.

Meanwhile, the illusion of the all-powerful commissioner evolved into a pretext to justify baseball's antitrust exemption. The commissioner, it was said, not only protected the owners from one another, but he also protected the fans from possible monopoly abuses by the owners.

One group whose interests Landis certainly did not promote was black ballplayers. With the manpower shortage of World War II and the remarkable success of the Negro Leagues, pressure to integrate baseball began to surface. Jackie Robinson got a tryout at the White Sox camp in the spring of 1942. Dodgers manager Leo Durocher declared that he'd be interested in managing black players. At the owners' winter meetings in December 1942, the great singer Paul Robeson appealed to the owners to integrate their game, but Landis cut him short and ruled that the subject would not be pursued. The Pirates gave Roy Campanella a tryout the next year. The Senators gave tryouts to Josh Gibson and Buck Leonard, and Bill Veeck announced his intention to buy the Phillies and hire black ballplayers.

But none of these initiatives broke baseball's color barrier. Leonard Koppett attributes the lack of progress during 1942–1944 to Landis:

> The source of all the backstage pressure was Landis. He was not only a bigot but also a hypocrite, making public statement that "no regulations" barred Negroes from Organized Baseball while making it clear that any club trying to hire one would have to deal with him.[27]

While there is no evidence that Landis moved baseball forward in this regard, it may be that his position simply reflected that of the large majority of owners.

Landis, for all of his failings, played his part properly. He was rewarded with four seven-year contracts and to this day is baseball's longest-serving commissioner. At age seventy-eight, Landis died of a heart attack on November 25, 1944, while serving his fourth term. The owners had already voted to extend a fifth term to Landis from 1946 through 1953, when he would have been eighty-seven. Landis was the game's commissioner for twenty-four years. Baseball did not have an easy time finding his replacement.

4

The Undistinguished Middle I
From Chandler to Eckert

Whatever his deficiencies, Commissioner Landis did succeed in establishing himself as the final arbiter for disputes between leagues, between teams, and between teams and players. Together with cleaning up the game's image, that's precisely what baseball needed him to do. Disagreements among distempered owners no longer paralyzed the administration of the sport.

But twenty-four years of making imperious decisions creates some hard feelings and some enemies. In November 1944, the owners wanted to preserve the positive contributions made by the commissioner but also wanted to clip the commissioner's wings a bit to assure that the owners remained in ultimate control of the industry. Upon Landis's passing, the commissioner's office was put temporarily under the control of the two league presidents, Ford Frick of the NL and Will Harridge of the AL. As Frick and Harridge performed their caretaker functions, the team owners set about to amend the Major League Agreement.

The barons made three principal changes with regard to the commissioner's powers. First, the commissioner's ability to invoke the "best interests" clause was now limited by a new paragraph in Article I, Section 3, that stipulated that the commissioner could not declare an action consistent with baseball's rules and regulations to be detrimental to the game's best interests. That is, the commissioner could not legislate but was bound by rules passed by a majority of the owners.

Second, Article I, Section 6, concerning the election or reelection of a commissioner, now required a three-fourths, rather than a simple majority, vote of the owners.[1] This provision would require any commissioner wanting to keep his job to be especially careful not to alienate needlessly any owner. Not surprisingly, some owners felt they were whimsical targets of Landis and wanted some safeguards for the future.

Third, the owners deleted a clause from Article VI, Section 1, that stated that the leagues and the owners "severally waive such right of recourse to the courts as would otherwise have existed in their favor" regarding decisions by the commissioner. In other words, henceforth if the owners were unhappy with a commissioner's judgment, they could take the matter to court.

Although not directly about the commissioner's authority, the owners agreed to return the annual salary to $50,000—where it had been for Landis's first term but $15,000 below Landis's salary after 1927.[2] The term remained at seven years. Finally, the original replacement clause that anticipated selection of the new commissioner by the president of the United States was scrapped in favor of a more modest approach: if the commissioner dies, resigns, or is otherwise unable to perform his duties, the functions would be carried out by a council consisting of the presidents of the AL and the NL and a third person whom the two presidents would appoint (in other words, the same structure as the old National Commission).[3] The new Major League Agreement was adopted just two months and one week after Landis's death on February 3, 1945.

Commissioner Happy Chandler

The owners gathered in Cleveland on April 24 to choose their next commissioner. Larry MacPhail, then the co-owner of the Yankees, suggested the Democratic U.S. senator from Kentucky Albert B. "Happy" Chandler. He seemed a good choice at the time. Members of Congress had been grousing about baseball's antitrust exemption, and the barons felt that they could use an experienced and well-connected politician.

Indeed, in a sense, Happy Chandler's entire life seemed to prepare him for the job. Chandler was born on April 18, 1898, in Corydon, Kentucky. His family was poor. His father was a hardworking farmer and an avid reader. His mother, raised in an orphanage and ten years younger than her husband, abandoned the family (Happy, then four, and his two-year-old brother, Robert) to seek a more glamorous life in a big city. Chandler remembered his mother's departure: "I followed mother out to the buggy, crying. . . . She gave us two boys a quick kiss, and Robert a long, long hug. The buggy wheels crunched off toward the depot. I sat down at the gate and tears rolled down my cheeks."[4]

Perhaps partially as a defense against abandonment, Chandler grew up a gregarious and accomplished student. Chandler credited his success and ease with people to his father's good nature, and he graduated valedictorian of his class. Beneath his picture in the high school yearbook was the prophetic observation: "Work hard and study while you wait, and you'll be governor of the state." Chandler went to Transylvania College, where he joined the glee club and the theater club and played on the school baseball, football, and basketball teams. Academic success again in college led him to the Harvard Law School. After one year, he transferred to the University of Kentucky, earning his law degree in 1925. After practicing law for a decade, he served two terms as Kentucky's Democratic governor from 1935 to 1939. He was elected U.S. senator in 1939.

Chandler, who had played a year of semipro ball with future Hall of Fame outfielder Earl Combs on his team, was an avid baseball fan. He often traveled up to Cincinnati to watch the Reds. There he struck up a friendship with Larry MacPhail, then the general manager of the Reds. Chandler seemed to embody all of the characteristics that team owners sought in a commissioner: he was smart, affable, garrulous, entertaining, prestigious, well-spoken, and, above all, well-connected.

Thus, on MacPhail's recommendation, the owners took a vote at their April 24, 1945, meeting. On the first ballot, Chandler received support from eleven of the sixteen owners—one short of the three-quarters approval needed for election. On the second ballot, he received the necessary twelve votes. Then the owners used the common public relations ruse: they took a third ballot that unanimously acclaimed Chandler as baseball's second commissioner.

Although Chandler assumed the commissioner's post on July 12, 1945, he was allowed to continue to serve as Kentucky's senator until his term expired on October 29 of that year. Despite removing the clause that disallowed legal challenges to the commissioner's decisions, the owners restored the same "loyalty pledge" they had made to Landis that stated they would accept Chandler's rulings, mistaken or otherwise.

Chandler's reign was bumpy, almost from the start. Chandler's first pose for a public photograph was with baseball clown Nick Altrock. The baseball historian Lee Lowenfish comments that Chandler "tried to adopt Landis' stance against gambling, yet his family was frequently photographed at the Churchill Downs racetrack in Louisville."[5] Chandler's next gaffe was telling AL umpire Ernest Stewart that he was interested in hearing the grievances of the men in blue. Stewart, inspired by Chandler's expression of concern, began union organizing, for which he was summarily fired by AL president Will Harridge. Harridge had to remind Chandler that the umpires were under the league president's jurisdiction, not under the commissioner's.

Chandler didn't do himself any favors by not adapting his homey Kentucky ways to the big city. Although he set up the commissioner's office in Cincinnati (his office window looked out over the Ohio River into Kentucky), Chandler made frequent trips to New York and other cities. At a sportswriters' dinner in his honor in Newark, New Jersey, on February 3, 1946, Chandler gave a speech that he described in his autobiography as follows: "I made pretty much my usual kind of informal, down-home speech. I told them how much I love Kentucky and her wonderful people, talked about fishing. . . . I told them I would wind up my remarks by singing. Of course, I have always loved to sing. . . . My choice that night was *My Old Kentucky Home*. Well that went over like a lead balloon. Instead of pleasing, it antagonized."[6] Chandler writes that

Happy Chandler, the
commissioner of baseball
from April 24, 1945, to
July 15, 1951.

his relations with the big city press never got any better. Given that
a large part of the commissioner's job has to do with image and
public relations, this was not an auspicious sign.

On August 28, 1945, Branch Rickey of the Brooklyn Dodgers
signed Jackie Robinson to a minor league contract to play for their
Montreal farm team in 1946.[7] Chandler let Rickey's signing stand,
though it was not yet a major public issue—Robinson would be
playing below the major league level and in Canada. But it augured
conflict ahead.

Chandler's first major affirmative action was in April 1946,
when he declared that all major leaguers who jumped to the new
Mexican League would be suspended for five years. Chandler
attempted to justify this restraint of trade before the U.S. Congress
on the grounds that if he did nothing, players would continue to
leave for the Mexican League, and it would bring chaos to baseball's labor market.[8]

One of the jumpers was Danny Gardella, a twenty-seven-year-
old outfielder who had been offered a signing bonus of $5,000 to

play for the New York Giants in 1946. The Mexican League offered Gardella an $8,000 signing bonus plus a $5,000 salary. Gardella opted for Mexico, but, like the other U.S. ballplayers who went south of the border, he found the playing conditions there intolerable and tried to return to the major leagues. Gardella and the others, however, were shut out by the Chandler ruling. Gardella sued baseball for $300,000. After losing the first ruling in July 1948, Gardella appealed. The Second Circuit Court of Appeals found in Gardella's favor, ruling that the advent of radio and television had involved baseball in interstate commerce and, thus, contrary to the Supreme Court's 1922 ruling in *Federal Baseball*, baseball was subject to the country's antitrust laws. The appeals court's ruling in *Gardella* stated that baseball's reserve clause is "shockingly repugnant to moral principles that . . . have been basic in America . . . [since] the Thirteenth Amendment . . . condemning 'involuntary servitude' . . . for the 'reserve clause' . . . results in something resembling peonage of the baseball player."[9] Damages of $300,000 were awarded to Gardella, and the 1922 Supreme Court decision was, in effect, reversed—at least, in the second circuit.

Baseball was sent into a tizzy. Its exemption and its reserve clause appeared to be terminally threatened, and many owners were questioning their new commissioner's tactics. Adumbrating McCarthyism, Branch Rickey stated that the reserve clause was opposed only by people with communist tendencies. Baseball appealed the Gardella ruling. With a new trial date set for November 1949, Chandler announced an amnesty for Mexican League jumpers in June 1949. Four months later, Gardella and baseball reached an out-of-court settlement.

But the fallout from the Mexican League went further. According to the testimony of Pee Wee Reese (Brooklyn Dodgers Hall of Fame shortstop during the 1940s and the 1950s) before the 1951 congressional hearings on organized baseball, the opportunity for players to sign with the Mexican League spurred the organization of the Players Guild in 1946 and the subsequent agreement on player benefits. The guild was organized by the labor lawyer Robert Murphy. Murphy attempted to form a players' union to engage in collective bargaining, but several false steps and effective intervention by Chandler thwarted the effort. The threat, however, made Chandler aware that some concessions had to be made. A joint owner/player committee was formed, and a package of new benefits was agreed upon, including the players' first pension fund, with both owner and player contributions; a minimum salary of $5,500; and spring training expense money of $25 a week, among other concessions. Chandler used both the carrot and the stick to hold labor at bay. Most credited Chandler for his successful maneuvering, though some owners felt he gave too much away to the players.

The 1946–1947 off-season kept Chandler busy. One brewing scandal concerned the Dodgers' famous manager Leo Durocher. Durocher was an outspoken figure who was constantly under fire for his fights with umpires and fans, his divorce, his lifestyle, his consorting with undesirable characters, and his visits to the racetrack. Chandler had called Leo to his office on more than one occasion to ask him to moderate his behavior. Then, after the 1946 season, Larry MacPhail of the Yankees hired away two of Durocher's coaches from the Dodgers, and there were rumors that he wanted to sign Durocher to manage. It seems that Branch Rickey of the Dodgers would not have minded if Durocher were hired away. At a spring training game in Havana in early March 1947, Durocher told some sportswriters that there were prominent gamblers sitting in MacPhail's box, presumably as his guests, and that if he [Durocher] were caught sitting with those people, he'd be suspended from the game. MacPhail demanded that Chandler take action against Durocher. Obligingly, Chandler held hearings on March 24 and March 28, and then, on April 9, just before the season was to begin, he suspended Durocher for one year. Durocher's transgression was spelled out by the commissioner: "an accumulation of unpleasant incidents . . . detrimental to baseball."[10]

Time magazine remarked that "Commissioner Chandler has done the seemingly impossible. He has made Durocher a sympathetic figure."[11] In his memoirs *Rhubarb in the Catbird Seat*, the legendary baseball announcer Red Barber summed up the incident:

> You have to understand that it was a war between Rickey and MacPhail. After Landis died, the owners had to come up with a new commissioner. Rickey wanted Ford Frick, a trained baseball

man. Well, if Rickey wanted Ford Frick, MacPhail was dead certain it wasn't going to be Frick. Whatever Rickey wanted, Rickey wasn't going to have. And MacPhail, a very powerful and persuasive figure, came up with Chandler.

Leo [Durocher] was caught in the middle. I thought it was an injustice. He is a much maligned man. I don't think anybody in baseball thought he should have been suspended. Rickey said to Chandler, "Happy, what have you done?" Even MacPhail, who had blown the whistle on Leo, was shocked.[12]

It seemed that no one came to Chandler's defense in the Durocher suspension. Arthur Daley, of the *New York Times*, commented, "It's like running a red light and being given the electric chair."[13] But even Daley may have given the benefit of the doubt to Chandler. In fact, Durocher was suspended for exercising his right to free speech and asserting that his behavior was being subjected to a double standard. Thus, in his effort to be Landis-like and wield the "best interests" clause via suspension, Chandler fell flat on his face.

Chandler's next challenge that off-season also involved Branch Rickey. The stakes, though, were considerably higher. Rickey had decided to bring Jackie Robinson, who had a spectacular season in Montreal, up to the major league club for the 1947 season. He was already up against an apparently overwhelming ownership vote against integrating baseball. The usual story goes something like this.

Larry MacPhail headed a committee made up of Ford Frick, Will Harridge, Sam Breadon (the owner of the St. Louis Cardinals), Philip Wrigley (the owner of the Chicago Cubs), and Tom Yawkey (the owner of the Boston Red Sox). The committee's charge was to write a report on baseball's labor problems and what to do about them. One section of the report, dated August 27, 1946, was entitled the "Race Question." In this section, the committee speculated that black ballplayers would bring black spectators to the park. This, in turn, would chase white spectators away from the game and ultimately reduce the value of the franchises. The authors might as well have been suburban real estate agents in the 1950s raising concerns about block busting. The report went

on to suggest that black players lacked "technique," "coordination," "competitive attitude," and "discipline," and that the Negro
Leagues failed to provide the proper training.[14]

Some three weeks after the report was circulated, the owners
met on September 16, 1946, at the Waldorf Astoria Hotel in New
York City. After discussing it, the owners voted 15 to 1 to endorse
the report's position against integrating the major leagues, with
Rickey being the sole dissenter.[15]

National League president Frick apparently asked that all
copies of the report be returned to him, so that he could burn them.
Except the commissioner's copy, which Chandler put in his file,
where it was not discovered until after his papers were donated to
the University of Kentucky library.

In his autobiography, Chandler tells a tale about Branch Rickey
visiting him at his home in Versailles, Kentucky.

> We faced each other in my walnut log cabin in my backyard. We
> sat on opposite sides of the big, old desk, in the cabin's book-
> lined study. Logs blazed and cracked in my great stone fireplace.
> We needed that fire. It was a cold, raw January day.
>
> Rickey was as emotional as I've ever seen him. He said he
> didn't know if he could do this in light of the opposition of his
> partners.
>
> I said "Branch, that 15–1 turndown at the Waldorf meet-
> ing—I think that was supposed to be mainly for my guidance,
> wouldn't you say?"
>
> Rickey nodded.
>
> I told Branch, "They'll never agree. . . . I am the only person
> on earth who can approve the transfer of the contract from Mon-
> treal to Brooklyn. . . .
>
> "I've already done a lot of thinking about this whole racial
> situation in our country. As a member of the Senate Military
> Affairs Committee I got to know a lot about our casualties dur-
> ing the war. Plenty of Negro boys were willing to go out and
> fight and die for this country. Is it right when they came back to
> tell them they can't play the national pastime? You know, Branch,
> I'm going to have to meet my Maker some day and if He asks
> me why I didn't let this boy play and I say it's because he's
> black that might not be a satisfactory answer."[16]

So, in Chandler's version, the owners cast a 15 to 1 vote against integration, and it was only Rickey's initiative and Chandler's fortitude that broke the baseball color line.

The owners have a different story. They deny that a vote was taken at the Waldorf meeting and state that many of them wanted to sign black players for their teams. In his memoirs, Ford Frick even claims that MacPhail had written a paragraph urging integration in his report, but that it was taken out because the owners feared the public's reaction.[17] Frick devotes an entire chapter in his memoirs to integration and never once mentions Happy Chandler. Given that Frick tried to burn all copies of the MacPhail report and that he was the NL president from 1934 to 1951 while nothing was done to integrate the game, it seems probable that his account is riddled with revisionist history. It also seems likely, however, that Chandler's account romanticizes his role in the matter. Baseball, after all, had no legal right to remain segregated. Both Landis and Frick had earlier stated that baseball had no rule against signing black players and that any owner was free to do so. So really all it took was an owner who was willing to stick his neck out. That was Branch Rickey. Rickey himself may have had mercenary motives, but it was he who made the first move. Once he did, there was little baseball could do to stop him. Still, here again, Chandler's acquiescence was bound to bring him a few more detractors among team owners. At least, Chandler thinks it did. In his autobiography, the chapter on integration is titled "Jackie Robinson, and My Downfall."

Chandler was not done alienating the owners. In 1949, Chandler inked baseball's first World Series television contract with Gillette, a six-year deal worth $1 million annually. Underscoring what a bad deal it was for baseball, Gillette turned around and sold its rights to NBC for $4 million a year. In reaction, Cardinals owner Fred Saigh dubbed Chandler the "bluegrass jackass."[18]

Along the way, Happy Chandler also managed to irritate individual owners. Back in the 1940s and 1950s, it was still commonplace for team owners to subsidize the reporters who covered their teams, providing transportation, room and board, and even handsome gratuities at Christmastime. Chandler made it known that he disfavored this practice, which seemed to compromise journalistic independence. Chandler irked other owners when he fined them for violating the player option rule and declared the affected players to be free agents. He commissioned an investigation of Del Webb, the Yankee owner whom Chandler called "the most refreshingly ignorant sonofabitch I ever met in my life,"[19] for his possible ties to the gambling industry. In short, it should have surprised no one that Happy Chandler did not receive the necessary twelve votes for reappointment in either December 1950 or March 1951. He resigned in June 1951, effective July 15, nine months before the official end of his first term.

Chandler left embittered at ownership, particularly his detractors. In his autobiography, *Heroes, Plain Folks and Skunks*, the last word refers to baseball's barons. The day he was installed as baseball's second commissioner, Chandler relates that he was cornered at the Mayflower Hotel in Washington, D.C., by then Cleveland Indians owner Alva Bradley. Bradley told him, "We all cheat, if we have to. This fellow cheats, that fellow cheats. I cheat, too. . . . In fact, we all cheat." Chandler reports that he responded, "Well, Mr. Bradley, I wish I'd known that before I signed on for this voyage."

One month after leaving office, Chandler testified before the Celler Committee hearings in the U.S. House of Representatives. He had these reflections about what was wrong with baseball, what should be done, and what the proper role of the commissioner was:

> These fellows are very fortunate that they own franchises—the 16 major-league club owners—and some of them think they own the game. They do not own baseball. They do control it. They think they own it, you understand, and they sometimes get delusions of grandeur and power.
>
> I would have loved to organize a third major league, or even a fourth, and I think a third could be organized very easily in the country.
>
> I thought I was bound to represent the American people first, then the baseball players and the umpires, and last the club owners. I mean because they own their own business, you understand.[20]

There is little doubt that in Happy Chandler's case, part of his difficulty with the owners came from this unrealistic and grandiose perception of his role.

Commissioner Ford Frick

On May 31, 1951, Cubs owner Philip Wrigley sent a memorandum from an owners' committee he chaired to the other owners. The memorandum began, "At some time in the not-to-distant [sic] future and certainly not later than May 1, 1952, the 16 major-league baseball club owners are going to be called upon to select a new commissioner of baseball."[21] It was the task of Wrigley's committee to consider how that job should be modified and what kind of person would best fill it. Parts of the memorandum are quite revealing.

> In an effort to make a dramatic move to restore public confidence, as well as to prevent a recurrence of a gambling scandal, the idea of having a commissioner was evolved and put into effect. This action was taken in an atmosphere verging on panic on the part of many club owners, but it proved to be a sound move and its intended purpose was accomplished. The commissioner, largely as a result of the personality and the reputation of the man selected, served as a symbol of baseball's desire to be honest.
>
> At the time the office was established, baseball as a business was relatively uncomplicated. Baseball as a whole was a much smaller entity. . . . Competition from other forms of recreation has become a factor of great importance over the last 32 years. At the time the commissioner's office was started, there was relatively little in the way of organized, aggressively promoted recreation, sports or otherwise. . . . All of these new forms of sports and recreation [golf, bowling, horse racing, football, basketball, and hockey] compete in some degree with baseball for a share of the consumer's recreation dollar. . . . It all means, of course, that baseball must be on its toes and up to date in its promotional methods to successfully meet this competition from so many sources.
>
> In actual practice, the commissioner's office has in effect become the central headquarters of a baseball trade association. From a one-man office, it has developed into a beehive of admin-

istrative operations, handling huge funds. . . . As the administrative operations of the commissioner's office have developed in
response to the new conditions, the main purpose for which the
job was set up has diminished in importance. The integrity of
baseball today in the public mind is at a high point, and has been
for many years.

Here, Wrigley and his colleagues are signaling some very important developments in the entertainment industry and presciently
calling for a new, more aggressive approach to marketing the game.
Although not explicitly stated, the implication is that the commissioner's office needed to become involved with business aspects of
the game and its promotion. Wrigley suggests that the czar who
protected the game's integrity was now an anachronism and perhaps baseball needed something more like a CEO. Had baseball
heeded the call of the Wrigley committee, the next fifty years might
have been much different in the baseball world. Instead, baseball
became tied up with congressional inquiries into the sport's presumed antitrust exemption, the exemption's relation to the historical role of the commissioner, and more internal bickering among
owners, as the NFL and, to a lesser degree, the NBA came to be
well-managed leagues that began to soar in popularity.

It didn't help that baseball chose Ford Frick as its next commissioner—a man who was singularly unprepared to take the office
to the next level. Indeed, he was not even able to maintain its traditional function. Many owners had had enough of the aggressive,
intrusive, and somewhat arbitrary styles of Landis and Chandler.
They were more interested in a commissioner who would either
stay out of their way or do their bidding, than in a commissioner
who would lead the industry as if it were a real business.

Landis and Chandler each had made major professional careers
for themselves before they came to baseball. Not Frick. He was a
lowly sports journalist before he became first a public relations
man for the National League in 1933 and then the NL president in
the same year. Frick was a baseball man through and through and
a rather mild-mannered one at that. He was the man whom the
backward-looking owners wanted, not some maverick who would
lead the industry forward in the post–World War II era. When Happy

Chandler asked who was going to fill the vacancy he was leaving in the commissioner's office and was told that the owners' choice was Frick, he commented, "It looks to me like the office of the commissioner is still vacant."[22]

Ford Frick was born in 1896, one of five children to Jacob and Emma Frick. Jacob was a grain farmer in northeast Indiana. Frick recalled his childhood years: "We had the whole world to ourselves. Woods to play in and lakes to swim in. We skated in the winter and played baseball in the summer. We made our own recreation. I suppose by modern standards we were underprivileged. But we never thought of ourselves as underprivileged."[23]

Frick worked his way through Indiana's DePauw University by being a waiter in a student boardinghouse and as a stringer for the *Chicago Tribune*. He played on his school's baseball team but was a self-described ordinary first baseman with a weak arm. After college, Frick moved to Colorado Springs and married a local woman. He taught English at Colorado College and wrote editorials and covered sports for the *Colorado Springs Gazette*. After five years in Colorado, in 1921, he moved to New York City, where he was a sportswriter for the Hearst paper the *New York American* and later for the afternoon Hearst paper the *New York Journal*. Covering the Yankees, Frick struck up a relationship with Babe Ruth, for whom he did some ghostwriting, and many other players and managers. He eventually became a part-time baseball and classical music radio broadcaster.

New York Giants manager John McGraw convinced Frick to take the new job as director of the NL's Public Service Bureau in 1933, and when NL president John Heydler resigned, Frick became the NL president on November 9, 1934. Although league presidents had a good deal of authority in those days, Frick did not put his mark on many events. But two stand out.

The first suggests the hand of a weak leader. On June 2, 1937, Frick suspended the pitching great Dizzy Dean indefinitely for comments "detrimental to baseball." Dean's transgression stemmed from a game between his Cardinals and the New York Giants on May 19. Dean was called for a balk by umpire George Barr. A week later, a local paper in Belleville, Illinois, purported to quote Dean as saying that Barr and Frick were "the two biggest crooks in baseball." Following the suspension, Frick asked Dean for an apology. When none was forthcoming, Frick summoned Dean to his office, where Dean stated that he was misquoted and had said nothing of the sort. Dean went back to St. Louis, and Frick continued to demand an apology. A few days passed with Dean denying that he made that statement. And before Dean could miss a turn in the rotation, Frick recanted in the third person as follows: "The president of the National League was not present at the time of these occurrences and therefore he can have no definite proof. Under the circumstances he is willing to accept the statement of Mr. Dean at its face value. He considers the case closed."[24]

The second event was the opening of baseball's Hall of Fame in 1936. Frick is generally credited with the idea, and, indeed, Frick said that starting the hall was his proudest accomplishment in his thirty-two years in the baseball industry. Describing Cooperstown, Frick stated, "There's a portrait of me up there which I don't like. It says I was father of the whole thing. Judge Landis never liked the idea, never warmed up to it, probably because he didn't think of it first."[25]

Frick's tenure as NL president coincided, of course, with the second half of Landis's reign, when the commissioner was resisting overtures to integrate the game. Frick was a silent partner during this period. In his memoirs, Frick recounts a supportive role he played toward integrating baseball during 1947. Basically, he told players who resisted integration that their behavior would not be tolerated. To the extent that Frick's account is accurate, it should be understood as supporting a decision that had already been made by Rickey and Chandler. Frick chose the Hall of Fame, not his support for integration, as his most important contribution to the game.

Frick became the commissioner at a complicated time. Suburbanization, the automobile, and the television set were assaulting America, with profound implications for the state of both minor and major league baseball. The U.S. Congress's simmering concern over baseball's antitrust status boiled to the surface with several hearings and numerous proposed pieces of legislation throughout the 1950s. By his own count, Frick testified seventeen times before

Ford Frick, the commissioner
of baseball from September 20,
1951, to November 16, 1965.

congressional committees. In 1952, the Toolson case attacking baseball's antitrust exemption was heard by the Supreme Court. Beginning in 1953, baseball was also confronted for the first time in its
modern era (since the 1903 agreement) with (1) relocating franchises, (2) its first prospective rival league since the 1914 Federal
League in the Continental League in 1959, and (3) its first expansion since 1903 in 1961–1962, among other things. Baseball navi-
gated most of these challenges successfully, and the industry was,
by any reasonable reckoning, stronger in 1965 when Frick left
office than it was in 1951 when he entered.

Also by reasonable reckoning, however, Frick did little affir-
matively to guide the ship. Frick had uttered "that's not in my
jurisdiction" so many times that the mocking tagline followed him
around like Ron and Hermione follow Harry Potter. Leonard Koppett commented on Frick's commissionership: "Frick was the first
(and I would argue the last) baseball commissioner who really
understood the job's function and limitations. He held office for 15
years and was often vilified by outsiders for knuckling under to
club-owner demands."[26]

Thus, it was not without irony when Ford Frick testified before the U.S. Congress on July 31, 1951, that the office of baseball's commissioner was established in order that there "could be no possible concern about the independence and impartiality of baseball's commission."[27] Of course, the implied comparison was to baseball's ruling National Commission from 1903 to 1920, the three-man body that had been controlled by Ban Johnson, the AL president, and Garry Herrmann, the owner of the Cincinnati Reds. Frick was not an owner, but many thought he might as well have been.

A few years earlier, in 1946, Bert Bell had been named as commissioner of the National Football League. Bell immediately sold his ownership interest in the Pittsburgh Steelers. Bell may have had the owners' interests in mind, but at least no one could accuse him of a conflict of interest—a problem that was to plague Bud Selig a half-century later, until he sold his interest in the Milwaukee Brewers in 2005, nearly thirteen years after he effectively took over as commissioner.[28]

When Frick took office in the summer of 1951, pressure had been building up for major league expansion. The Pacific Coast League (PCL) wanted to be declared an open classification league with the ultimate goal of becoming a third major league. Once Happy Chandler was out of office, he told Congress that he supported a third top league to join the AL and the NL. Frick was more guarded. Without the PCL becoming a major league, the population and the industrial growth on the West Coast made it inevitable that some existing teams would want to move there. But before this could happen, the fifty-year-old tradition of franchise stability had to be ruptured. Several medium-size cities had two teams in the early 1950s, and these would be the first to give. Not surprisingly, Bill Veeck, who owned the St. Louis Browns at the time, was out ahead of the curve in 1953. He applied to the AL to be able to move his team to Baltimore. The AL owners voted him down, 5 to 2, on March 16, 1953. Though Frick was not at the league meeting, he made it clear that he opposed Veeck's plan. Veeck, with his maverick ideas for eliminating the reserve clause, revenue sharing among the teams, and innovative team marketing, was a thorn in

Frick's side. Frick did not want Veeck to be the first owner to benefit from a team relocation.

However, on March 18, 1953, the NL owners convened again to grant their unanimous permission to Boston Braves owner Lou Perini to move his team to Milwaukee—a move that was to have a profound impact on the future development of the commissioner's office. Following the 1953 season, after Veeck had sold off his ownership interest in the Browns, the NL finally approved the team's move to Baltimore—and the era of peripatetic franchises and public stadium subsidies was in full swing. In 1954, the Philadelphia Athletics moved to Kansas City (only to move to Oakland thirteen years later). After the 1957 season, the Brooklyn Dodgers and the New York Giants moved to Los Angeles and San Francisco, respectively. Then in 1961 and 1962, the AL and the NL each expanded by two teams.

The AL expansion provided another occasion for Frick to thumb his nose at Veeck. Veeck had resurfaced with a controlling interest in the Chicago White Sox in 1959. He hatched a plan to move his team to Los Angeles and had lined up the necessary votes in the AL to support the relocation. But Frick, who had all along proclaimed Los Angeles to be "open territory," changed his tune and ruled that L.A. was now the territory of the Dodgers and Walter O'Malley. If the White Sox wanted to move there, the team would have to indemnify O'Malley. O'Malley demanded that the new team play first at Wrigley Field in Los Angeles, then move to his new park in Chavez Ravine and pay him $350,000 in territorial damages. Needless to say, the feisty Veeck was not happy. He and his co-owner, Hank Greenberg, tried to convince other AL owners to reject the demand for territorial damages and force the matter to a vote of all sixteen owners. With the two leagues each providing eight votes on either side of the issue, Frick would be forced to cast the tie breaker. Here's what Veeck wrote about the issue in his book *Veeck—as in Wreck*:

> The last thing Frick wanted to do was to vote. Frick was so anxious not to vote that he looked ill. Frick has a slogan of his own, a slogan that has served him throughout the years. It goes: "You boys settle it among yourselves." For that he gets paid $65,000 a year.[29]

In 1961, the AL admitted the Los Angeles Angels into the league as an expansion team. The team moved to Anaheim in 1965 and changed its name to the California Angels. (In 1997, pursuant to an agreement with the city of Anaheim, which invested some $30 million in the renovation of the Angels' stadium, the team changed its name again to the Anaheim Angels. In 2005, the team owner is trying to have his cake and eat it, too, keeping the team at its refurbished stadium in Anaheim and reclaiming the team's original name, the Los Angeles Angels. The matter is in litigation.)

Frick was questioned about baseball's suddenly footloose franchises at congressional hearings in 1958. His answer rationalizes the 1950s moves but fails to justify subsequent moves and move threats:

> There is demand for major league baseball around the country. Now when two clubs or three clubs are in a town and one of them moves, it still leaves that town with baseball. As commissioner of baseball, I think that is good, because you are taking baseball to a new community without leaving the old town barren.
>
> However, when the time comes that you start moving a club from a one-club city to another one-club city merely for the sake of moving, then the commissioner is very definitely opposed. . . .
>
> I think the removal of a club from Washington would be catastrophic. I don't think organized baseball can afford not to be in the nation's capital.[30]

While Frick's 1958 comment on baseball in D.C. may have been prophetic, his policy on recognizing Roger Maris's 1961 home run record was not. Frick, an old friend of and a ghostwriter for Babe Ruth, decided that Maris's sixty-one home runs in 1961 could not be compared to Ruth's sixty home runs in 1927 because the season had 162 games in 1961 and only 154 games in 1927. Thus, Frick, in perhaps his only imperious decision, declared that Maris's feat would enter the record books with an asterisk. Frick did not bother to ponder the effects of the 1961 Yankees having to do more traveling, put up with more media pressure, or face more physically imposing pitchers. Nor did Frick's decision account for its effect on baseball fans' obsession with records and the urge to make cross-generational comparisons. In what may have been his most popular move as commissioner, in 1992 Fay Vincent undid the curse of the asterisk.

Still, Frick's decade-and-a-half reign is most notable for what he didn't do. Baseball was in a period of transition. Enormous opportunities were available to promote and market the game. Television exposure was growing and, with it, possibilities for tie-in sales, creating and selling logo products, and making package deals with advertisers, among other things. Exploiting these potentials, however, would have required a lively and creative commissioner's office, staffed with marketing experts. Frick preferred the old, sleepy office of Landis's day. Meanwhile, the NFL went marching on. Between 1961 and 1972, for instance, the percentage of Americans stating that pro football was their favorite sport rose from 21 to 36 percent, while those identifying baseball fell from 34 to 21 percent.[31]

An internal report on baseball's problems, prepared by a committee of owners, league executives, and an outside consultant, suggested that the industry's governance problems were more widespread than just inadequate initiative in marketing. Here are some of the report's findings.

1. Owners used to have the public's respect. "Today we find the term 'major league magnate' invariably used in a derogatory manner."

2. "[An] unwillingness on the part of men in authority to establish policy or determine goals and their methods of attainment."

3. "Lack of cooperation between [sic] clubs . . . A lack of planning and a failure to measure tomorrow's effect of today's hasty statement is responsible for most errors in public relations judgment. . . . A principal reason for this lack of anticipation is the almost complete absence of cooperation between [sic] the member clubs."

4. "Lack of united front on policy questions . . . From time to time it appears that half of the club owners or officials are public dissenters on one or more matters of overall policy. . . . This disunity has been one of the blacker spots of present public policy methods."

5. "There is evidence that during the past few years there has grown up a suspicion that the office of the commissioner is overly dominated by the owners and operators. True or not, that is bad. We must remember that the commissioner is the representative of the public. In meetings, in his discussions, in conferences he must advocate for these unrepresented groups."[32]

Frick announced his retirement in 1964, making him the only commissioner to leave the job on his own accord at the end of his term. In his last formal communication to the owners, Frick finally opened up and made it clear that the problems referenced in the 1950s report had not abated:

So long as the owners and operators refuse to look beyond the day and the hour; so long as clubs and individuals persist in gaining personal headlines through public criticism of their associates; so long as baseball people are unwilling to abide by the rules they themselves make; so long as expediency is permitted to replace sound judgment, there can be no satisfactory solution.[33]

Speaking about the commissioner's job in a 1972 interview, Frick stated, "Good Lord, I didn't want it. My name had been bandied about but I wasn't interested."[34] As we shall see, Frick is not the only commissioner to profess no interest in taking the job. One wonders whether Frick and the others were ever told that they could just say no.

Even though Wrigley and his colleagues felt that upholding the integrity of baseball was no longer an important function in the 1950s, Frick's own initial conception of the job was precisely to safeguard the perceived honesty of the game. He told the House Judiciary Committee in 1957, "Since the establishment of the office of the commissioner, the commissioner's primary concern has been and should be the preservation of the integrity and honesty of the game on the field."[35] Somewhat curiously, just seven years later in his November 1964 communication to the owners, Frick sang a different tune: "The . . . problem that led to the creation of the commissioner's office no longer exists. Public faith and confidence in the honesty of the game and the players has [sic] been restored. Today, it is the conduct of the owners and the operators themselves that is being questioned by the press and public."[36]

While it seems clear that Frick attended to few matters other than integrity, it is unclear how well he managed the few integrity issues that did arise. Yankees co-owner Del Webb was in the construction business. In 1947, he built the Flamingo Hotel in Las Vegas, the first of that town's luxury gambling hotels, for Bugsy Siegel. Webb's company also took an ownership interest in the hotel. Bill Veeck wrote that it was generally understood among the team owners that Frick would require Webb to divest himself of his ownership in the hotel as soon as it was financially feasible.[37] Not only did Frick not do this, but he stood idly by as Webb bought another Las Vegas gambling hotel, the Sahara, in August 1961.

Frick also favored Webb in on-field matters in a manner that brought baseball's competitive integrity into question. At the end of the 1954 season, Webb and his co-owner, Dan Topping, arranged for their business associate Arnold Johnson to buy the Philadelphia Athletics and move them to Kansas City.[38] In his autobiography, Hank Greenberg, the former star player and baseball executive, wrote about the resulting relationship between the Kansas City A's and the New York Yankees: "They traded some forty or fifty ballplayers back and forth between the clubs so the Yankees, instead of losing a ballplayer, would trade him to Kansas City and he'd play there and develop then come back and play for the Yankees again. This, of course, created unfair competition."[39] That is, the A's served as a de facto farm team for the Yankees, enabling the Yankees to get around optioning rules on their players. Through this pipeline passed such Yankee notables as Roger Maris, Ralph Terry, Art Ditmar, and Hector Lopez. Commissioner Frick watched in silence.[40]

By doing little, diverting his attention from wrongdoing, and defending baseball in Congress, Frick made few enemies among team owners, with the exception of Bill Veeck. That was the key to his longevity in office.

Despite the festering problems, baseball in 1965 seemed to appreciate the laissez-faire posture that Frick had brought to the commissionership. In the barons' next selection, they did Frick one better.

Commissioner William Eckert

Nobody really knows what possessed the owners to elect General William Eckert as the sport's fourth commissioner. Perhaps Ford Frick's parting communication scared them. In it, not only did Frick lambaste the owners for their selfishness, but he claimed that the old powers of the commissioner's office urgently needed to be restored. Frick was referring to the two changes in baseball's constitution made in 1945: the first removing the clause that forbade owners from taking their grievances against the commissioner to court, and the second stating that the commissioner could not contravene articles of the baseball constitution in implementing his "best interests" powers.[41] In truth, neither of these changes would have prevented Frick from being an assertive leader had he the will and the ability to be one. (The owners did restore the prohibition on suing over the commissioner's decisions, but, as we shall see, this did not deter some aggrieved owners from legal action.)

Following an owners' meeting in November 1964, the *Sporting News* interviewed Arthur Allyn, the Chicago White Sox owner, about the process of finding a new leader. Allyn was expansive in answering, sometimes heavy on spin and sometimes revealing:

> The new commissioner will be selected not as a representative of the owners, but as a representative of the public. . . . It was generally agreed that no politicians and no person connected with baseball would be considered. . . . It cannot be someone in baseball, because no matter who he is and no matter how unimpeachable his character, there are some ties and associations from which he cannot divorce himself. And even if as commissioner he made every decision fairly and without prejudice, nobody would believe it if it happened to involve a club or a league office in which he previously had a position.[42]

Eckert was certainly not a baseball insider. Far from it. And he was not a politician. Baseball had its man.

Eckert was born on January 29, 1908, in Freeport, Illinois. His father owned an animal feed store. Young William enlisted in the National Guard at age fifteen and went on to study at West Point, where he finished 128th in a class of 241. He had a distinguished Air Force career, though, winning several medals during World War II. Eckert had been comptroller of the Air Force when he retired at age fifty-three in 1961, following a mild heart attack. He settled in Washington, D.C., and worked in management at several electronics companies between 1961 and 1965.

Baseball's barons were originally considering a list of 156 potential candidates to replace Frick. When the list was cut down to 15, Eckert's name was not on it at first, but later, apparently on the urging of Tigers owner John Fetzer, his name was restored. Fetzer, who was convinced that baseball needed strong business leadership, promoted Eckert's candidacy because of his business experience. Fetzer was right about the need for effective business leadership but wrong about Eckert.

Clark Griffith, the former owner of the Minnesota Twins, was at the meeting that elected Eckert. He recalls that Cardinals owner Gussie Busch and Dodgers owner Walter O'Malley were strong supporters of Eckert's, but "later it turned out that they were thinking of another general with a similar name"—General Eugene Zuckert, the former secretary of the Air Force.[43]

The announcement of Eckert led one New York columnist to exclaim, "My God, they've elected the unknown soldier."[44]

Eckert knew little about baseball. At the announcement of his appointment, a reporter inquired when was the last time that the new commissioner had seen a game. Eckert allowed that he had been to a Dodgers game in Los Angeles a year or two earlier. On follow-up, it became apparent that Eckert did not know the Dodgers had previously played in Brooklyn. As the gaffes continued, baseball created a five-man cabinet of insiders to tutor Eckert.

It didn't seem to help. During his first tour of spring training camps, Eckert opined publicly on the similarities of baseball to the Air Force: "First, you have highly competitive units—different

William Eckert, the
commissioner of baseball
from November 17, 1965,
to November 20, 1968.

teams, just as you have squadrons. Then you have rules and regulations in both, rules to be made and interpreted and changed. And
third, you have franchises, like Air Force bases, being opened and
moved to fill needs."[45] Apparently, one morning Eckert's special
assistant, John McHale, came into the commissioner's office and
noticed that he seemed somewhat distressed. McHale inquired
whether anything was wrong, and Eckert responded that the Yankees had been sold without anyone notifying the commissioner's
office. McHale checked out the story and discovered that the com-
edy team Bob and Ray had put on a skit that morning about one of
them buying the team. At a joint owners' meeting, Eckert referred
to the Cincinnati Cardinals, a nice alliteration perhaps but one that
went unappreciated by those in attendance. And so it went.

Eckert got the standard seven-year, $65,000 annual salary con-
tract. And it looked like the owners would have to endure. The first
important challenge came immediately. The Milwaukee Braves and
the National League were being sued by the state of Wisconsin

because the Braves' ownership intended to move the team to Atlanta for the 1966 season. The Braves would be the first team to violate the Frick rule, moving out of a city with only one franchise. Bud Selig worked on the case for Wisconsin and was a witness for the prosecution—a story to be told in greater detail in chapter 6. Eckert stayed away from the trial and left matters up to baseball's attorneys, led in the court room by Bowie Kuhn. The Braves and the NL lost at trial, but the decision was reversed in the Wisconsin Supreme Court, which ruled that baseball's exemption protected it from the state's antitrust suit.

Two years later, Eckert stood by as Charlie Finley announced his intention to move his Kansas City Athletics to Oakland, which he did for the 1968 season. In 1968, the NL added two new teams in Montreal and San Diego, and the following year the AL added teams in Seattle and Kansas City. In April 1968, Martin Luther King Jr. was assassinated, and two months later Robert Kennedy was shot. Baseball suffered bad press because Eckert issued no directives and no games were canceled. The barons had had enough. Less than halfway through his term, Eckert was dismissed on December 6, 1968.

5

The Undistinguished Middle II
From Kuhn to Vincent

On February 4, 1969, Bowie Kuhn was elected baseball's fifth commissioner. The owners had been searching for a replacement for Eckert for two months, and successive votes produced deadlocks. The three finalists were Lee MacPhail, the general manager of the Yankees and the son of Larry MacPhail; John McHale, the president of the expansion Montreal Expos; and Chub Feeney, the vice president of the San Francisco Giants. None could garner the necessary three-quarters support.

McHale went to Bowie Kuhn, the NL attorney, seeking advice. Kuhn, who had his own ambitions for the job, told McHale that he had an obligation to the Expos and should withdraw his name from consideration. Which he did. Soon thereafter, Kuhn was chosen as a compromise candidate and given the job on an interim basis, for one year at $100,000.

Commissioner Bowie Kuhn

Unlike his predecessor, Kuhn had grown up a baseball fan. During his high school years, he worked the outfield scoreboard at the old Griffith Stadium for Washington Senators games. For his efforts he was paid one dollar a day—a remuneration that only the late Calvin

Griffith would have seen fit to offer. Still, that was good enough for young Bowie; of it, he wrote, "I have had only a few jobs in my life, but the best was scoreboard boy at Griffith Stadium."[1]

Kuhn's father was the son of a Bavarian farmer and had come to America in 1894. Though he had little formal education, he worked his way up to become a top executive for a D.C. power company. His mother had a pedigree bloodline. Her family tree included five governors, two senators, and the frontiersman Jim Bowie, the inventor of the Bowie knife. Kuhn was born on October 28, 1926, and had two older siblings. He writes that "My mother and father took enormous pride in the academic achievements of their children. Good report cards were received with jubilation, which inspired the student in us."[2] He was the president of his senior class in high school and was voted the "most popular" and "most likely to succeed."

Although he had an imposing physical presence, reaching six feet five inches, by his senior year, Kuhn had little athletic talent. The basketball coach at his school was Red Auerbach, the future Hall of Fame coach of the Boston Celtics. In his 1987 autobiography, *Hardball: The Education of a Baseball Commissioner*, Kuhn recounts an experience he had with Auerbach:

> The only varsity sport I attempted was basketball. . . . Coach Auerbach stopped me in the hall one day, looked up and said, "Son, you're the tallest boy in the school. How come you're not out for the basketball team?"
>
> "Because I'm a lousy player," I replied.
>
> "You let me be the judge of that," he answered, and suited me up for a week of workouts under his guidance. After a week, he took me aside and said, "Son, you were right, and I was wrong. You won't have to come back tomorrow."[3]

Kuhn went on to college at Franklin and Marshall and then transferred to Princeton, where he got his B.A. in economics. He received his law degree from the University of Virginia and took a job for $4,000 annually at the large D.C. firm Willkie, Farr & Gallagher, in large part because it had the NL among its clients. He was involved in the preparations for some of the baseball executives who testified before Congress in the 1950s and was the lead lawyer in defending the Milwaukee Braves and the NL in the state of Wisconsin's antitrust suit against baseball. In his book, Kuhn states that he had little sympathy for the Braves because he believed that teams should move only when in dire straits. Kuhn writes that his heart was not in the case, which might help to account for the defeat of the NL and the Braves in trial court.

Kuhn was vacationing with his wife during the 1968 Christmas holiday in Dutchess County, New York, when he received a phone call from Yankee president Mike Burke. Kuhn explained that Burke told him the owners were hopelessly stalemated in their effort to select a new commissioner and asked him whether he would be interested in the job. Like Frick before him and Selig after him, Kuhn disclaimed any interest: "I told Mike that I was flattered but that I was not interested. I said, 'Mike, I am a very private person and I like it that way and I want to leave it that way.' "[4]

Whether this disavowal was a bargaining stance or not, it seems to have had little bearing on reality. Later in his book, Kuhn states that Commissioner Landis was his boyhood hero. At his inaugural press conference, Kuhn told the media, "Every American boy dreams of being commissioner and I'm no different. I'm honored and delighted to take over this important job."[5] And for the next fifteen years, Bowie Kuhn did not spare an effort to continue in the job.

Kuhn certainly brought a new image to the office. Not only was he a giant in physical stature next to Commissioner Eckert, but he carried himself with a regal air. The former sportswriter par excellence Red Smith described Kuhn: "There has never been a commissioner who stood more erect, wore better clothes, or kept his shoes more meticulously polished than Bowie Kuhn."[6] To this he might have added: or managed to never have a single hair on his head out of place.

Kuhn's hyper-organized life was challenged almost from his first day in the commissioner's office. In the spring of 1969, baseball was facing the prospect of its first player strike. The union wanted the owners' pension contribution to increase commensurately with the increase in baseball's new national television contract. The baseball historian Robert Burk wrote, "Kuhn, seeking ratification as Eckert's permanent replacement, recognized that his brokering a deal and 'saving the season' would raise his as-yet microscopic stature and force his coronation upon the magnates."[7] Kuhn convinced the owners to meet the players' halfway and thereby averted the strike. He won round praise in the media and was off to a good start.

His next intervention did not go as well. Don Clendenon and Jesus Alou had been selected by the expansion Montreal Expos in the player draft. The Expos then packaged the two players in a trade to the Houston Astros for the emerging young star Rusty Staub. Shortly after the trade was announced, Clendenon said that he was going to retire from the game. Under baseball's rules, Clendenon's retirement would nullify the trade. But Kuhn, showing his interventionist penchant, decided that it was in the best interests of baseball for Staub to play for John McHale's Expos, whether or not Clendenon was part of the deal. Kuhn reasoned that the Expos were a new team and they needed a young star. Not even Landis had been so bumptiously dirigiste in regulating player movement. Many wondered whether Kuhn might not have been attempting to repay McHale for dropping out of the commissioner's race.

Not surprisingly, Houston's owner denounced Kuhn for abusing his powers and went on to sue the Expos. Meanwhile, other players were substituted for Clendenon and Alou in the trade. Then, on April 3, Clendenon reversed course and agreed to play for Montreal for $50,000 a year, instead of the $36,000 he was to be paid in Houston. Unwittingly, Kuhn had established a fad. On April 19, when the Red Sox traded outfielder Ken Harrelson to the Cleveland Indians, Harrelson announced his retirement. He explained that he did not want to leave Boston because he was a popular figure in New England and was able to earn hundreds of thousands of dollars in nonbaseball income. Kuhn encouraged Harrelson to accept the trade, and Harrelson saw his $50,000 salary in Boston doubled to $100,000 in Cleveland. New York Mets first baseman Ed Kranepool was catching on. He told the press, "Great, if I'm traded, I'll retire before I report."[8]

Kuhn's admiration of Commissioner Landis was on full display by June 1969. He had learned that three owners of the Atlanta Braves—Bill Bartholomay, John Louis, and Del Coleman—were also directors of the development company Parvin-Dohrmann. Not only was Parvin-Dohrmann suspected of having mob connections, but it had begun buying into Las Vegas casinos. A's owner Charlie Finley owned stock in the company. Kuhn summoned them all to his office and asked them to sell their interests in the company. Only Coleman opted for Parvin-Dohrmann over baseball.

In July, Kuhn pulled off a major PR coup. Professional baseball had begun in 1869 with the barnstorming Cincinnati Redlegs. It was the one-hundredth anniversary of professional baseball. So Kuhn convinced Richard Nixon to host a baseball centennial celebration at the White House the day before the All-Star Game. Nixon turned the White House over to baseball for an evening and a day. Kuhn stood side-by-side with the president as he introduced over a hundred baseball celebrities who were present at the festivities.

All in all, it was a successful first year for Kuhn. The owners were sufficiently satisfied to offer Kuhn the real job for seven years, at $150,000 annually.

Year two was not as smooth. It began with Curt Flood, the slick fielding centerfielder of the St. Louis Cardinals, bringing an antitrust suit against baseball over its reserve clause. Then, in late January, the Wharton School presented its study on the organization of baseball, which had been commissioned after the dismissal of Eckert. Wharton recommended centralizing the management structure by requiring administrative committees, such as the Player Relations Committee (PRC), to report to the commissioner. The owners rejected the Wharton report, believing that it put too much power in the hands of the new commissioner. (Though over time virtually all of its recommendations were adopted.)

On February 19, based on a story in *Sports Illustrated*, Kuhn suspended Tigers pitcher Denny McLain indefinitely for his alleged involvement with a Michigan gambling ring. Kuhn admitted he had no hard evidence but, his legal background notwithstanding, decided to suspend McLain while he conducted an investigation.

Bowie Kuhn, the commissioner
of baseball from February 4,
1969, to September 30, 1984.

McLain was allowed to return on July 1, but his behavior was
bizarre and violent, leading to two more suspensions before the
1970 season ended. Three suspensions in one season stands as a
baseball record, but not one that opened the doors at Cooperstown.

Meanwhile, the expansion Seattle Pilots were failing. The team
was unable to pay its bills, and several lawsuits were filed against
it. Kuhn couldn't stop the bleeding or find new buyers for the team
in Seattle. On March 31, 1970, the team was awarded by a bankruptcy referee to a group in Milwaukee headed by Bud Selig and
Ed Fitzgerald for $10.8 million. Opening day was a week away.
The city of Seattle was soon to bring an antitrust suit against baseball for taking away its team.

In his autobiography, Kuhn made a perceptive comment about
Seattle and other host cities: "Some baseball people came in time
to conclude that Seattle was a bad baseball town. I do not think
that is a correct assessment of Seattle or that there is such a thing

in North America. Ineffective ownership is usually the problem in places where baseball struggles."[9] Unfortunately, Kuhn, despite serious efforts, was unable to implement this philosophy in the case of the Washington Senators, who fled to Texas before the 1972 season. Equally unfortunate, subsequent commissioners have not hesitated to state that certain cities would not be suitable for baseball if they did not build a new stadium with public funds.

Not deterred by his problematic handling of the McLain situation, Kuhn found another target when *Look* magazine published excerpts from Jim Bouton's book *Ball Four* in May. Bouton wrote openly about the sometimes sordid life in the Yankees' clubhouse and his various misadventures with teammates as Peeping Toms when the team was on the road. Kuhn's puritanical instincts were offended, so he called Bouton into his office to advise him of his displeasure. Bouton's publisher couldn't let the occasion pass, beginning a publicity campaign under the slogan: "The book baseball tried to ban."

But May 1970 brought a more important development for the commissioner's office. Under pressure from Flood's antitrust suit, team owners were inclined to exhibit goodwill toward the players. They agreed with the union to have player grievances reviewed by an independent arbitration panel. Up to this point, such review was the sole province of the commissioner, yet it was a power that most commissioners would be content to abandon. Adjudicating player grievances often meant player suspensions or free agent designations, which served only to alienate one owner or another. Commissioners like Kuhn wanted to keep their jobs and avoid making unnecessary enemies.

The Flood case was heard in federal district court in June 1970. In August, the presiding judge ruled in baseball's favor, stating that only Congress or the U.S. Supreme Court could undo the sport's antitrust exemption. The U.S. Court of Appeals upheld the district court's ruling in April 1971, and then, in a 5 to 3 vote on June 19, 1972, the Supreme Court closed the book on Flood. The decision, written by Justice Blackmun, however, left some ambiguity in the scope of baseball's business activities that were covered by the exemption. This ambiguity has been the grist for many challenges to baseball's exemption and to contradictory judicial decisions in different circuits in recent years.[10]

In trial, one of the arguments adduced by baseball executives was that any needed changes in the reserve system could be adequately addressed in collective bargaining. Kuhn repeated this view in a statement after the district court judge's ruling.[11] Though the argument may have been effective in court, it proved counterproductive, as it also inspired the future efforts of the Players Association (PA).

While Kuhn's role in the PA's challenge to the reserve clause was not central, the advent of free agency did transpire on his watch. In his memoirs, the former head of the PA Marvin Miller credits Kuhn with being so hostile to the players that he motivated them for the struggle.

> While the total failure of that effort stemmed from the owners' blunders, Kuhn must be singled out as the most important contributor to the successes of the Players Association. His moves consistently backfired; his attempts at leadership created divisions. His inability to distinguish between reality and his prejudices, his lack of concern for the rights of players, sections of the press, and even of the stray, unpopular owner—all combined to make Kuhn a vital ingredient in the growth and strength of the union. To paraphrase Voltaire on God, if Bowie Kuhn had never existed, we would have had to invent him.[12]

Briefly, the struggle against the reserve clause advanced as follows. In 1974, star pitcher Catfish Hunter signed a two-year contract with Charlie Finley's Oakland A's. One contract provision called for Finley to put half of Hunter's compensation into an annuity. During 1974, Finley made no payments into the annuity, violating the terms of the contract. Hunter filed a grievance, and the three-person arbitration panel, headed by Peter Seitz, ruled that Hunter was no longer bound by the contract. That is, he was a free agent. Hunter went on to sign a lucrative multiyear deal with the Yankees in 1975.

Seeing the cracks in the reserve clause system, pitchers Dave McNally of the Expos and Andy Messersmith of the Dodgers refused to sign the 1975 contracts offered by their respective clubs. Their clubs exercised the renewal clause in the standard player contract, unilaterally signing them to the option year. After the season, McNally and Messersmith claimed that they had played out their option year under the reserve clause and hence were now free agents. The owners disagreed, and the case went before Seitz's arbitration panel. After four weeks, Seitz wrote a sixty-one-page decision, ruling on behalf of the players and urging that the two sides establish reasonable principles for free agency through collective bargaining. The owners summarily fired Seitz and then appealed his decision at federal district court. After a defeat in district court, the owners appealed to the circuit court of appeals, where in March 1976 they lost again.

According to Marvin Miller, during the four weeks that Seitz deliberated on the McNally/Messersmith matter, Seitz went to Kuhn and Miller and urged them to reach a compromise agreement on free agency. Not only did Kuhn spurn such suggestions, when Seitz finally ruled on behalf of the players, Kuhn proceeded to litigate the case to death. Although these maneuvers were largely out of the public's eye, they were crucial decisions by baseball's leadership that came at a pivotal turning point in the game's history. Had Kuhn been more foresighted and accepted the inevitability of some form of free agency, he would have compromised on the issue with the Players Association. The work stoppages and bitterness that ensued might have been avoided, and a better-designed system may have resulted. Of course, the opportunity for constructive and cooperative relations that was undermined by Kuhn in 1976 was then compounded many times over ten years later by Ueberroth, when he led the owners in collusion. Together, these two events, more than any others, are responsible for the historical distrust and dysfunctionality in the relationship between baseball's barons and the players.

Back in 1976, the owners took out their frustration over the Seitz decision on the fans, as well as on the players, by locking out the players from spring training camps. In a more productive effort, Kuhn persuaded the owners to reopen the camps on March 17. The season proceeded without a basic agreement until an accord was reached in July.

When the 1976 agreement expired after the 1979 season, however, the owners had regrouped and were geared for battle. They wanted teams losing a free agent to be compensated with a major league player from the signing team. Marvin Miller correctly perceived that this would substantially lower the value of free agents, and he resisted the owners' compensation proposal tooth and nail. A strike in 1980 was averted only when the owners accepted Miller's suggestion for a joint study committee to look into the compensation issue. The study committee made a proposal that the owners rejected. The owners then declared that they would implement their own system, and the players went on strike in the middle of the 1981 season. The strike began on June 12, 1981, and lasted until August 1, just seven days before the owners' insurance policy was to exhaust its funds. In the end, the owners suffered through fifty days of a regular season strike, the longest in professional sports to that point, and they accepted a compensation proposal similar to the one that had come out of the study committee. In short, the owners lost the skirmish, and many blamed Kuhn for not providing better leadership.

Meanwhile, Kuhn had been fighting other battles. One of the most publicized was his blocking the attempted sale of Oakland A's players by Charlie Finley in June 1976. Suspecting that he would not be able to re-sign his star players Vida Blue, Rollie Fingers, and Joe Rudi in an era of free agency, Finley agreed to sell Blue to the Yankees for $1.5 million and Fingers and Rudi to the Red Sox for $1 million each. Players had been sold by owners to other teams from time immemorial, and no one ever stopped them. The most renowned sale, of course, was in 1919 when Babe Ruth was sold by the Red Sox to the Yankees for $125,000 and a $350,000 loan. (Without considering the loan, the $125,000 in 1919 dollars was worth $411,000 in 1976 dollars.)

The lack of precedent and of a rule prohibiting such transactions did not stop Kuhn. He didn't like Finley, and he didn't like the smell of the deal. Kuhn argued that he was protecting baseball's competitive balance, and his action was therefore in the best interests of baseball. Baseball's constitution to the contrary, Finley sued Kuhn for $10 million. The trial began in federal district court in Chicago on December 16, 1976. Finley's lawyer made a cogent opening statement:

> Your honor, the evidence will show that the sales of outfielder Joe Rudi and pitcher Rollie Fingers to the Boston Red Sox, and Vida Blue to the New York Yankees were, in fact, consummated without any rule violation. There was no dispute between the teams involved, or between any other teams in baseball with regard to these player sales. There was no moral turpitude problem involved, and there was no dishonesty.
>
> The evidence will also show that under those circumstances there is no authority whatsoever for the defendant, Bowie Kuhn, to induce the breach of these substantial contracts, and for the only reason being what he unilaterally believed to be, as he termed, acting in "the best interests of baseball."[13]

Finley's lawyer called AL president Lee MacPhail, who testified that he had advised Kuhn not to interfere with the sales because they violated no regulation. Kuhn's lawyer called a gaggle of owners to the stand, each of whom supported the commissioner. Finley himself testified that the player sale would not hurt competitive balance because it was his intention to use the proceeds to rebuild his team with strong, young players. Moreover, the sold players would eventually move to big-market teams anyway once their contracts were up at year's end. By selling them in June, at least the A's, as a relatively small-market team, got something back for them. Finley had economic logic on his side, but the judge ruled that economic logic was not what mattered. After deliberating for two months, the presiding judge ruled on March 17, 1977:

> The fact that this case has commanded a great deal of attention in the vociferous world of baseball fans, and has provoked widespread and not always unemotional discussion, tends to obscure the relative simplicity of the legal issues involved. The case is not a Finley-Kuhn popularity contest. Neither is it an appellate

judicial review of Bowie Kuhn's actions. The question before the court is not whether Bowie Kuhn was wise to do what he did, but rather whether he had the authority.

The judge went on to rule that Kuhn did have the authority, based on the best interests clause and Article VII, Section 2 (waiving the right to recourse to the courts), of the Major League Agreement. The judge then clarified that the waiver of the right to judicial review could be negated only if the commissioner contravenes the law of the land, violates the charter of the organization, or fails to follow the basic rudiments of due process.[14] He closed by questioning whether it was prudent to grant the commissioner such broad and unfettered discretion. A poll taken by the *Sporting News* at the time suggested that fans may have had similar concerns: only 12.7 percent thought Kuhn was right in disallowing the player sales.[15]

But Kuhn's troubles with Finley were not over. After the trial, Finley sold Paul Lindblad to the Rangers for $400,000. Kuhn, it seems, had wearied of bumping heads with Finley and decided to allow this one. In fact, he used the Lindblad sale as a precedent, proclaiming henceforth that he would allow no player transactions that involved more than $400,000 in cash. This principle of cash limitation remains today, with the threshold raised to $1 million—though it seems to be invoked somewhat arbitrarily. To be sure, Finley continued to unload players over the next few years, prompting Kuhn to pass a special rule for Finley only: no cash amounting to more than $50,000 in player deals.

Finley, of course, was not the only owner who gave Kuhn trouble, nor was he the only owner to sue Kuhn. Braves owner Ted Turner joined the act. Turner, after a few drinks at a cocktail party in October 1976, told Giants owner Bob Lurie that he would go as high as necessary to sign Gary Mathews. When Turner signed Mathews in the first free agent draft on November 4, Lurie signed a tampering complaint (Turner was making a move toward Mathews while he was still under contract with the Giants—if you can call such cocktail banter making a move). Kuhn jumped right on it, suspending Turner for one year and stripping the Braves of an amateur draft pick. Then Turner jumped on it and sued Kuhn. The judge ruled that Kuhn's power was not impregnable; he had gone beyond his authority in taking away a draft pick on the grounds that such a sanction was not contemplated in Article II of the Major League Agreement. The one-year suspension, however, stuck.

Kuhn was not done cleaning up baseball. In 1979, the Hall of Famer Willie Mays signed a $100,000 contract with an Atlantic City hotel/gambling casino. Kuhn summoned Mays and told him that he'd have to stop working for the New York Mets if he took the job in Atlantic City. Mays protested that his job for the hotel had nothing to do with its gambling operations. He would be doing community work, visiting children in hospitals, playing in golf tournaments, and so on. Kuhn wasn't persuaded, and Mays left baseball.

Later that year, Kuhn decided to reach out to Steinbrenner, whom he had already suspended several years earlier. Kuhn put him on the owners' Executive Council. At the time, MLB was negotiating an extension of its contract with the umpires. According to Kuhn, he was soon to learn that Steinbrenner, currying favor with the men in blue, was leaking bargaining information to Richie Phillips, the head of the umpires' union.[16]

The next year the developer Edward DeBartolo Sr. had a deal to buy the Chicago White Sox. Because DeBartolo's portfolio included racetracks, Kuhn held up the sale. Never mind that George Steinbrenner, John Galbreath, and George Argyros owned horses. The White Sox were sold the next year to Jerry Reinsdorf and Eddie Einhorn.

Mickey Mantle was on deck. In 1982, Mantle, who was working as a spring training instructor for the Yankees, was offered a $100,000 a year job at the Claridge Hotel and Casino, in Atlantic City. The commissioner gave him the Kuhnian choice. Mantle, too, left baseball.

And so it went. Kuhn, trying desperately to please the owners, though trying a bit harder for Walter O'Malley than for the others, was unable to suppress his sanctimonious, czarlike instincts. Complicating matters further was that the owners were leery of Kuhn and gave him contradictory signals: one moment he was responsible for labor relations, the next he was to step aside. Kuhn was intelligent and had some important insights into the game. One such insight was that he observed football's popularity passing baseball by and concluded that baseball needed to enter the modern era. Among other things, this meant converting his job into a type of CEO and introducing serious marketing and promotion efforts at the team and central levels. But Kuhn was schizophrenic in this regard—he wanted to be a modern business leader, yet he clung to the notion that his first responsibility was to raise baseball's ethical standing, and close behind was the thought that he needed to protect all constituencies of the game.

Properly construed, the commissioner must appear to be looking out for all interests, but he must attend first and foremost to the interests of those who hired him. As in all industries, looking out for the owners' profit means paying attention to the consumer, but the bottom line is always the bottom line. Baseball's marketing made very few strides under Kuhn, and the industry's need to get beyond crisis management saw little, if any, progress.

Leonard Koppett added another layer to understanding Kuhn's dilemma:

> Through all these developments, Kuhn developed another pattern that would eventually undo him. He plunged full-bore into internal politics. A commissioner is the creature of the owners, and owners fall into factions, and Bowie became enmeshed in playing one group against another in seeking support for his position on various matters. Since you can never please all of them, your support must come from whichever group or individual seems more potent at the time. The trouble is, alliances and interests shift from time to time and issue to issue, so you wind up displeasing almost everyone at some time on some point. And people, especially powerful people, tend to remember being thwarted more than favors, so that vindictiveness lasts longer than gratitude. . . . But Kuhn's insensitivity and arrogance . . . led him to make more enemies than necessary and create fewer loyalists than he needed.[17]

In his autobiography, Kuhn described at great length the denouement of his commissionership and the search for his successor. At one point, Kuhn reflected, "The most interesting story of all was that my friend Bud Selig wanted the job. When I heard it the second or third time, I called Bud."[18] Selig was chairing the commissioner's search committee and denied having any interest in the job. Kuhn continued, "I liked the idea of Bud, who had the necessary experience and following among the owners to be effective. Besides, we had never had an owner-commissioner, and perhaps the time had come to try one."[19]

Yet, curiously, in the postscript to the 1997 edition of *Hardball*, Kuhn seemed to have forgotten what he wrote in the first edition ten years earlier. Describing the ascension of Selig, Kuhn wrote,

> What followed was the election of an owner-commissioner, Bud Selig, the boss of the Milwaukee Brewers. Baseball hadn't seen the likes of this since the disastrous rule of the National Commission in the early part of the century, which expired in the ignominy of the Black Sox. . . . Had the owners collectively lost their minds? My first reaction was to think they had. The owner/leader was discredited by our own history. . . . [Yet] perhaps, I came to think, it might make some sense as a temporary measure for one reason and one reason only: to create a level playing field for the imminent collective bargaining with the Players Association.[20]

Kuhn ended his 1997 postscript with an idealistic vision of what the commissioner's office might become:

> I envision a national game where the commissioner once again stands for something beyond the ordinary; where the public interest counts; where commercial immediacy can be put aside; where baseball dares to become something more than just another segment of the entertainment industry and where the game is a real model of virtue for the public and for kids in particular.[21]

It seems that Kuhn might have spent more energy on the ethical standards of the law firm he joined after leaving baseball. The firm was sued for various improprieties by its clients. After the suits were filed, Kuhn moved from New Jersey to Florida, allegedly to protect himself and his multimillion-dollar investments from his creditors.[22]

Commissioner Peter Ueberroth

Peter Ueberroth was born in Evanston, Illinois, on September 2, 1937. His father, Victor, was an aluminum-siding salesman. His mother, Laura, passed away when Peter was four, and his father remarried a year later. The family was always on the move, and Peter attended six different primary schools and three secondary schools. By the time Peter was in high school, he was pretty much self-supporting. He left home his sophomore year to work as the director of recreation in an orphanage for children from broken homes, earning $125 a month.

Peter earned a partial scholarship as a water polo player to attend San Jose State University. He financed the rest of his college education by working as a traveling seed salesman and as a chicken-farm egg selector. After graduation and marriage, he moved for two years to Hawaii, where he went to work for a non-scheduled airline owned by the financier Kirk Kerkorian. Kerkorian made Ueberroth, twenty-three years old at the time, a vice president of the company and gave him 3 percent of the stock. In 1963, Ueberroth set up a travel agency company, with one employee and a $5,000 capitalization. He then returned to California and grew his business to be the second-largest travel agency in the country, with two hundred offices and $300 million yearly in revenues.[23]

A highly successful entrepreneur, Ueberroth was still a relative unknown until 1979, when he was chosen to head up the Los Angeles Olympic Organizing Committee (LAOOC) for the 1984 summer games. After several successive games that were financial flops, Ueberroth worked the L.A. games like a charm. Four years before the L.A. Games, the winter Olympics were held in Lake Placid, New York. Corporate sponsorships for those games sold for $10,000. Ueberroth sold sponsorships for the L.A. Olympics at $4 million a piece. He enlisted thousands of volunteers and worked his paid employees to the bone. Together with some clever promotional stunts, the L.A. games were a smashing success, yielding a reported $200 million profit for the LAOOC. Ueberroth was turned from a nobody into *Time* magazine's man of the year.

And baseball wanted to hitch its wagon up to Ueberroth's coattails. Bud Selig, who chaired the commissioner search committee, commented on Ueberroth: "He's effective, he's articulate, he's good-looking. He fits this marvelous American dream of a guy who started with nothing, became a millionaire and is about to become commissioner of baseball."[24] What Selig did not say is that there was considerable controversy about Ueberroth's management style. Many employees at the LAOOC believed that he was excessively controlling and manipulative and enjoyed keeping people off-balance. One former LAOOC executive stated bluntly that Ueberroth's style "doesn't work. It causes insecurity and unrest. Experienced people won't put up with it."[25]

But baseball could not be too picky. Many prospective candidates removed their names from consideration. One such person was John McHale of the Montreal Expos. McHale commented, "Let's face it, the commissionership is less attractive than it used to be. In past years, the dignity of that job was next to that of the presidency of the United States, but it has diminished." McHale went on to warn that the next commissioner would be getting a clear message from the owners: "You work for us; we really own the game."[26] Somebody forgot to tell Peter Ueberroth.

Ueberroth agreed to assume the commissionership under certain conditions. First, he wanted his maximum fining authority to increase from $5,000 (the level set in 1921) to $250,000. Second, he wanted to be a CEO with all departments, including the NL and the AL presidents, reporting to him. Third, he wanted the reelection provision to be changed from a three-quarters vote of ownership to a 50 percent vote (providing he had at least five votes of support in each league). Fourth, he wanted Kuhn to extend his term so that Ueberroth would not assume the commissionership until October 1, 1984. The owners agreed, along with a $300,000 salary for their new leader (double Bowie Kuhn's last salary).

In baseball, Ueberroth saw an industry that was more mismanaged than the Olympics and that needed harsher medicine. One problem was that baseball had done an abysmal job of marketing itself. Decades of being alone on the national sports pedestal and of being protected by the judicially conferred antitrust exemption had encouraged a precarious complacency and laxity among the owners and the central office. Although baseball had established the MLB Promotions Corporation in 1968, by 1984 the licensing and merchandising revenue per club was only $40,000, less than one-tenth the amount in the NFL at the time. Ueberroth brought in LAOOC alumnus Joel Rubenstein to ramp up baseball's merchandising effort. At $5 million a pop, baseball sold sponsorships to IBM (the "Tale of the Tape" measuring home run distances), to Arby's for the RBI leader, and to Equitable Life for Old-Timers Day games, among others. Ueberroth also informed Rawlings, which had been selling equipment and uniforms to baseball's teams, that it would now have to pay baseball $1 million and supply the equipment and the uniforms free of charge. In return, Rawlings would be designated the game's official equipment supplier. By the end of Ueberroth's term in 1989, baseball's licensing and merchandising revenues exceeded $36 million annually.

Ueberroth's chutzpah, then, worked out well in the marketing arena, but it proved problematic elsewhere. The trouble started literally on day one. On October 1, 1984, the umpires announced that they would not work the postseason unless they had a new contract. Round one of the postseason was played with replacement umps—and not without some embarrassing moments. Then, on October 7, the owners and the umps agreed to submit their dispute to binding arbitration by the commissioner, and the umps went back to work. Eight days later, Ueberroth handed down his verdict. The umpires had asked for an average salary and benefits package of $340,000. Ueberroth gave them $480,000. In one blow, Ueberroth had not only stripped the NL and the AL presidents of one of their only remaining significant functions (control over the umpires), but he had also slapped the owners in their faces by giving the umps more than even the men in blue had demanded.

Having shown some incipient disdain for the owners, Ueberroth then heaped some disdain on his predecessor. On March 18, Ueberroth reinstated Willie Mays and Mickey Mantle, who had been banned from baseball employment by Bowie Kuhn due to their promotional contracts with Atlantic City hotels.

Next, the imperious commissioner slapped the owners in the face again. The players went on strike in August over a dispute in the terms of a new collective-bargaining agreement. Ueberroth suf-

Peter Ueberroth, the
commissioner of baseball
from October 1, 1984, to
March 31, 1989.

fered from the same professional delusion as his predecessors and
saw himself as the fans' commissioner. More important, he didn't
want the blemish of a work stoppage on his record. Despite the
widespread perception, among owners at least, that the players
would not be able to hang together over the relatively minor issues
on the bargaining table, one day into the strike Ueberroth called
the head of the owners' Player Relations Committee (PRC), Barry
Rona, into his office and ordered him to reach an agreement with
the Players Association in twenty-four hours. At noon, Ueberroth
showed up at the office where Rona and Don Fehr were negotiating, sealed a compromise agreement, and called a press conference
at 1 P.M. The strike would last only two days, and *Time* magazine's
man of the year was now the man who saved baseball.

The owners were none too pleased. Ueberroth had announced
the agreement before it was even approved by the owners on the
PRC, let alone by the rest of the owners. The final agreement contained few of the salary containment reforms that the owners sought.

At the time, the barons did not know that Ueberroth had in mind a different mechanism to contain salaries. As one owner later put it: "The thing that was called collusion grew out of the failure to get what we wanted in 1985 [collective bargaining]."[27]

Ueberroth had set the stage for ownership collusion in the players' market. He changed the management process. Under Kuhn, the owners had two plenary meetings a year, and they were almost entirely ceremonial. Indeed, owners often sent surrogates to the plenaries. Any important decisions were made by the executive council. Ueberroth decided the owners would hold four plenaries a year and that the owners themselves needed to attend. His reasoning: how could they act like partners if they didn't even know one another?

Ueberroth berated the owners at the meetings, often calling them "dumb" and "stupid" in their decisions. He also scorned them outside the meetings. Peter O'Malley, the owner of the Dodgers and a close associate of Kuhn, said of Ueberroth that "[he] loved to put the owners down, embarrass them any way he could." Ueberroth said of O'Malley, "The only thing he really cares about are his two tickets to the opera."[28]

Ueberroth himself seemed to care about a lot of things other than baseball. Between the quarterly owner meetings, he spent much of his time at home in Newport Beach, California, playing golf or working on other business deals. There were so many packages going between 350 Park Avenue and Newport Beach that some began to refer to him as the "FedEx commissioner." During his four and a half years in baseball, Ueberroth served on a number of corporate boards and did some outside consulting. He negotiated the merger of the brokerage houses E. F. Hutton and Shearson, yielding a slick side income of $900,000 for his efforts.

But Ueberroth's real legacy had nothing to do with FedEx or brokerage firms. He was the ringleader of ownership collusion during 1986–1988 that ultimately cost the owners $280 million in damages and a deepening distrust in their relations with the players. At the September 1985 ownership meeting, Ueberroth lectured the barons about how player contracts longer than two years didn't make any sense. He also had Lee MacPhail deliver a report that argued that players on long-term contracts displayed diminishing performance. The owners congregated again at the October World Series in St. Louis. Czar Peter harangued the owners once more on long-term contracts. He then took a page from Mao's cultural revolution book and instructed the owners to do criticism/self-criticism about the foolish player contracts they had signed. The mea culpas got a slow start, but pretty soon it was like a religious revival meeting. Ueberroth then asked the owners to go around the room and state whether they planned to sign any free agents during the coming off-season. He explained to the owners that it was legal for them to talk about not signing free agents as long as they did not make an agreement not to sign them. According to the testimony from the collusion hearing transcripts, Ueberroth then ended the meeting by saying, "Well, you are smart businessmen. You all agree we have a problem. Go solve it."[29] And they did; the only problem was that they got caught.[30]

Ueberroth brought his magisterial ways to other matters. After several players were revealed to be addicted to cocaine, in the spring of 1986 Ueberroth unilaterally ordered mandatory drug testing of all players four times a year. The players' union brought a grievance that such matters were subject to collective bargaining and won. The major leagues were not to have their first drug testing agreement until 2002, and even that agreement was rather limited.

Ueberroth also used the commissioner's powers to reward owners who followed his path. As baseball's licensing and sponsorship revenues soared, Ueberroth kept a substantial chunk of these monies in a separate fund to be disbursed at his discretion.[31] His acolytes benefited.

Ueberroth announced in June 1988 that he would not seek a second term. Most owners breathed a sigh of relief. Bud Selig knew who baseball's next leader would be.

Commissioner Bart Giamatti

In June 1983, Bud Selig was heading up the search committee to replace Bowie Kuhn. Selig had been interviewing several candidates. On June 6, he met Bart Giamatti for dinner at the Helmsley

Palace Hotel in New York City. Following dinner, they walked the
city's streets talking about baseball, the favorite games they'd seen
or listened to, the great pennant races, beloved players, and contro-
versial calls until the early hours of the morning. Selig was smit-
ten. He had his man and wrote a ten-page letter to his committee
members explaining his preference for Giamatti. The trouble was
that Giamatti was in the middle of his term as president of Yale
University, and Yale was in the middle of a rancorous dispute with
its labor unions. He was interested in the commissionership, but he
couldn't take it right away. Baseball couldn't wait, so it anointed
Ueberroth.

However, when Chub Feeney retired as NL president in 1986,
Giamatti was then free to take Feeney's job, with the understanding that he was the likely successor to Ueberroth.[32] And when the
latter announced his prospective retirement in June 1988, the owners readily tapped Giamatti to succeed him.

Giamatti was born in Boston on April 4, 1938. He was raised
in western Massachusetts in the town of South Hadley. His father
was a professor of romance languages and Italian literature at Mt.
Holyoke College and a leading authority on the works of Dante.
Bart's mother graduated from Smith College and had been taking
her junior year abroad in Italy when she met her husband.

Bart spent his summers in South Hadley riding his bike and listening to Red Sox games on the radio. When he was about eight
years old, his father and his uncle took him to his first game at
Fenway Park. The visit made an indelible mark on his memory. In
one of his published books, *Take Time for Paradise*,[33] Giamatti
argues that "we have always envisioned [paradise] as a garden,
sometimes on a mountain top, often on an island, but always as
removed, an enclosed, green place." This is what Fenway Park was
to young Bart—a removed, enclosed, green place amid the concrete blocks of Boston . . . a paradise. And the game itself was no
less magical:

> [It] functioned occasionally as a part of religion but much more
> expansively and powerfully as part of our artistic or imaginative
> impulse . . . [as] a medium for self-transformation . . . thinking

about baseball will tell us about ourselves as a people. . . . Baseball, in all its dimensions, best mirrors the condition of freedom for Americans that Americans ever guard and aspire to. . . . All play aspires to the condition of paradise . . . to a freedom we cannot recall, save as a moment of play in some garden now lost.[34]

Giamatti's childhood hero was Sox infielder Bobby Doerr. When asked why it was not Ted Williams, Giamatti explained that he could imagine himself playing second base but couldn't see hitting .400. Yet even second base was a bit of a challenge for young Bart. When he didn't make the cut for his high school team, the coach nonetheless loved his enthusiasm for the game and made him the team manager.

What he lacked on the field, he made up for in the classroom. He received a bachelor's degree, magna cum laude, from Yale University in 1960 and a Ph.D. in comparative literature from Yale in 1964. His first teaching job was at Princeton, but he was hired back by Yale after two years. After an extremely productive life as a popular teacher and a scholar, he became Yale's president in 1978. At Yale, Giamatti developed a reputation for taking a stern stand against its unions, a reputation that could not have been a matter of indifference to baseball's barons.

With a $200,000 salary, Giamatti became the NL president in December 1986. There were not many functions left for league presidents when he took office, but Giamatti stood out as a strict enforcer of baseball's ethical and disciplinary code. On September 1, 1987, the Astros' Billy Hatcher became the first player to be ejected for coming to the plate with a corked bat. Hatcher claimed that the bat belonged to a pitcher on the team and that he used it only for batting practice. Giamatti was unimpressed with Hatcher's excuse and suspended him for ten games. On April 30, while serving as the Reds' manager, Pete Rose shoved umpire Dave Pallone in the ninth inning of a close ballgame with the Mets. Giamatti suspended Rose for thirty games, the stiffest penalty ever given a manager for an on-field incident. Three weeks later, Giamatti suspended Dodger slugger Pedro Guerrero for four games after Guerrero was hit by a pitch and reacted by throwing his bat toward the pitcher. Then, Giamatti suspended Phillies pitcher Kevin Gross for ten days for having implanted a piece of sandpaper in his glove, which he used to scuff the ball and alter its flight.

To Giamatti, baseball stood on high ground. He was not going to let anyone knock it down. He could handle the ethical transgressions well enough on his own, but he was less secure about the business side of baseball. When Giamatti met Fay Vincent at a dinner party in 1978, the two intellectuals and baseball lovers became fast friends. Vincent was a Yale Law School graduate who had worked at the Securities and Exchange Commission (SEC) and served several years as the CEO at Columbia Pictures. Giamatti thought that Vincent would be his perfect complement as deputy commissioner.

So, with Vincent at his side, on April 1, 1989, Bart Giamatti became the seventh commissioner of baseball. Though they had different professional skills, Vincent and Giamatti shared a moralist predilection and a conviction that the commissioner's main duty was to preserve the integrity of baseball. Two months before taking office, Giamatti and Vincent were meeting with Ueberroth to talk about the transition to a new commissioner. Rumors had been circulating that Pete Rose, the Cincinnati Reds' manager and baseball's all-time hit leader, was betting on games. The three decided together to call Rose and his lawyers into the commissioner's office to get his side of the story and also to hire the investigative lawyer John Dowd to look into the allegations. After several months of sleuthing at a cost of $3 million, Dowd found lots of evidence that Rose was gambling on baseball games. Giamatti called a hearing, but before the proceedings began, another ugly matter surfaced.

Giamatti had signed a letter on behalf of the convicted felon and bookie Ron Peters. Peters had provided very useful information to Dowd about Rose, and Dowd drafted a letter to the sentencing judge acknowledging Peters's constructive role. Dowd gave the letter to Giamatti for his signature, and the new commissioner obliged him. The problem was that the letter contained language that suggested Giamatti may have already been convinced of Rose's guilt.[35] Rose's lawyers seized on this and went to a Cincinnati court to ask that Giamatti's hearings be enjoined and the commissioner be obligated to pay an indemnity to Rose for be-

Bart Giamatti (center), the commissioner of baseball from April 1, 1989, to September 1, 1989, with Bud Selig and Selig's childhood friend Senator Herb Kohl.

smirching his reputation. The Cincinnati court agreed to grant an injunction on the hearings. During the summer months, Giamatti was embroiled in nasty and debilitating depositions and court hearings. He was chain-smoking, eating heavily, and sleeping poorly throughout.

Finally, in mid-August, the two sides began to discuss a settlement. Giamatti and Vincent first offered a ten-year banishment from the game, then a seven-year ban. Rose's lawyers wanted language stating that the accused admitted no offense. On August 23, they reached an accord: Rose would be put on the ineligible list, and although his status would be termed a "permanent suspension," he would be able to apply for reinstatement after one year.[36] The agreement included an ethically inane, but legally meaningful, sentence: "Nothing in this agreement shall be deemed either an admission or a denial by Peter Edward Rose of the allegations that he bet on any major league baseball game." Eight days later, exactly five months after taking office, Bart Giamatti suffered a fatal heart attack at his summer home on Martha's Vineyard.

Thus, Giamatti's commissionership was consumed with one event. Leonard Koppett reflected on what might have been:

> What kind of commissionership he might have had, and where he might have led baseball in the 1990s, can never be known. My own opinion, which reflects the conventional wisdom of the time and the general impression of insiders, is that his tenure might have been very good indeed. He would have shed, or at least tempered, his romanticism. He had persuasive powers, people skills, the ability to establish positive relationships, and certainly the intelligence to deal with the real difficulties. His public persona was ideal, his rhetoric would be on the fan's wavelength instead of mindless like Eckert's, transparently self-serving like Kuhn's, or coldly distant like Ueberroth's. He might have become the best of all the commissioners.[37]

Commissioner Fay Vincent

Baseball was in shock over Giamatti's sudden death. The next in line was Fay Vincent. When he was interviewed by Bud Selig and Jerry Reinsdorf about how he would approach the job, Vincent responded, "Bart's agenda is my agenda."[38] A few owners were concerned that they didn't know enough about Vincent and that they shouldn't pick Giamatti's successor hastily. According to Reinsdorf, he left the owners' meeting and went to Vincent's room at Milwaukee's Pfister Hotel, where the owners had assembled. He told Vincent that some owners were concerned that he was a newcomer to the game and wondered whether Vincent would support an amendment to the Major League Agreement that would provide a way to fire a commissioner. Vincent said that he would rather not add such a provision but stated that it would not be a problem because if he lost the owners' confidence, he would resign. Reinsdorf returned to the meeting, and Vincent was chosen by acclamation. Baseball's eighth commissioner would receive an annual salary of $650,000.

It didn't take long for Vincent to earn his keep. At 5:04 P.M. on October 17, 1989, a powerful earthquake jolted San Francisco. Vincent was already in his field box at Candlestick Park before the start of game three of the World Series between the Giants and the Oakland A's. When word came that the jolt they had felt at the stadium caused part of the upper level of the Bay Bridge to fall to the lower level; that a mile-and-a-half stretch of the Nimitz Freeway collapsed, crushing cars below; and that fires raged throughout the city, Vincent promptly called off game three. San Francisco's worst tremor since 1906 would cause sixty-seven fatalities.

The next day Vincent spoke at a press conference at the St. Francis Hotel, which was still without power.

> It has become very clear to all of us in Major League Baseball that our concerns, our issue, is a modest one in this tragedy. Baseball is not the highest priority to be dealt with. We want to be very sensitive as to the state of life in this community. The great tragedy is, it coincides with our modest little sporting event. . . . We know our place, and it would be totally inappropriate to think of playing right now, even if we knew about the condition of the park. Of course, we want to do everything in our power to finish this World Series, but we will not intrude on the dignity of this community.[39]

The series resumed on October 27, after a ten-day hiatus. Baseball had done the right thing, and Vincent was off to a marvelous start as commissioner.

Fay Vincent was born in Waterbury, Connecticut, on May 29, 1938, the same year as Bart Giamatti. His father worked for the telephone company, and his mother was a schoolteacher. Vincent's father was the captain of the Yale University football team and also of the baseball team and later became an NFL game official.

Young Fay followed in his father's footsteps. He went to Hotchkiss private school on a scholarship, where he, too, played on the football team. Fay was a hulking tackle, six feet three inches tall and 240 pounds. Fay's teammate was George H. W. Bush's younger brother, William (Bucky) Bush. Bucky Bush said of Vincent, "Half the plays we ran behind Vincent. He was so strong he could take out two men."[40]

Fay Vincent, the commissioner of baseball from September 13, 1989, to September 7, 1992.

After graduating from Hotchkiss, Vincent went with Bucky to work in his brother's oil fields in Texas. They shared a one-room apartment. Bucky, who went on to become an investment banker in St. Louis, commented that the other oil workers that summer were in awe of Vincent because "Fay's IQ was higher than the rest of them combined."[41]

Vincent enrolled at Williams College the next fall. He played tackle on the Williams football team until December 10. That day, one of his roommates, as a prank, locked Vincent in his room. Vincent fell asleep for two hours, and when he awoke, he had to go to the bathroom. The fact that Vincent's room was up three flights of stairs and that the roof's ledge and gutters were icy did not deter the young Vincent. He decided to go out the window and crawl over to the next room and continue on to the bathroom. Instead, once outside he lost his footing and fell three stories. Halfway down, he hit a steel railing, slowing his fall but breaking his back.[42] The injury left Vincent partially crippled.

Vincent graduated from Williams cum laude in 1960. He had thoughts of going on to the priesthood but was told that his disability would prevent him from celebrating mass. His next choice—opposites attract—was Yale Law School. Between 1963 and 1978, he practiced corporate law in New York City and Washington, D.C. He then went to the Securities and Exchange Commission for a brief six months, when a college friend, whose family controlled Columbia Pictures, asked him to run and bring integrity back to the film company. In 1982, Coca-Cola purchased Columbia Pictures and named Vincent chairman of the board and executive vice president of Coca-Cola. When he left Coca-Cola in 1988, he carried lucrative stock options with him, making him a multimillionaire.

Vincent joined Ueberroth as the only other commissioner who was independently wealthy when anointed as baseball's czar. Each comported himself with a bit more independence and hauteur than the other commissioners. Perhaps more notable, however, was that with Vincent, baseball had its fourth commissioner within the previous five years. That kind of turnover is never auspicious for managing, let alone for strategic planning in, an organization. It yields less continuity, less experience, more adjustment, and more misunderstanding.

The October 1989 earthquake, in hindsight, was a harbinger of the stormy times that lay ahead for Vincent. The immediate problem was labor. Baseball was about to reap the rewards of the new 1990–1993 television agreement with CBS, doubling the yearly central TV revenues to $14 million per team. Dumping large piles of money in the lords' laps was always a dangerous thing to do—it seemed to inevitably find its way into higher player contracts. The 1989 off-season was no exception, and this gave the hawkish owners more reason to seek new labor market restrictions in the collective-bargaining agreement (CBA) under negotiation.

The owners put a pay-for-performance scheme on the bargaining table, but the players weren't biting. The owners then voted to lock the players out of spring training during February and March 1990. With negotiations going nowhere and under pressure from the dovish, mostly high-revenue owners (Fred Wilpon of the Mets,

Eli Jacobs of the Orioles, Peter O'Malley of the Dodgers, and Walter Haas of the A's), Vincent inserted himself into the bargaining process. He took the pay-for-performance plan off the table and replaced it with his more moderate plan. Eventually, he pushed the Player Relations Committee to reach a deal with the union, and the camps were reopened on March 20. Similar to Ueberroth, the new commissioner did not want a prolonged work stoppage on his watch, especially at the beginning of his reign. Fans were happy, but the coalition of owners wanting to dump Vincent was already beginning to crystallize.

For Vincent, something else was at stake in the 1990 labor negotiations. The distrust and bitterness from the collusion experience had badly polluted relations with the Players Association. Vincent believed that constructive labor relations were a key to the sport's future. Largely for this reason, Vincent hired Steve Greenberg, who had served many years as a successful player agent and had an excellent relationship with Don Fehr, as his deputy commissioner. Greenberg was the one who actually negotiated the final details of the March 20, 1990, agreement with Fehr. But Greenberg's conciliatory attitude toward labor was another point that helped to turn some owners against Vincent.[43]

Vincent's next challenge came quickly. Howard Spira, a small-time gambler with mob connections, was paid $40,000 in hush money by George Steinbrenner in January 1990, after digging up some dirt on Yankee slugger Dave Winfield and Winfield's foundation. Spira threatened to release negative information to the press about other Yankees, as well as the tapes of his conversations with Steinbrenner about Winfield, unless Steinbrenner gave him an additional $110,000. At this point, Steinbrenner reported Spira to the FBI, and on March 23, 1990, a Florida grand jury indicted Spira on eight counts of extortion. Vincent was unhappy that Steinbrenner was consorting with such a lowlife and hired John Dowd, who had done the report on Pete Rose's gambling activities, to investigate the Spira case. On July 5–6, 1990, Vincent held hearings on the matter. On July 30, Vincent put Steinbrenner on baseball's ineligible list. Steinbrenner's banishment lasted just over two years, and Vincent had made another enemy. Meanwhile, other owners were dismayed when Vincent unilaterally decided to include former Negro League players in MLB's health plan.

It didn't get any easier. In 1991, the NL announced that it was going to expand by two teams for the 1993 season. Prior to this time, expansion fees were always divided among the teams in the league that was expanding. But the previous expansions were all announced before player free agency, and the fees involved were trivial relative to what was about to come. The last NL expansion had been in 1969 (Montreal and San Diego), when each team paid $12.5 million to enter the league. The last AL expansion was in 1977 (Seattle and Toronto), when each team paid $7 million. The 1993 teams (Colorado and Florida) were each going to pay $95 million.[44]

The AL wanted its share of the booty. Among other things, it saw the expansion monies as helping both leagues pay off the exorbitant collusion bill of $280 million. The NL told the AL owners that if they wanted expansion money, they should expand their own league. Bud Selig, representing the AL owners, and Doug Danforth, representing the NL owners, negotiated with each other for several months but could not reach an understanding. The AL argued that it would be contributing 50 percent of the players in the expansion draft, so it should get 50 percent of the fees. The NL demurred but made a final offer to share 30 percent of the expansion revenue. The leagues were having no more success negotiating with each other than they had together negotiating with the players' union. Furthermore, the AL owners thought they could do better than the NL's 30 percent offer by referring the issue to Vincent. So Selig and Danforth agreed to bring the matter to Fay Vincent for resolution. Vincent had been resisting involvement, knowing that it was a no-win situation for him; no matter what he decided he would alienate half of the owners. But with Selig and Danforth getting nowhere, he finally consented. After a three-hour hearing in June 1991, Vincent issued his ruling. It was prefaced with these familiar words:

> I am disturbed by the apparent unwillingness of some within base-
> ball to rise above parochial interest and to think in terms of the
> greater good of the game. The squabbling within baseball, the

finger-pointing, the tendency to see economic issues as moral ones . . . all of these are contributing to our joint fall from grace.

The ruling itself appalled the AL owners. They would get 22 percent of the fees ($3 million per team), yet they would contribute 54 percent of the players (three per team) to the expansion draft. (At the time, the AL had fourteen teams and the NL had twelve.) Furthermore, Vincent ruled that in the future, expansion fees would be split 50/50 between the leagues.

Whatever Vincent's ruling in this matter, he was going to make enemies. This time they happened to be AL owners.

In November 1991, the owners' PRC hired Dick Ravitch to be its lead negotiator. Ravitch's salary was $750,000; Vincent's was $650,000. This was not an auspicious beginning, and things only got worse. Most owners were wary of Vincent's involvement in labor issues because of the role he played during the 1990 lockout. They further believed, reflecting back on what happened with Kuhn in 1976 and Ueberroth in 1985, that it was undermining their bargaining position to have any commissioner overseeing collective bargaining. Ravitch reaffirmed this belief: if the commissioner stepped in and forced the owners' hands in order to avoid a work stoppage, then the owners lost all their leverage.

The chair of the PRC was Bud Selig. Ravitch convinced Selig that baseball needed to change the language in the Major League Agreement to ensure that the commissioner would not interfere in labor negotiations. They would need Vincent's approval for the change, but Vincent wouldn't give it. In his view, there was clear, irrevocable language in the agreement stating that the commissioner's powers could not be diminished while he was in office. Vincent believed that this was a crucial principle because it was the only thing that protected the commissioner from the whims of self-interested owners.

Vincent did, however, agree to three conditions. First, he would not independently discuss bargaining issues with executive officers of the union. Second, he would not comment to the press on matters pertaining to bargaining. Third, he would stay out of any labor action by the owners.

The owners accepted Vincent's compromise—for a while. When Vincent showed up at the June 1992 PRC meeting, several owners began calling again for a change in the agreement. Vincent maintained that the three conditions did not preclude his involvement in the labor agenda and that he couldn't imagine an organization whose CEO was not participating in the most important matter confronting it. So the owners and Vincent were again at loggerheads, but Vincent was able to defuse the matter temporarily with a forceful speech. In it, Vincent declared that player salaries were too high, that baseball's labor market needed new significant restraints, and that he would not get in the way of the owners taking a strong stance.

Meanwhile, still another issue was pressing. The NL had long talked about the need to realign its divisions in accordance with a team's location and time zone. For instance, it had the clear mismatch of Cincinnati in the West and Chicago in the East. In 1992, realignment was being actively discussed in the NL. Chicago did not want to go to the West because it meant playing more games late at night and would hurt the team's television ratings. The NL voted 10 to 2 in favor of realignment, but Chicago's negative vote was all that was needed to prevent it from going forward. Vincent, however, stepped in with his "best interests" powers and mandated realignment. He had made a new enemy.

The Cubs sued Vincent, claiming that he exceeded his authority as limited by Article VII of the Major League Agreement, which only allowed the commissioner to settle disputes between clubs whose resolution was not expressly provided for in the MLA or through collective bargaining. In her July 23, 1992, decision, district court judge Suzanne Conlon (northern district, Illinois) concluded that the commissioner's Article I "best interests" authority was preempted in this case by Article VII:

Under Illinois rules for construing contracts, it is clear that the broad authority granted the Commissioner by Article I of the MLA is not boundless as he suggests. Giving language of Article I its common sense and ordinary meaning, the Commissioner's authority to investigate "acts," "transactions" and "practices" to determine and take "preventive, remedial or punitive action" does not encompass restructuring the divisions of the National League. There has been no conduct for the Commissioner to investigate, punish or remedy under Article I. The veto exercised by the Chicago Cubs as a matter of contractual right merely resulted in the maintenance of long-standing divisional assignments reflected in the National League Constitution.[45]

Vincent appealed the decision, but seventeen days after he resigned, the executive council, led by Bud Selig, rescinded Vincent's order to realign the NL. Baseball's lawyers then asked the Seventh Circuit Court of Appeals to dismiss Vincent's appeal and Judge Conlon to vacate her decision.

Vincent had also locked horns with the Cubs' ownership over the Tribune Corporation's superstation WGN. Both WGN and WTBS, the Braves' superstation, were broadcasting their clubs games to more than 50 million households across the country. One study suggested that by eating into baseball's national television markets, these superstation broadcasts were costing baseball $250 million a year in television revenue. Yet the clubs were making combined payments of only $20 million to baseball. Vincent was pushing to sharply increase these payments. Neither the Tribune Corporation nor Ted Turner felt ingratiated by Vincent's perseverance.

Vincent created another detractor in San Francisco. Giants owner Bob Lurie had been trying to get some public funding in the Bay Area so that he could move his team out of the hellish edifice known as Candlestick Park. Four referendums resulted in four rejections. Lurie wanted to move his team to Tampa Bay and apparently received Vincent's blessing to pursue the potential. When Lurie had a $115 million offer in hand from a group led by Vince Naimoli, MLB came under pressure from San Francisco politicians to prevent the sale. Major League Baseball obliged, and Lurie felt he had been double-crossed by the commissioner.

Vincent also had the misfortune of presiding over the beginning of a new era of growing revenue inequalities among the teams. In the late 1970s, the revenue disparity between the top and the bottom team hovered around $18 million. By 1985, the disparity was around $30 million, and by 1991, the gap had grown to more than $60 million. The sharp increase was due to two main factors: rapidly growing local television revenues (mostly from cable contracts) and new, revenue-laden stadiums in Toronto, Chicago, and Baltimore. Throughout the 1990s and early 2000s, these new revenue sources continued to grow and create ever more vast revenue inequalities. In 2004, for instance, the top to bottom gap had increased to a whopping $267 million before revenue sharing. (After revenue sharing, it was a more modest, but still huge, $166 million.[46])

But Vincent caught the beginning of the wave. It was on his watch that the small-market clubs began to coalesce around the need for revenue sharing. As the gap widened, the small-market caucus became more strident. The low-revenue owners wanted to see the commissioner promote revenue sharing more actively, but all they saw was a committee to study the issue. This created a still broader group of disaffected owners.

At an owners' meeting in Chicago on September 3, 2002, the anti-Vincent forces felt that they had reached a critical mass. Doug Danforth, of the Pirates, expressed views that were held by many:

> I personally have no confidence in Fay's leadership. Players' salaries are too high; clubs are on the verge of collapse; and there's no planning. Media leaks come out of his office, and he's intervened in areas he had no business getting involved in. The commissioner is the leader. He has to take the blame for how bad things are. Baseball cannot move forward under his leadership. The office is in disarray and he is not able to build consensus among owners.[47]

Danforth's expectations were no doubt unreasonable. Baseball's economic problems could not be fairly laid at Fay Vincent's feet. But this was not a court of justice; it was an owners' meeting. They passed a no-confidence-in-the-commissioner motion with a two-thirds margin (18 to 9). The owners presented this to Vincent, thinking that it would cause him to resign. But Vincent responded that the Major League Agreement prohibited any diminution of the commissioner's powers while in office. He claimed that dismissal was the ultimate diminution of his power and hence was a violation of the agreement. As a matter of principle, Vincent said he would never resign. Within a few days, however, Vincent relented, having decided that a drawn-out legal battle was in no one's interest.

The owners met again in St. Louis on September 8. They were in no mood to look for another meddlesome commissioner or one who thought he represented the fans and the players rather than the owners. So, they voted in one of their own, Bud Selig, the owner of the Milwaukee Brewers, as baseball's acting commissioner.

6

Bud Selig
A Lifetime in Preparation

The Early Years

Allan H. "Bud" Selig was born on July 30, 1934, in Milwaukee, Wisconsin. His father, Ben, had come to the United States from Romania when he was four years old. He was a hard-working, ingratiating man who believed strongly in the value of education. Ben Selig's first job was as a salesman for a Milwaukee newspaper, then known as the *Journal*. The job created personal contacts and led to his working for an established car dealership. After a few years, Ben Selig seized an opportunity to open his own dealership and later pioneered in developing an auto-leasing business. Eventually, Selig's business became the largest car dealership in the state.

Ben Selig, however, had little interest in baseball. Young Bud's interest came from his mother. Herself an immigrant from the Ukraine, Marie Selig attended college, a rare accomplishment for a woman in the early twentieth century, and became a schoolteacher. When Bud was only three, Marie began taking Bud and his older brother, Jerry, to Borchert Field, where the triple-A farm team of the Chicago Cubs played. The field was in a German neighborhood of Milwaukee and had the distinction of being the only ballpark in the country where there was no seat from which a spectator could see both foul poles.

By the time Bud was in the third or the fourth grade, he was exhibiting all the telltale marks of a true baseball fanatic. He got up in the morning, grabbed the paper, turned immediately to the sports pages, and scrutinized the box scores. When not at Borchert Field, he avidly listened to the Cubs (and occasionally to the White Sox) games on the radio. Like most boys, Bud also loved to play baseball, participating in various sandlot leagues during his youth and spending countless hours playing a game called Strikeout (played with a bat and a tennis ball against a wall) with his childhood friend Herb Kohl. By age eleven, the two friends often took the local bus to Borchert Field together. Neither Kohl nor Bud had the talent to play competitively, but each did all right for himself nonetheless. Kohl went on to become a U.S. senator from Wisconsin and the owner of the NBA Milwaukee Bucks.

Ben Selig did allow himself one escape from hard work. He loved to fish. One Saturday, Ben and his friend took Bud and Jerry on a fishing trip. They took a boat out onto Lake Michigan and promptly at 2 P.M., Bud pulled out his transistor radio to listen to the Cubs game. Ben's friend complained about the disruption to the lake's serenity, and they ended up returning to shore to drop Bud off. Bud sat alone on land and contentedly listened to the game, while the others resumed their fishing expedition. Bud had found the passion of his life.

Bud also loved to read players' biographies and team histories. One day Bud's sixth-grade teacher, Ruth Schlieben, was talking to Marie Selig and told her, "You know your son, all he wants to do is read sports books." Marie responded, "What's wrong with that? He's reading, isn't he?"

Marie was an art and music buff, in addition to being a baseball fan. She took Bud to the symphony and art museums, and Bud got her to take him to baseball games. After Bud's group acquired the Brewers in 1970, Bud said, "The first 18 years of Brewers baseball, she never missed a game, never. She'd sit in the box next to mine, bring her friends, keep score. If you didn't know how the Brewers did, her face would tell the whole story."[1]

Bud Selig, with his mother, Marie, at his fiftieth birthday party, July 30, 1984.

On Bud's eleventh birthday, July 30, 1945, Marie took him to a game at Borchert Field. At the time, Bill Veeck owned the minor league Cubs team (called the Brewers) that played there. It turned out that Veeck, ever the innovative promoter, had decided to honor the birthday of one of his pitchers by having a huge cake brought out onto the field. Bud thought that his mother had arranged a birthday surprise and that the cake was for him, until the Brewers' pitcher jumped out of the giant dessert.

Sometimes Bud went to major league Cubs games in Chicago. His dad attended business meetings, and Bud would meet his uncle at Wrigley Field. As Bud got older, his father dropped him off at Wrigley and came back to get him after the game. If Ben arrived before the game ended, he simply sat down next to Bud and took out a copy of *Time* magazine to read.

Once Ben Selig dropped Bud off at a game at Comiskey Park to watch the White Sox. When Ben returned to pick Bud up toward the game's end, Bud was not in the proper seat. Bud had moved down to a seat closer to the field. Ben's voice boomed out from the public address system: "I'm Ben Selig from Milwaukee, and my boy is here." Perhaps young Bud was impressionable and began to get the idea, between the birthday cake and the public address announcement, that baseball would be his calling.

If so, the impression must have only been reinforced by the present his mother gave him for his fifteenth birthday—a baseball trip to New York. Bud's hero was Yankee great Joe DiMaggio, and his favorite team, his fondness for the Cubs notwithstanding, was the Yankees. Marie took Bud and his brother by train to New York, where they went to Yankees, Giants, and Dodgers games on successive days. On his birthday itself, July 30, 1949, they went to Yankee Stadium to watch the Yankees play the Indians. It turned out that Casey Stengel was fifty-nine years old on that day, and the Yankees had arranged for a huge birthday cake to be brought out onto the field. Bud, sitting in the upper deck, turned to Marie and exclaimed, "Mom, what did you do?"

When Marie and Ben were not indulging Bud's baseball habit, they made sure that he was attending assiduously to his studies. In 1952, Bud enrolled at the University of Wisconsin. Bud had a wide reputation as a hard-working, if not compulsive, student. Bud's younger daughter, Wendy, relates that his college buddies used to joke that they could always recognize Bud's books because every line would be marked with highlighter.

The one thing that distracted Bud from his studies was the relocation of the Boston Braves to Milwaukee before the 1953 season. As a teenager, Bud had often visited the site to witness the construction of County Stadium, and he traveled from Madison to Milwaukee to attend the Braves' first game at the new field. Bud recalled, "When Billy Bruton hit the home run off St. Louis outfielder Enos Slaughter's glove to win the game, it was just wild. It became a love affair with the intensity that no one could have predicted."

Bud graduated from Wisconsin in 1956 and went into the service. As it happened, Bud's first day in the service was October 8, 1956. A young Yankee pitcher that day led his team to a 2 to 0 victory over the Brooklyn Dodgers in the fifth game of the World Series. Don Larsen pitched the first perfect World Series game. Bud missed it.

Bud, however, was back in Milwaukee when the Braves drove for the first pennant during the final weeks of the 1957 season. Bud was sitting in the upper deck when Hank Aaron hit his dramatic home run off the Cardinals' Billy Muffet in late September. Bud remembered, "When Hank hit that home run, I remember sitting there and crying. I was so happy. It was really one of those great moments you never forget."[2]

When Bud left the service, his first instinct was to study U.S. history in graduate school. His father, however, prevailed upon him to work in the family business. Ben Selig told his son: give me a year at the dealership and if you don't like it, you can go to graduate school. Bud today says that there wasn't anything that he wouldn't do for his father. He tried his hand in the car business and, as with baseball and his studies, became totally involved. Bud worked mostly in management, overseeing sales, leasing, and the family's emerging real estate holdings. He did little work directly with customers and says that contrary to many media accounts, he never sold a used car.

Selig described his work at the dealership:

I was doing more leasing, but I was really in management stuff. I did a lot of accounting and things. I would help on occasion in the new car department, but I never sold anything. It was a large dealership, and I learned. During high school and college I drove a parts truck and so I learned all phases of the business. I worked six days a week, five nights a week. Finally, in 1961 my mother complained that I was working too much and demanded that I take a night off. I took off Wednesday night because there was a program called "Naked City" that I loved on that night.

Back in Milwaukee, of course, Bud took full advantage of the fact that his hometown now had a major league team. Bud went to games regularly and loved every minute of it. So much so, in fact, that when the new Braves' owners, in response to concerns about absentee ownership from Chicago, decided to do a limited public stock offering in March 1963, Bud snapped up two thousand shares at $11.38 each. He sold off seventeen hundred of these shares at a profit prior to the Braves' departure to Atlanta after the 1965 season and then sold his final three hundred shares at $32 a piece in January 1966.[3]

The Braves' first years in Milwaukee were enormously successful. Team attendance was 1.83 million in 1953, when the team finished in second place in the NL. In each of the next four years, attendance exceeded 2 million, with one first-place and two second-place finishes. In 1958, the Braves won the pennant again, and attendance reached 1.97 million. The team was generating handsome profits.[4]

But after 1958, team performance trailed off, and the Braves discovered an iron law of baseball: in any city, fans like winners and dislike losers. After winning the pennant by 8 games in 1958, the Braves finished in second place; 2 games out in 1959, and their attendance dipped modestly to 1.75 million. In 1960, the team finished 7 games out, and attendance fell to 1.5 million. In 1961, the Braves slipped to fourth place and 10 games out, with an attendance of 1.1 million. In 1962, the team finished 15.5 games out of first place, with the turnstile count dropping to a nadir of 767,000. In November 1962, owner Lou Perini had had enough, selling the team for a nifty capital gain of almost $6 million to a group from Chicago, headed by Bill Bartholomay.

The Battle for Milwaukee

Despite being the smallest host city to a major league team, Milwaukee had proven itself to be a good baseball town. Indeed, taking the whole period of the Braves' stay in Milwaukee, 1953–1965, the team had the second-highest attendance of all major league franchises at 19.55 million (topped only by the Brooklyn/Los Angeles Dodgers). But the falling attendance led many to question whether Milwaukee continued to be a baseball-worthy city. The new owner, Bill Bartholomay, claimed that the addition of the Minnesota Twins in 1961 accounted for the lion's share of the 400,000 attendance skid that year. He cited evidence suggesting that the team had lost most of its support base from western and northwestern Wisconsin to the Twins.[5]

The 1963 Braves were no better than those of 1962, finishing fifteen games out. Attendance stagnated at 773,000. By July, rumors began to circulate that Bartholomay's group was having conversations with Atlanta officials about moving the team. It was at this time that one particularly passionate baseball fan from Milwaukee decided to take matters into his own hands. Bud Selig formed a group called Go-to-Bat-for-the-Braves and apparently spent a good part of the 1963–1964 off-season helping the team sell season's tickets. The team actually played a little better in 1964, though still finishing in fifth place, and Selig's work seemed to aid attendance, which rose to 910,911.

Bartholomay's negotiations, however, had proceeded to his liking, and shortly after the end of the 1964 season, he called a meeting of the franchise's board of directors. At the meeting, the board voted 12 to 6 to ask the NL for permission to move the team to Atlanta. The six nay votes were from local investors, each of whom held less than 1 percent of the team's stock. One of the nay votes came from the local businessman and the future Milwaukee Brewers co-owner Ed Fitzgerald.

If the NL approved the move, it would mark the first time in baseball's modern era that a team abandoned a major league city that had only one team. Commissioner Frick had testified in Congress on more than one occasion that he would be against such a team relocation. Frick notwithstanding, the NL voted to approve the move at its meeting on November 7, 1964.

A few days later, Ed Fitzgerald and Bud Selig formed a new organization, Teams, Inc. Teams, Inc. had two goals: first, to do whatever it could to keep the Braves in Milwaukee and, failing that, to attract another major league team to the city. By January 1965, Selig or Fitzgerald had spoken with Commissioner Frick, NL president Warren Giles, and officials from nine of the ten NL teams. In that month, Teams, Inc., issued a report that detailed its strategy for retaining the Braves. The Braves' lease at Milwaukee County Stadium ran through the 1965 season, so Selig and Fitzgerald had at least one more season to mobilize fan interest in the team. Selig, who still owned three hundred shares of Braves stock, convinced the ownership to stop making calls to sell season's tickets. He reasoned that the fans were angry at the ownership, and his organization would have better success. Selig stated that he would spend most of the 1964–1965 off-season trying to sell season's tickets. Fans were indeed alienated from the team, and Selig's success was modest at best. Final attendance for 1965 was only 555,584.

With attendance failing, Selig and his childhood buddy Herb Kohl, now a successful and wealthy local businessman, decided to make an offer to Bill Bartholomay to buy the team. They did not make a specific offer but guaranteed a price that would give him and his partners a good return on their investment. Bartholomay saw greener pastures in Atlanta and was not interested.

It was time for another strategy. With encouragement from Teams, Inc., the state of Wisconsin filed an antitrust suit against the Braves and the other NL teams on August 6, 1965. In its trial brief of November 1965, the state asserted that "Milwaukee is an excellent baseball town, that it is a disgrace to all baseball that it no longer has a major league team, that baseball is a monopoly, and that if it can't behave better than it has, it deserves to be regulated."

The thirty-one-year-old Bud Selig provided logistical support for the state's suit, he helped to prepare some of the state's witnesses, and he himself testified as a state's witness. Yet the suit posed a conflict for him. He wanted the state to win to force the Braves to return to Milwaukee for the 1966 season, but he also knew that it was likely that the team would be allowed to leave. That being the case, Selig's next goal was to bring a new team to Milwaukee, and to succeed in doing so would require at the very least that he remain in the good graces of the NL owners. Thus, when Selig testified during the trial, he stated that he was not in support of the suit.

Ralph Andreano, an economist at the University of Wisconsin in Madison and the state's expert witness on the baseball monopoly, recalled his interactions with Bud Selig when he was preparing for his testimony:

> My memory of Bud was that he was part of the team, with John Hanson and then Bill Veeck, who prepared me for testimony. He was always somewhat in the background and was not always

accessible to the press, though the *Milwaukee Journal*, which covered the trial extensively, did report his involvement, though they didn't quite know what he was doing. Bud's primary task was preparing me for testimony, and then helping Willard Stafford, who was going to actually try the case, through the labyrinth of the baseball agreements, etc. My memory of Bud was that he was so gung ho about the case and wanted major league baseball in Wisconsin so badly, that he latched on to anything to defeat Bill Bartholomay, the lead owner of the Braves, who wanted to move the Braves to Atlanta. My relations with Bud were fine and he really did help me with a lot of details. Bud did help me verify parts of my chart, which proved very decisive at the District Court level and almost at the Supreme Court level, and in general helped me prepare for my testimony. After each day, we would meet at the Pfister [Hotel], and Bud and Willard would go over my testimony, help me anticipate questions, and give criticism of what I did right and what wrong. On the whole it was a good relationship with Bud and I think he really did help the team prosecute the case well.[6]

Selig's role at the trial itself was to share his report on the economic viability of Milwaukee as a major league city. To prepare his report, Selig interviewed numerous baseball executives and traveled to Los Angeles to study the experience of the Angels, an AL expansion team. Based on the Angels' numbers, Selig prepared rudimentary pro formas to show that a new Milwaukee club would be profitable.

Many baseball executives were called to testify at the trial. Commissioner Frick figured prominently. In his pretrial deposition, the commissioner engaged in the following exchange with the state's lawyer:

Q. What do you consider the Commissioner's authority to be with respect to the transfer of franchises or the expansion of the league?

A. I think he has no authority whatsoever except the influence that he can use, the persuasion. . . .

Q. Will you tell me what plans for expansion the major leagues have at the moment?

A. I can't answer that question because I do not know. I do not sit in the league meetings. . . .

Q. Do you think Milwaukee is a good baseball town?
A. I've always thought it was a good baseball town. . . . If I were looking at expansion, Milwaukee would be on my list. . . .

Q. Do you think it's justification to move if the owners come to a conclusion that they might make more money in some other place than where they are currently located?
A. I couldn't answer it.[7]

Then, in trial, the state's attorney quoted a November 17, 1958, letter that Frick had written to the Phillies' owner. The letter read in part:

> If we refuse to consider the interest of the public in the development of our game; if we insist on being completely monopolistic in our organization, we will lose the public esteem which presently exists. . . . We will be the victims for every crackpot congressman in the country and we will, by our own shortcomings, pave the way for the breakdown of our structure.

Frick was asked whether he still held that opinion, and he stated that he did. Then he was asked whether he believed a shortage of playing talent was an impediment to the expansion of the major leagues. He answered that it was not.

Bowie Kuhn was the lead attorney for the NL. He later admitted to not having his heart in the case. In the end, it showed. The state of Wisconsin prevailed in trial court. But the Braves and the NL appealed to the state Supreme Court, which heard the arguments on June 9, 1966.[8] On July 27, in a split decision, the court held that it was true that baseball was acting monopolistically but that its behavior was protected under the U.S. Supreme Court's *Federal Baseball* decision of 1922.

Selig described what the team's flight meant to local fans in his 1993 testimony before the U.S. Congress:

> The city of Milwaukee and the state of Wisconsin were traumatized by the loss of that franchise. The people in my home state felt hostility, bitterness and a deep sense of betrayal toward major league baseball for allowing the Braves to abandon us. The years of drawing more than 2 million fans per season were forgotten.[9]

Anticipating likely defeat in the courts, Selig had begun a new initiative, Milwaukee Brewers, Inc. (MBI). Selig extracted pledges from ten local businessmen who each would put up $150,000 and a $1.5 million loan commitment from two local concessionaire companies. With a prospective capitalization of $3 million, Selig and Fitzgerald traveled to the NL owners' meeting in Miami Beach on December 2, 1965. Selig made a formal presentation, including his financial projections for a future Milwaukee team, and handed out a glossy booklet that MBI had produced with the support of the *Journal* company.

In his March 1966 trial testimony, Selig recounted some of the questions and comments made during his December 1965 presentation to the owners. The Dodgers' Walter O'Malley "asked [Selig] if the political situation in Milwaukee had improved [and] said that he personally wasn't in favor of granting the application unless it had." The Astros' Roy Hofheinz queried whether the prospective Milwaukee team owners "were in sympathy with the lawsuit against the league." And the Mets' Donald Grant stated that "he was not in favor of awarding a franchise to someone who was suing the league." Selig assured them that he was not a party to the lawsuit.[10] But his assurances seemed to be of no avail. Two hours after Selig's presentation ended, the NL issued a press release stating, "It is the considered judgment of the League that none of the applicants would be able to operate a franchise in 1966 and that League expansion in 1966 is not feasible." Selig himself opined, "There was so much anger towards us. I'd go to a meeting and people wouldn't even talk to us. It was like we had leprosy. They hated Milwaukee, hated Wisconsin."[11]

But Bud was tenacious. Bud's group made applications for expansion franchises in the AL in 1967 and the NL in 1966, 1967, and 1968. They lost out to Montreal, San Diego, Kansas City, and Seattle. They unsuccessfully attempted to make a deal with Bob Short to purchase his Washington Senators. He and his MBI partners then pursued purchasing the Chicago White Sox from Arthur Allyn in 1969. They offered $12.4 million for the team, but that deal fell through at the last minute when Allyn's brother, a 50 percent shareholder, decided that he did not want to sell. Selig

Bud Selig in his Brewers' office in the early 1970s.

commented, "When that deal went up in smoke, my heart sank. I knew we were coming to the end, that I couldn't hold this group together much longer."[12]

But they still didn't give up. The owners of the expansion Seattle Pilots had paid $5.25 million for the team, in addition to forfeiting certain annual revenue streams for several years. The team performed abysmally on the field in its first year, 1969, and its attendance fully reflected the team's performance. The owners were bleeding cash and were interested in finding new investors or selling the team. They reached an oral agreement with Bud Selig's Milwaukee group in October 1969 to sell the team for $10.8 million. (Selig himself put up only $300,000 of that money.[13]) The AL, however, refused to approve the sale and instead tried to find a way to recapitalize the team. When these efforts failed, on March 8, 1970, Selig and the Pilots' owners signed a formal buy/sell agreement. With Seattle's King County trying to block the team from moving for the 1970 season, the AL still refused permission for the sale. Selig's lawyers recommended to the Pilots' owners that the team file for bankruptcy, which it did. The bankruptcy court ordered the sale of the team by April 1, 1970. The truck driver who loaded his vehicle in Arizona with the team's equipment was told to drive to Utah and await further instructions. On the evening of March 31, the Seattle bankruptcy referee, Sidney Volinn, decided that the team would be sold to Selig's group and the truck driver was told to head east. The Milwaukee Brewers began their first season six days later. Selig reflected, "Of all the marvelous things that have happened to me, including becoming commissioner of baseball, that will always be my proudest accomplishment because the odds were stacked up tremendously against Milwaukee."[14]

Selig Enters Major League Baseball

Selig and Fitzgerald finally had succeeded in restoring major league baseball to Milwaukee. The problem was that it had almost been a full-time job for the previous seven years. Few people would have had the energy, the confidence, the patience, and the grit to have stayed the course. Indeed, it seemed as though Selig was not to be denied and that the pure force of his will brought major league baseball back to Milwaukee.

But Bud's dedication to baseball meant that his work at the car dealership was partially neglected. At the 1965 trial, Selig was asked by the NL attorney to describe his activities on behalf of saving baseball for his hometown. It was clear from the description that it was a more-than-forty-hour-a-week job. Then the lawyer asked how Bud could be vice president of the car dealership at the same time. Bud's answer was evasive.

His family life also suffered. Bud had married Donna Chaimson, a shopkeeper's daughter from northern Wisconsin, in 1956. The couple's first daughter, Sari, was born in 1957 and their second daughter, Wendy, was born in 1960. In 1975, after nineteen years of marriage, Bud and Donna were divorced. Donna explained that Bud's love for baseball left little time for her: "From the day Bud became involved in baseball, he divorced me and married baseball."[15]

Bud Selig, with his wife, Sue, and his granddaughter Natalie, at Miller
Park, Milwaukee, on Father's Day, 2004.

Bud remarried Sue Lappin less than two years later in 1977.
Sue also had a daughter, Lisa, born in 1959, from her previous
marriage. Life in the family, as it had been with Donna, remained
focused on baseball. Wendy reports that there were no family vaca-
tions or trips other than traveling with the team for an occasional
away series. Such trips were usually made to Baltimore because
Bud had a close relationship with Orioles owner Jerry Hoffberger.
On such jaunts, days were spent hanging around at the ballpark, discussing the good and the bad plays of the night before, and evenings
were spent at the game.

At home in Milwaukee, other than an occasional game of tennis that Wendy played with her dad, family leisure time was still
dedicated solely to baseball. There were no family outings for a

picnic, a hike, a museum visit, a play, and no games of *Monopoly*, *Yahtzee*, or *Concentration*. There were only visits to the ballpark.

During the off-season or when Bud did not travel with the team on a road trip or when the team played a day game, Wendy remembers that her dad was at the car dealership until at least 9 P.M. every night—except Thursday night when it closed early. And when he was home, baseball usually filled the air. Wendy commented, "When I really think about what we did as a family, I can tell you even, I remember Sunday nights, there was a sports talk show and invariably he would put it on during dinner on Sunday nights—God forbid we miss something that was said on this radio show." Wendy adjusted well to her circumstances, becoming a baseball aficionado herself and having a very close relationship with her dad.

Of course, as his parents had been with him, Bud was very interested in his daughters' success in school and often did homework with his girls. And girls are all he had—his three daughters produced five daughters of their own.

But that was okay because Bud was around men all day long. When Milwaukee landed the AL Brewers in 1970, Bud and Ed Fitzgerald took over control of the team. Anyone who has ever spent more than five minutes with Bud Selig knows him to be amiable, engaging, and garrulous. He can be that way in person or on the phone. Some people in baseball joke that Bud spent his first twenty-two years in baseball on the phone 24/7. As soon as Bud became a member of the elite club of baseball team owners, and there were twenty-four of them back in 1970, he was on the phone getting to know each and every one of his partners in the industry.

Bud became particularly friendly with an elder statesman in the game, John Fetzer, the owner of the Detroit Tigers. He credits Fetzer with educating him on the importance of cultivating a cooperative relationship among the owners and the need to be patient in building a consensus for change. Fetzer also recommended Bud for service on several of the ownership committees that are involved in assisting the commissioner's office in setting policy.

Yet during the early years of the Milwaukee Brewers, Bud and Ed Fitzgerald had a division of labor. Although Ed was the biggest investor in the franchise, Bud mostly handled the day-to-day operations of the team.[16] At first, Ed played a larger role representing the team on ownership committees. Ed, for instance, served as the chair of the important Player Relations Committee during much of the Kuhn commissionership. Bud served on a few lesser committees in the early years. His initial reluctance to get more involved in baseball's central administration was due to the natural caution of a neophyte, but it also had to do with how intimidated he was at his first owners' meeting.

> My first owners' meeting came a week after I got the team. Bowie [Kuhn] called me up and said we've got a meeting in New York. You've got to come. I didn't know what it was about. I was excited. I mean, are you kidding me? This was hard to believe. I was sitting right in between [Cardinals owner] Gussie Bush, who had broken an ankle and was pounding a cane, and [Cubs owner] Phil Wrigley, who was a very quiet, thoughtful man. The meeting was all about labor and the pension plan. And if I told you what they were arguing about, you wouldn't believe it. This was one of our problems. I thought at one point I was going to get caned by Gussie Bush. But I was stunned when I left there, because of the hatred and the anger. And I've often said to people that it never got better until two or three years ago. There's no question about it. The anger and the mistrust—it was really quite sad, and the sport itself suffered.[17]

As the 1970s wore on, Bud became inured to baseball's peculiar management style and began to participate on more owners' committees. Then, in 1980, when Ed Fitzgerald moved to Tennessee and resigned from the Brewers board, Bud became even more active and more central to baseball's governance committees.[18] In part, Bud's prominent role was because most owners shunned the administrative responsibilities. In part, it was because Bud loved being involved in all aspects of the game. When he was not rooting for his Brewers with all his heart and soul, he was spending hours upon hours talking on the phone with other owners. He listened and listened and always seemed to be on the side of whichever owner he was speaking to.

Bud Selig with Bowie Kuhn,
in 1984.

While some were derisive about Bud's perpetual phone mara-
thons, Selig was actually beginning to do something that had never
been done before in baseball. He was creating a common denomi-
nator for ownership cohesion. Of course, Peter Ueberroth did this
as well, but he did it with negative energy and led the owners
down the illegal path of collusion. Bud was a one-man polling and
counseling service, identifying the owners' common problems and
interests. They all felt that they could talk to him.

In Milwaukee, Bud had cathected both his team's competitive
fortunes and the industry's economic prospects. He managed the
team with a tight budget and generally succeeded in eking out a
modest profit. His staff often referred to him as "Budget Bud."[19]
He befriended the players and loved being around the game as
much as anyone did. His mood swings, like those of all intense
fans, were pronounced and followed the team's success or failure.

Mike Bauman followed the Brewers for years as a reporter for the *Milwaukee Journal-Sentinel* and then became a reporter for mlb.com. In a 2005 retrospective, Bauman described Selig's emotional investment in his team this way:

> He was, above all else, a fan. When the Brewers won, he was gleeful. When the Brewers lost, he was often, well, angry. . . . He didn't hide his emotions. "You watched all my temper tantrums— you were witness to them. You know that's no exaggeration," the Commissioner said with a smile that wasn't exactly sheepish.[20]

While Bud's emotions may have been out of control when it came to the game on the field, when the industry's problems were on the agenda, Bud was the consummate politician. As Fitzgerald's role on ownership committees faded, Selig's role, already appreciable, just kept expanding.

One of Bud's early committee assignments was to chair a committee of four owners to study and recommend a policy on interleague play. At the owners' summer meetings in August 1973, Bud's committee recommended in favor of interleague play, but the proposal was voted down by the NL owners on the executive council.

The following summer Bud, somewhat uncharacteristically, vented publicly at the baseball establishment. Two Brewers players (Don Money and Darrell Porter) were selected as alternates for the 1974 All-Star Game. Neither, however, entered the game. Selig called it "a disgrace that we [the Brewers] did not have anybody performing in the All-Star Game" and threatened to file a protest with the AL office.[21] Selig's beef was really with Earl Weaver, who managed the AL all stars that year, and the matter blew over.

In July 1975, Bowie Kuhn was up for reelection. On the first ballot he received only eight votes in the AL, but procedures at the time required that he receive three-quarters support in each league. Kuhn was one short. Selig and Fitzgerald, who had by then forgiven Kuhn for his role as defense attorney for the NL in the 1965–1966 Braves case, were key figures lobbying on behalf of Kuhn's candidacy for a second seven-year term.

Kuhn was reelected, but the next few years were rocky for baseball's leadership. Major League Baseball lost the Messersmith/

McNally arbitration and the two federal court cases that followed. Then Kuhn pushed the owners to end their lockout in 1976. By 1978, a bloc of disgruntled owners were looking for a scapegoat and began to organize an oust Kuhn movement. Selig was one of the prime movers of a resolution to endorse Kuhn that was eventually signed by twenty of the twenty-six owners.

In 1980, Selig, one of four owners on the executive council at the time, led the opposition to Edward DeBartolo Sr.'s purchase of the White Sox. DeBartolo owned three race tracks and lived in Youngstown, Ohio. Selig told the press, "Absentee ownership was the basic problem. Look, I lived through it when the Braves left Milwaukee for Atlanta in the 1960s."

In the summer of 1982, Selig took part on another committee that ultimately came out in support of revenue sharing from big city to small city teams. In November of that year, Selig was chosen as the chair of the search committee to replace Bowie Kuhn.[22] The following month Selig and William Williams of the Cincinnati Reds filed a report on debt policy to MLB's finance committee. The report recommended that baseball adopt a 60/40 debt rule, meaning that no team could have more than 40 percent debt in its capitalization. The rule was contested by the Players Association on the grounds that it would be used indirectly as a means to control salaries. The owners argued that the rule was intended only to preserve a sound financial structure for the industry. The owners prevailed in arbitration.[23]

In June 1983, the owners appointed Lee MacPhail to replace Ray Grebey as the president of the Player Relations Committee. At the time, Selig was one of six owners on the PRC board. Selig's centrality to MLB's governance was already apparent.

Selig and the IRS

Three days after MacPhail's appointment, on June 21, 1983, MLB received some terrific news from a federal district court in Wisconsin. Bud Selig had won his tax case against the IRS. When Selig and his partners bought the Milwaukee Brewers in 1970 for $10.8 million, they allocated $10.2 million, or 94.4 percent, of the purchase price to the value of the players' contracts they acquired. According to tax practice at the time, Selig and his partners were then able to amortize the $10.2 million over five years, thereby deducting $2.04 million from their operating profit each year before calculating taxable income.

Since the Brewers were held as a Subchapter S corporation, any reported team losses could then be carried over to the individual income taxes of the team's part owners. This scheme provides an important tax-sheltering opportunity to the owners of sports teams.

The Selig case was an important test of this tax shelter. In 1979, the IRS informed Selig that his amortization deductions were not allowed. Selig paid the taxes and sued for recovery. The month-long trial finally took place in May 1983; Selig and his partners had home-field advantage. The case was heard before Judge John Reynolds in Milwaukee. The judge's decision had all the impartiality and dispassion of Tom Delay opining on abortion rights. In his decision, for instance, Judge Reynolds wrote, "Baseball is good for Americans (who can argue with this)."

But the real problem with Judge Reynolds's decision was that he didn't understand the matter before him. A player's contract has asset value only if he produces a value greater than he is paid. In the pre-1977 (advent of free agency) days, many players were indeed paid less than the value they produced, and their contracts thus had asset value. The problem here is that this value does not diminish over time, because before 1977 the players eventually were replaced by new players who also were paid below their market value. That is, player contracts in the aggregate were nonwasting assets, and, therefore, they did not depreciate. The team's ability to exploit the player rested in the monopoly condition and the rules of baseball and was derived from the team's garnering a berth in a monopoly sports league. In any given year, a particular player's value might depreciate, but other players' value may appreciate, and, on average, there is no loss of value.

Beyond this, amortization of player contracts makes no sense because player salaries are already expensed (counted as costs) on the team's books. To both expense and amortize the same thing is to double count one's costs—artificially inflating costs and deflating profits. Some people argue that teams should be able to amortize players' contracts because they are using up the value invested in the players' development. But here, too, the cost (minor league player salaries, scouting, and training) of player development is already expensed.

Judge Reynolds, confused and addled by his love of baseball, found for Selig (who owned approximately 12 percent of the Brewers at the time). The IRS had to refund to Selig $151,608, plus interest and legal fees, for overpayment of taxes during 1970–1976.

The IRS appealed the decision, but in July 1984 the Seventh Circuit Court of Appeals upheld the Reynolds ruling. The appeals court decision suffers from the same curious economic logic and an even more romantic attachment to the game. Literary allusions are prevalent throughout the appeals court's ruling, which closes with the following:

Oh! somewhere in this favored land the sun is shining bright;
The band is playing somewhere, and somewhere hearts are light.
And somewhere men are laughing, and somewhere children shout;
But there is no joy in Mudville—mighty Casey has Struck Out.

There should be joy somewhere in Milwaukee—the district court's judgment is upheld.

Of course, with free agency it is no longer the case that the average player produces a value greater than he is paid. At best, this situation may apply to the small minority of players during their first two years in the majors—before they become eligible for either salary arbitration or free agency. Yet not only does the amortization of player contracts continue, it was extended in October 2004 legislation to include all intangible assets.[24] (The 1976 tax reform, however, did establish the presumption that no more than 50 percent of a team's value is allocable to player contracts. Selig's case preceded the reform.)

Notwithstanding its weak intellectual underpinning, Selig's victory against the IRS was really a victory for all of Bud's fellow owners. Selig's value to the industry just kept growing. Indeed, in

June 1983, several owners reportedly began to urge Selig to become a candidate to replace Bowie Kuhn. Selig's refrain at the time was heard many times later on: "I don't want to be commissioner. Under no circumstances."[25]

Besides, Selig was chairing the commissioner's search committee. After Giamatti, Selig's first choice, made it clear that he had to remain as Yale's president for the time being, Selig's committee recommended Peter Ueberroth. According to several reports, Selig and his close friend Jerry Reinsdorf, now the owner of the White Sox, were among the more enthusiastic supporters of Ueberroth's choreography toward collusion. Whether Selig was a main collusion cheerleader, he did serve as the chair of the PRC from 1985 through 1992 and must have played an important role in setting the path of labor relations during that time.

To this day, Ueberroth, Selig, and most owners still refuse to acknowledge that there was any collusion during 1986–1988. Fay Vincent and Richard Ravitch, the PRC chief during 1991–1994, both assert there was collusion and believe that the owners' refusal to acknowledge it remains an important source of distrust between the players' union and MLB.

When Ueberroth announced that he would not seek a second term as commissioner, Selig again was chosen to chair the search committee. In February 1991, Selig was appointed to the board of directors of the Cooperstown Hall of Fame, on which he continues to serve. In May of that year, Selig was chosen as the AL's negotiator over how to divide the $180 million of expansion revenues with the NL.

After the owners forced Vincent to resign in September 1992, Selig was elevated from member to chair of MLB's executive council. As chair, Selig began to fill the duties of the commissioner. By the time Selig ascended to the throne, he had served or was serving on the following owners' committees, several of which he also chaired: executive council, ownership committee, legislative affairs and government relations committee, realignment committee, board of directors of MLB Properties, relocation committee of the executive council, PRC, superstation committee, big-market/small-market committee, planning committee, interleague play committee, expansion committee, owners' representative to 1990–1992 economic study committee, television committee, AL board of directors, search committee AL president, joint league expansion committee, finance committee, audit and budget committee, restructuring study committee, board of directors of MLB promotion corporation, three division study committee, commissioner search committees, and board of directors of the Hall of Fame.

After Selig was selected as the chair of the executive council in 1992, Dodgers owner Peter O'Malley asked, "How can he be in charge of so many things?"[26] A good question. Selig was probably the most powerful man in baseball even before he became acting commissioner.

7

Baseball's Acting Commissioner, 1992-1998

Bud Selig was in his Milwaukee office on September 8, 1992, looking forward to the game that day when Robin Yount would be going for his 3,000th hit. Yount didn't get it. After the game, Selig flew to St. Louis for the owners' meeting. Once in his hotel room, he got a call from Eli Jacobs, the owner of the Baltimore Orioles and one of the owners who had supported Fay Vincent to the end. Jacobs told him, "The guys have been talking. You've got to take over tomorrow."[1] Selig responded, "We'll discuss it tomorrow." Moments later, another call came from Chicago Cubs executive Stan Cook with the same message. Selig gave the same answer.

The next morning, Selig was elected 10 to 0 (eight owners and the two league presidents) by the executive council to be its chair. After the meeting, Selig flew back to Milwaukee with Rangers owner George W. Bush, Padres owner Tom Werner, and AL president Bobby Brown to watch Yount get his 3,000th hit that evening. The four then flew back to St. Louis for the continuation of the owners' meetings the next day.

The Major League Agreement stipulates that the commissioner serves as the chair of the executive council. Until September 9, 1992, the chair of the executive council was always the commissioner. By making Selig the chair and not making him the commissioner, the owners were moving into uncharted waters—a circumstance that created more than its share of ambiguity in future years. The press came to refer to Selig as the acting commissioner.

Some suggested that Jerry Reinsdorf, Selig's close associate and the owner of the White Sox, was the éminence grise of baseball. Reinsdorf rejected any notion that he was the puppeteer: "There is only one powerful owner in baseball, and that's Bud Selig. He's the only one who can get votes out of the other owners. It's because he's such a nice guy, and he works at staying in touch with the rest of us." At the time, Selig told the press, "I probably talk with every owner at least once a week, and some many times more than that."[2]

When Bud told his wife, Sue, of his new position, she inquired, "What does this mean?" Bud responded, "It's two to four months, not more. Don't worry about it. It won't affect anything." He told the press the same thing: two to four months.

While Bud's title and his permanence may have been hazy, the monumental challenges that lay before him were strikingly clear. The realignment issue and its impact on the Chicago Cubs were still in litigation. National television revenues, which had been growing by leaps and bounds, were poised to take a severe dip (as it turned out the next year, by more than 50 percent). Attendance at games fell by 1.6 percent in 1992, with eighteen of the twenty-eight teams experiencing drops. A 1992 Gallup survey showed that MLB now lagged the NFL in popularity by a more than 2 to 1 margin. With the emergence of local cable TV revenues and new ballparks, team revenue disparities were growing rapidly and engendering consternation among the owners. Average player salaries had just passed the $1 million level for the first time. And MLB had serious image problems, most notably from the messy dispute with, and the resignation of, Fay Vincent.

One of the first matters on Selig's agenda was to deal with the realignment suit that the Cubs filed against Vincent. Bud explained the approach he would take to this and other issues: "We can move forward to resolve the realignment issue through consensus rather than confrontation, which is the approach I would like to take to each and every problem confronting the game today."[3] After consulting with the executive council, Selig then rescinded the order to realign the divisions.

At the winter owners' meeting in December 1992, the magnates voted 15 to 13 to reopen the collective-bargaining agreement (CBA) with the players. Many expected that this was a harbinger of a lockout for spring training camps in March. Dick Ravitch, the PRC chief, called Don Fehr with the message that he should prepare for urgent talks. There was no lockout in 1993, and there were no serious collective-bargaining talks for nineteen months.

After the December meeting, Selig met the press and was asked whether baseball had made any progress toward selecting its next commissioner. Two months, after all, had already elapsed. Selig opined, "We need a strong commissioner, and we expect to have our man [soon]. We need a strong commissioner like Bart. Bart said: 'My job is to lead by suasion.' He understood that there were 26 owners with sometimes 26 different agendas. It was up to the commissioner to bring us together." And, responding to one query about whether he was the man for the job, Selig reiterated, "As for me, that part isn't even worth talking about because I have zero interest in the job."[4]

One person who did have an interest in the commissioner's job was the Ohio senator and the chair of the Committee on the Judiciary Howard Metzenbaum. In particular, Metzenbaum wanted to know how the historical function of the commissioner to protect the game's integrity and the fans could continue to be exercised if the acting commissioner were also a team owner. Senator Metzenbaum, who formerly owned a share of the Cleveland Indians, convened Senate hearings on baseball's antitrust exemption in December 1992. In his opening remarks, the senator stated,

> Fay Vincent understood that the antitrust exemption placed a special obligation on the commissioner to govern the sport in a manner that protected the public interest. Vincent had independent authority to put the interest of the fans and interests of the sport of baseball ahead of the business interests of the team owners.
>
> That's no longer the case. Jerry Reinsdorf, the owner of the Chicago White Sox and one of the key participants in Vincent's

Bud Selig and President George W. Bush on opening day of the
Washington Nationals at RFK Stadium, April 14, 2005. Bush was
a co-owner and a managing partner of the Texas Rangers before
becoming the governor of Texas. He is rumored to have some
interest in the commissioner's job. Bush and Selig both serve in
their present positions until 2009.

ouster, has stated that the job of the next baseball commissioner
will be to "run the business for the owners, not the players or the
umpires or the fans."[5]

When Selig testified, he assured Senator Metzenbaum and his
colleagues that baseball would soon have a strong commissioner.
The restructuring committee simply needed to finish its efforts to
redefine the parameters of the commissioner's job, and then MLB
would hire its new leader.

But before baseball's barons reassembled to decide these matters, one baroness from Cincinnati needed to be disciplined. Marge
Schott had been an almost constant embarrassment to the game

since she became the Reds' managing partner in July 1985. Schott knew little about baseball and seemingly even less about world events, and she rivaled the late Charles Comiskey in parsimony. In a 1988 interview with the *Cincinnati Post*, Schott shared the following ruminations about her team: "Q: Who do you see as your toughest competition? A: Well, I hope it's St. Louis. Q: I mean in the division. A: Let me see. I don't know. Maybe the Kansas City Royals. Q: I mean your division. A: Well, Pittsburgh's got some young coming, Los Angeles is going to come back."[6] To the surprise of everyone at CBS television, moments before the first pitch of the 1990 World Series at Riverfront Stadium in Cincinnati, Schott grabbed the microphone and called for a moment of silence for the U.S. troops "in the Far East."[7]

Accounts of her penny-pinching abound. During the 1990 World Series, she made the players' wives pay airfare on the team's chartered plane to California and then pay half of the hotel bill. On another occasion, she tried to sell doughnuts left over from an executives' meeting to her office employees.

But the real problem for baseball had to do with a different manifestation of her ignorance. She repeatedly uttered phrases that smacked of bigotry, using racial slurs, such as "niggers" or "dirty Jews," when addressing club employees. One time Schott declared that Hitler "had the right idea but he went too far." So, on February 3, 1993, Selig decided that baseball had had enough. He suspended Schott for one year and fined her $25,000 (or approximately 50,000 resold doughnuts) for "the most base and demeaning type of racial and ethnic stereotyping."

A week later, Selig appointed Bill Bartholomay, the Braves' owner who had moved the team out of Milwaukee seventeen years earlier, as head of the commissioner's search committee. On February 17, the owners convened in Phoenix for their sixth meeting in six months. There they made a fateful decision that many owners have rued ever since. Ravitch had argued to the owners that the players would not accept a salary cap without an owners' decision to share local revenue. What Ravitch left out of his pitch was that the players also wouldn't accept a salary cap even with revenue sharing. Nonetheless, Ravitch won the day, and the owners declared that there was a link between salaries and revenue sharing. Selig explained the owners' reasoning: "We're saying today there is a linkage between these two things. It's often been said by the Players Association: let them solve their own problems first. Let them go to revenue sharing. The clubs took a step today to acknowledge there is a direct linkage."[8] The longer-term problem created is that the declaration of linkage has made revenue sharing an obligatory subject for collective bargaining. Now, whenever the owners want to alter their revenue-sharing scheme, they have to get the approval of the Players Association.

Only two weeks went by before the owners met again. Selig seemed to be living up to his word that he wanted to develop a style of decision making by consensus. The March 3–4, 1993, meetings were eventful. The owners approved in principle three divisions per league with a wild card team for the postseason, interleague play, and league realignment. As a prelude to substantial discussions on revenue sharing and on Ravitch's urging, they also agreed to share full franchise financial information with one another. Furthermore, they announced an initiative to shorten games by twenty minutes. And Selig reported to the owners that the restructuring committee had concluded its report (on February 16) but said that it would not be distributed to the owners until the executive council had vetted it.

In any event, there seemed to be less urgency to see the report as several owners began to express a desire not to hire a new commissioner at least until the new television and collective-bargaining agreements were signed. Others were concerned that there had been four commissioners over the previous four years and six new owners had joined the game in the past year.[9] Without some continuity, baseball would never get its act together. The two- to four-month time frame for hiring a new leader had already elapsed, and Senator Metzenbaum did not seem unduly bent out of shape. When the owners met again in April, the executive council still had not released the restructuring committee's report. With no one pushing, baseball was prepared to wait.

The owners met again in May, when they concentrated on discussing the new television deal that had been negotiated by Bill

Giles, Eddie Einhorn, and Tom Werner with ABC and NBC. Guaranteed rights payments dropped precipitously, and regional broadcasts were substituted for national ones. At the time, it was the best they could do, and the barons approved the deal by a 25 to 2 margin. Selig tried to put a positive spin on it, proclaiming, "We are seizing control of our own destiny."[10] Baseball hoped to gain in incentive payments what it had lost in guarantees. It wasn't to work out that way, as national media revenue per team dropped from around $15 million to $5 million per year.

Meanwhile, the 1993 season was underway, and despite the urgent call from Dick Ravitch to Don Fehr back in December, no collective-bargaining talks were being held. The reason for the delay was that the owners couldn't agree with one another over the plan they would present to the union. They agreed that the salary system and revenue sharing were linked, but they couldn't agree on the details of either. PRC chief Ravitch had been spending his time politicking among the owners, trying to get them to share their books and to identify a sharing plan that three-quarters of the owners would accept. However, by the All-Star break, the only tune Ravitch heard the owners picking was dueling banjos.

In August, hoping to iron out a revenue-sharing consensus, Ravitch summoned the barons to a bucolic resort in Kohler, Wisconsin, sixty miles north of Milwaukee—a sufficiently isolated venue where he thought no reporters would bother them. Ravitch was wrong about the reporters and, more significantly, wrong to think that the owners could agree upon a sharing plan. Indeed, the two-day enclave at Kohler was the most rancorous and destructive meeting that anyone in attendance could remember. At the time, there was only minimal sharing of local team revenues in baseball. American League teams shared 20 percent of gate receipts with the visiting team, and NL teams shared less than 5 percent. In addition, there was negligible sharing of cable television revenues in the AL.

Tensions were building to share additional revenues ever since the Yankees signed their twelve-year cable deal with the MSG network for $493 million in 1988 (including a $50 million upfront bonus). The Orioles' revenue jump of more than $30 million from

Camden Yards, with other new stadiums in process, and the expected sharp decrease in the (equally shared) national television contract beginning in 1994 brought the pressure to a boiling point.

In preparation for the Kohler meetings, eleven high-revenue teams began caucusing weeks in advance, as did a larger group of low- and middle-revenue teams.[11] At Kohler, because of the acrimony, the two caucuses could scarcely meet in the same room. Ravitch, Selig, and others had to carry messages back and forth.

In a 2005 interview, Selig used some striking epithets to describe the atmosphere in Kohler.

> I've never seen anger like that. It wasn't just bad. It was vile. Kohler, Wisconsin, was probably the most painful three days I've ever been through. Everybody else who was there, including George W. Bush, had never seen anything like it. It was worse than terrible. People said things to each other that were awful.[12]

Understandably, Selig painted a considerably more benign picture of the Kohler confab to the press at the time: "It's seven or eight hours later and this is a highly complex subject. Today's discussion has been constructive and enlightening. Obviously, there is a difference of opinion."[13]

The high-revenue club owners had a mantra at Kohler: "You're not going to put your hands in my pockets." Paul Beeston, the president of the Blue Jays, said that *acrimony* was too weak a word to describe the tone at Kohler; *hatred* was more appropriate. Selig didn't know how the owners would ever be able to function collectively again.

> At Kohler we hit the bottom of the barrel. It was just heartbreaking. . . . I had to call a lot of people the next day. I had great relationships with them on both sides. I had to tell them: "Guys, please don't. Don't do this, because otherwise we'll never put this house back together again, and then what are we going to do?" I think that's what scared them and got them to understand. You can say "fuck you" and "I'll sue you" as many times as you like. It's like my father used to say to me years ago: "You're mad, so what, who cares, now what are we going to do about it?"[14]

Notwithstanding Selig's persistent therapy sessions with the choleric owners, the magnates were afraid that the game was being threatened by their disunity. They knew that some accommodation, some compromise had to be made. One final stimulus that pushed the high-revenue teams to accept revenue sharing was the coming expiration of the NL's television agreement. The small-market owners threatened not to sign a new agreement, which meant that teams would be able to televise their home games only in their local markets. Since U.S. copyright law gave the telecasting rights to the home team, large-market teams would be able to show only half the number of games in their local markets.

Although tempers had calmed down a bit, the owners were not ready to reopen the revenue-sharing discussion at their September 1993 meeting. Instead, they voted in favor of moving to three divisions with club realignment, accepting a new ESPN contract that was 36 percent lower than the existing one, and appointing Ken Schanzer to direct the new baseball television partnership with NBC and ABC. Perhaps to deflect revenue-sharing questions, the owners also told the press about progress in their search for a new commissioner. The search committee chair, Bill Bartholomay, stated, "I think we're on a fast course. I would expect we'll be done by the end of the year."[15] The names mentioned included Colin Powell, George Mitchell, George Bush, Dick Ebersol, and Bud Selig. Selig, however, continued to deny an interest in the job: "The answer is no, it's been no, everybody knows it's no. I'm not going to change my mind. I have no interest in the job."[16]

But Selig couldn't have been too unhappy with his situation. Bud was doing largely what he would do anyway—working the phones 24/7. In September 1993, the owners voted to give him a $1 million a year salary as acting commissioner ($350,000 more than Fay Vincent) and to allow him to handle MLB's business out of a new office in Milwaukee. He was also permitted to continue in his executive capacity with the Brewers, from whom Selig continued to earn between $450,000 and $540,000 a year during 1993–1997.[17] Selig's compensation from MLB was referred to as an honorarium. Since Selig was considered the chair of the executive council (as opposed to the commissioner) and the Major League

Agreement stipulated that executive council members could not be paid, this semantical twist was more than a nicety. It also meant that social security taxes did not have to be withheld. Selig's "honorarium" was raised to $1.25 million in 1994 and to $1.5 million in 1995.[18] These rapid rises, impressive though they seem, paled in comparison to what was to come. In Selig's final year as acting commissioner, he was reportedly being paid $2.5 million.[19]

A month later, Bartholomay and Selig were still singing the same tune. Bartholomay said the list was down to six and that the committee was doing deep background checks on the finalists. He predicted a decision by early December. Selig counseled reporters to pay no attention to the rumors circulating about his candidacy.[20]

At their December meeting, the barons considered expanding by two teams for 1997. Such a move would expand the number of players under major league contract and in the union by eighty, and some owners argued that this could be an inducement to the union in exchange for accepting a salary cap and revenue sharing.[21]

The owners met again in early January 1994, in the Chicago suburb of Rosemont. Bartholomay was doing his best imitation of a broken record, announcing that the commissioner's list was now down below five and that a decision was imminent. But the real news was that the owners were discussing revenue sharing for the first time since Kohler, five months earlier. There were still caucuses. In fact, what were two caucuses in Kohler had expanded into three in Rosemont: eight clubs in the high-revenue caucus, thirteen in the middle, and seven in the low one. But Selig continued working the phones and brokering compromises. This time, calmer heads prevailed. Dick Ravitch put forth a revenue-sharing/salary cap plan that received twenty affirmative votes. According to the Major League Agreement, it needed three-fourths support or twenty-one votes, but the owners were making progress.[22] In fact, the magnates were sufficiently heartened that they agreed to try again, ten days later in Ft. Lauderdale.

On January 18, 1994, in Ft. Lauderdale, the owners made history: they unanimously agreed on a plan that would move approximately $58 million (based on 1993 revenues) from high- to low-revenue teams. The sharing, however, would be contingent on the players accepting a salary cap. Basically, the high-revenue teams consented to surrender some of their revenue to their low-revenue partners with the expectation that they would save a roughly equal sum of money from the salary cap. Furthermore, the salary cap would also contain a payroll floor (around 75 percent of the cap), and the revenue transfers would enable the low-revenue teams to meet this floor.

The owners also attempted to bring closure to the commissioner search. According to various sources, Bartholomay's committee was prepared to recommend Arnold Weber, the retiring president of Northwestern University. Stan Cook of the Cubs and Jerry Reinsdorf of the White Sox each had been serving on Northwestern's board of trustees since 1987 and had a close relationship with Weber. Bartholomay, although an owner of the Braves, was also based in Chicago and knew Weber. Before Bartholomay could recommend Weber and call for a vote, however, he received a letter signed by eleven low- and medium-revenue club owners stating that they would not vote for a new commissioner until a new collective-bargaining agreement was signed. At least five additional clubs supported this position orally.[23] Selig explained that in the face of this overwhelming view among the owners, he would reluctantly agree to remain as acting commissioner but that "in no way, shape or manner do I want to be commissioner, or will I be commissioner."[24]

Significantly, in Ft. Lauderdale the owners also finally approved the restructuring committee's report that clarified the powers of the commissioner. Senator Metzenbaum, concerned that Selig's two to four months as interim commissioner was now approaching eighteen months, that the term would extend indefinitely into the future, and that the restructuring report diminished the commissioner's role, called new hearings in March. Metzenbaum, as would many other members of Congress in the coming years, treated Selig with near disdain.

Selig told the senator that the restructuring of the office did not limit the commissioner's prerogatives but rather clarified and redefined them. In fact, the restructuring did two things. First, it made the commissioner the permanent chair of the PRC, making him a direct participant and a partisan of the owners in the collective-bargaining process. This change constituted a sharp departure from the previous "neutral" role of the commissioner in labor matters. Second, to make sure that the experience with Kuhn in 1976, Ueberroth in 1985, or Vincent in 1990 (where the commissioner essentially compelled the owners to make a compromise in order to avoid or curtail a work stoppage) would never happen again, the restructuring rescinded the commissioner's "best interests" powers to act unilaterally to resolve a collective-bargaining dispute. That is, the commissioner could not force an end to a lockout or impose contract terms on the owners. This second point is undoubtedly what troubled Metzenbaum regarding the possible diminution of the commissioner's powers. The first point, if anything, strengthened the commissioner's hand.

Senator Connie Mack of Florida, who was disappointed that Tampa Bay did not yet have a major league team despite having built a domed stadium, went after Selig on the question of how the restructuring clarified whether the commissioner could be fired. Selig responded, "It's been left silent as it always was." Mack observed that this was no clarification at all.

Metzenbaum piled on. To Selig's claim that the office had been fortified, the Ohio senator asserted, "I think your answer is incredible. I don't think you're giving me a correct answer."

Yet Selig held his ground. He argued that the "best interests" clause was never intended to apply broadly to all business matters; it was conceived strictly as a unilateral authority to deal with integrity violations. Since this delineation was never made explicit, the restructuring clarified what in Selig's view was always intended.[25]

Seventy-year-old intentions are difficult to discern. To be sure, the circumstances of the 1921 agreement do suggest that the owners were granting the commissioner special authority over integrity issues. Yet the wording of the agreement states (Sections 2a and 2b): "To investigate, either upon complaint or upon his own initiative, *any act, transaction or practice* charged, alleged or suspected to be detrimental to the best interests of the national game of baseball. . . . To determine, after investigation, what preventive, remedial or punitive action is appropriate . . ." (italics added). The wording "any act, transaction or practice" seems to suggest that a broad interpretation of the "best interests" authority is appropriate.

The real issue, however, was not the intentions of the owners in 1921. The real issue was that there was an ongoing dispute and ambiguity about what the commissioner's authority should be. With regard to labor, the conundrum was well articulated by baseball's seventh commissioner, Bart Giamatti: "Why should I involve myself in a process in which I hold moral suasion over only one side?" Perhaps even more cogently, if the "best interests" authority were applicable, the commissioner would have power over the owners' position but not over the players'. The commissioner could force the owners to end a lockout but couldn't compel the players to halt a strike. In the end, with "best interests" authority in collective bargaining, the commissioner was providing added leverage to the players. There was no reason for the owners to accept such a predicament. And with the 1994 restructuring, the owners made it clear that they would not accept it.

Following Congress's well-established, effete, saber-rattling tradition, Metzenbaum huffed and puffed at baseball's governance and antitrust exemption, but he blew nothing down. In fact, he let the matter drop altogether.

Baseball had more urgent matters on its agenda—as did Congress, one would hope. The owners agreed in February on a revenue-sharing plan. Next, they had to agree on a salary cap plan to present to the players. On June 14, 1994, seventeen months and one week after they had reopened the collective-bargaining agreement and Ravitch had told Fehr to prepare urgently for talks, the owners were finally ready to put their proposal on the bargaining table.[26]

The owners proposed that the players would receive 50 percent of all revenues (approximately 3 percentage points below what they were receiving at the time) and each team's payroll would have to be between 84 and 110 percent of the average team's payroll. Predictably, the players were unwilling to discuss any kind of a cap, even if the owners chose to share revenue among themselves. The two sides also had disagreements over salary arbitration and the specifics of the revenue-sharing plan. With little progress being made, on July 28, 1994, the Players Association set August 12 as a strike deadline. Fans seemed undeterred by this quadrennial squabbling ritual. Average game attendance was at an all-time high.

Bravado, not common sense, prevailed. On August 1, the owners announced that they would cease making payments to the players' pension fund. Although the fund agreement had expired, the fund was traditionally financed from All-Star Game revenues. The players played in the 1994 All-Star Game and felt they were entitled to ongoing coverage. Moreover, the owners had given them no warning about their intention. The players filed an unfair labor practices suit, which they later won.

On cue, the players went on strike on August 12. On September 14, Selig called off the rest of the season, marking the first time since 1904 that no World Series would be played. With midterm congressional elections coming up in November, the Clinton administration saw an opportunity to intervene that, if successful, could garner the Democrats some additional support. On October 13, Clinton appointed Bill Usery Jr., probably the country's most noted labor mediator, to mediate the negotiations between the players and the owners. Usery did get the owners to substitute a stiff luxury tax on payrolls for their salary cap—thus breaking the linkage between revenue sharing and a salary cap—but the players resisted even the luxury tax.

Don Fehr argued that the revenue-sharing system itself would provide a substantial break on salaries. If shared revenue was generated by a tax on a team's local revenue of, say, 20 percent, then a player who generated $10 million of extra revenue for a club would now generate only $8 million net. Such a player may have been paid up to $10 million in the past but under this kind of revenue sharing would be paid only up to $8 million. Eventually, the players did consent in mid-December to a fixed 5.25 percent tax on payrolls, along with revenue sharing, but the owners were looking for much more.

Meanwhile, the owners' negotiators were in flux. Dick Ravitch, whose influence had been on the wane at least since June and who, in fact, felt that he was never given the authority he had been promised, resigned in early December.[27] Ravitch stated that he had never contemplated staying longer than his three-year term, but it was apparent that he was dissatisfied with his role, believing that he had been marginalized by Selig. Ravitch was nominally replaced by John Harrington, the managing partner of the Red Sox, but Harrington himself participated in only a few days of talks before he, too, appeared to be marginalized. Jerry McMorris, the co-owner of the Rockies, was the point man for the crucial negotiations that preceded the owners' declaration of a bargaining impasse on December 23. Whether the switching of the guard reflected an alternate ascendance of different ownership cliques or whether Selig was simply trying to keep the players off balance is unclear. Whatever the strategy was, it was not working.

Along with the declaration of impasse, the owners unilaterally implemented their salary cap proposal. The union immediately filed an unfair labor practices suit with the National Labor Relations Board (NLRB), claiming inter alia that negotiations were moving forward and there was no impasse. On January 13, the executive council voted to proceed with its plans to recruit replacement players from minor leaguers and retired veterans. After the meeting, Selig was asked why the owners were keeping details of the replacement player plan secret. He responded, "I don't know that there is a secret. All the details have yet to be worked out." According to the *New York Times*, when Selig made this statement, the executive council was in possession of seven pages of details, the last page of which read, in part, "The information contained in this memorandum is highly confidential. Under no circumstances should this memorandum be released to any member of the press."[28]

The two sides hadn't met since December 22. The thought of replacement players invoked images of chaos and all-out war. Even some owners appeared to be against such a move. Peter Angelos, the owner of the Orioles, for instance, was a labor lawyer who had no taste for such hostility. Furthermore, his star player, Cal Ripken, was on the verge of breaking Lou Gehrig's consecutive game record, and his feat would be undermined if the Orioles played games without him. Labor law in Ontario and Quebec made it very unlikely that replacement players would even be allowed to play on the Blue Jays' or the Expos' home fields.

On January 26, President Clinton ordered Bill Usery to bring both sides back to the bargaining table. When the talks resumed on February 1, the owners removed their demand for a salary cap and instead proposed a luxury tax on high payrolls: a 75 percent tax on payrolls between $35 million and $42 million, and a 100 percent tax on payrolls of more than $42 million. With these discussions proceeding, the owners unilaterally revoked the authority of teams to sign player contracts, eliminated salary arbitration, and terminated the anticollusion clause that had been negotiated in the last contract.

On February 7, Clinton summoned both sides to the White House and requested that they consider binding arbitration. The players agreed. The owners demurred.[29] The next day the players filed another unfair labor practices grievance in response to owners' unilateral actions the previous week. The NLRB agreed with the union and referred the case to federal district court in New York. As spring training went forward with replacement players, Judge Sonia Sotomayor heard the case. The owners claimed that their unilateral actions were not in areas that are subject to mandatory bargaining, and, hence, they were at liberty to do what they did. Sotomayor, however, agreed with the NLRB, claiming that any provision that affected wages was subject to mandatory bargaining. Sotomayor ruled on March 31 that each of the owners' actions (suspending the signing of new player contracts, abrogating salary arbitration, and ending the anticollusion clause) could impact player salaries, and she issued an injunction that compelled the owners to restore all the terms and conditions of the previous collective-bargaining agreement. With the old CBA restored, the players ended their strike. The owners were fearful of damage to the game and were in too much disarray to take unified, aggressive action. Thus, they chose not to lock out the players, and the regular season began almost a month late, on April 26. Major League Baseball was debilitated, but it was still alive.

It is easy to second-guess Selig and the owners for the way they conducted their negotiations. The initial seventeen-month delay in starting negotiations, the confusion over who was the commissioner and what was his role, the turnover of PRC chiefs, the imprudent implementation of unilateral actions that violated labor law, among other missteps, all seem foolish in hindsight. Perhaps a more rational and intelligent approach could have avoided the work stoppage, the cancellation of the 1994 season, and the ensuing severe popularity hit that baseball suffered. Yet the facts remain that the owners and the players had fundamentally different perceptions of the industry's problems and needs, the union was strong and intransigent, and the owners were acutely divided among themselves, notwithstanding a tentative agreement to carry out some additional revenue sharing. The owners' position was compromised further by the likelihood that their internal discussions were being leaked to the union by certain owners.

Judge Sotomayor also ordered the owners and the players back to the bargaining table. After several months of respite, low-level negotiations without either Selig or Fehr resumed, but little was accomplished. The owners hired a new PRC chief in late 1995, Randy Levine, the personable labor commissioner of New York City.[30] It was not until October 24, 1996, however, that the two sides reached a tentative agreement. On November 6, the owners voted 18 to 12 against the agreement, but a few days later Jerry Reinsdorf signed Albert Belle to a record five-year, $55 million deal. Reinsdorf, who had been a ringleader during the collusion and the ouster of Vincent, as well as a consistent hawk on labor matters, seemed to have abandoned his principles. The capricious owners were so moved by Reinsdorf's apparent duplicity that they voted again on the tentative deal on November 26. This time the vote was 26 in favor and 4 against, with Reinsdorf joining the quartet.

The new agreement contained some substantial reforms. Most prominently, MLB introduced its first revenue-sharing system. The system was phased in over the five years of the 1996–2001 agreement. By 2001, each team was taxed at 20 percent of its net local revenue (all local revenue minus stadium expenses).[31] Three-quarters of the collected revenue was distributed equally to all thirty clubs, and one-quarter was distributed only to clubs with below-average revenue (in proportion to how far each club was below the average). Approximately $168 million was transferred from the top half to the bottom half of teams via this system in 2001.[32]

The second significant innovation of the 1996 agreement was the introduction of baseball's first luxury tax. This tax on high-payroll teams was designed to substitute (albeit poorly) for a salary cap. From the perspective of the high-revenue clubs, there is a bitter irony in this substitution. These clubs agreed in January 1994 to share some of their revenues with small-market clubs, if and only if the Players Association agreed to a salary cap. Their expectation was that they would earn back in the salary cap what they were giving up with revenue sharing. The outcome, however, was that not only did they get no relief from a salary cap, they had an additional burden thrust upon them with the obligation to pay a luxury tax if their payrolls exceeded a certain threshold. The political skill of Bud Selig in maintaining the owners' willingness to move forward with revenue sharing without a cap should not be underestimated.

Under the new agreement, beginning in 1997 the teams with the top five payrolls paid a tax of 35 percent on the amount by which their payroll was above the midpoint between the payroll of the fifth- and sixth-highest payroll teams (the threshold). The 1998 tax was 35 percent on the top five payrolls on the amount they were above 1.078 times the 1997 threshold. The 1999 tax was 34 percent on the top five payrolls on the amount they were above 1.071 times the 1998 threshold.[33] There was no luxury tax in the last two years of the agreement.

A third noteworthy reform in the 1996 agreement was the introduction of an Industry Growth Fund (IGF) to promote the growth of the game in the United States, in Canada, and throughout the world. The players contributed 2.5 percent of their 1997 and 1998 salaries to this fund, and the owners contributed a matching sum (largely out of the proceeds from the luxury tax). The IGF was supposed to be jointly administered and signaled the desire of both sides to begin building a partnership between the owners and the players.

Finally, the agreement included an unprecedented element. The two sides agreed to go to Congress to seek a partial lifting of MLB's antitrust exemption as it applied to collective bargaining. Congress complied in the 1998 Curt Flood Act, which gives the players an

opportunity to sue MLB if the owners attempt to unilaterally impose restrictive conditions on baseball's labor market. The union
had argued that one of the reasons for baseball's tumultuous labor
relations was that players had only one means to defend their interests—the strike. If the players were also able to bring an antitrust suit (after union decertification), then they would have the
same legal recourse available as did players in other sports. Because
most unions are reluctant to call for a decertification, it is ques-
tionable whether the Curt Flood Act will have any impact on baseball's labor relations in the future.

Certainly, the introduction of revenue sharing, a luxury tax, and
a jointly managed Industry Growth Fund all indicated substantive
reform. Most significantly to the fans, baseball had an agreement
and the players were back on the field. Appearing on *Meet the Press*
in July 1996, Selig stated that after the new CBA was signed, the
owners would appoint a new commissioner and that it wouldn't be
him.[34] With a new agreement signed in November, the press and
the public began to wonder again how long baseball would have
only an acting commissioner.

At their January 1997 meeting in Scottsdale, Arizona, the owners went through the motions of reopening the search process. This
time, however, they declared that the executive council would be
the search committee. Selig repeated the old refrain: "My view on
my own situation hasn't changed since 1992, no matter what many
of them thought or said."[35]

In Scottsdale, the owners also created a committee to make a
report on realignment. Major League Baseball was planning to expand by two teams in 1998, leaving a total of thirty teams. If the
two leagues were of equal size, it would mean an odd number of
teams in each league and would imply an idle team for the majority of dates. Something had to be done. The committee was to
come back with the solution by June.

Meanwhile, a pesky but revealing little litigation landed on
Selig's desk. Marvin Goldklang, a minority partner of the New
York Yankees and the owner of several minor league teams (some
with the actor Bill Murray and Mike Veeck), was seeking substan-

tial compensation from the Florida Marlins for taking over his baseball territory in Miami. Goldklang operated the single-A Miami Miracles when the Marlins came to town. The Marlins, as a higher classification–level team, had the right under baseball's rules to preempt the territory, but they then also had to compensate Goldklang for his territory. The compensation sum was to be determined by an arbitration panel, with the panel's swing vote being decided by an individual appointed by the commissioner or by the commissioner himself, according to the rules. In this case, however, the swing voter was appointed by the executive council, because MLB had no formal commissioner. Goldklang argued that the executive council was conflicted because it was a body of owners who would naturally support the position of a fellow owner—in this case, the owner of the Marlins at the time, Wayne Huizenga. Goldklang claimed that the rules entitled him to an appointment from the commissioner who, in conception anyway, was a neutral party, and that Bud Selig was the de facto commissioner. What Goldklang really wanted was to invalidate the traditional process and define a new one to ensure a neutral panel.[36]

What followed was a seven-hour deposition of Selig, wherein Bud had to argue that he was no more than the chair of the executive council. In the deposition and in the trial, Goldklang's lawyers did a good job of establishing that Selig looked, walked, and acted like a commissioner. Selig himself referred to the commissioners of baseball as his predecessors in the job. He also received compensation well in excess of prior commissioners, and mere members of the executive council were prohibited from being compensated. In addition, it was established that many team executives and owners had sent letters to Selig referring to him as commissioner and that even Selig had referred to himself as "acting commissioner." Nonetheless, during the trial Selig persuaded the judge that he was never elected commissioner by the requisite three-quarters vote of ownership and that he did not make unilateral decisions but rather ruled with the consensus of the executive council.[37] Goldklang lost his suit, but he set up a victory for George Steinbrenner in his coming Adidas case.

On March 3, 1997, the Yankees signed a ten-year, $95 million sponsorship deal with Adidas. The Yankees had not signed the MLB Properties agreement and hence believed that they were free to enter this deal. Major League Baseball thought otherwise and, in fact, reaffirmed this position by taking a three-quarters vote of ownership. The Yankees then brought a suit against MLB, claiming that they were being stripped of the value of the team's historical logos and marks and that MLB was engaging in an unlawful restraint of trade. The Major League Agreement provides for such disputes to be resolved by the neutral commissioner, but Steinbrenner's lawyer, David Boies, argued that baseball had no commissioner, as MLB itself had just argued in the Goldklang case, and that, in any event, Selig was conflicted out because he was also a team owner. If MLB was allowed to curtail the Yankees' sponsorship deal, baseball itself could sign the deal, and the Milwaukee Brewers would be entitled to one-thirtieth of the money—more than $3 million. One week after the suit was filed, nine of the ten members of the executive council met to strip Steinbrenner of his membership on the council and other ownership committees. Major League Baseball, however, was not anxious to have its antitrust exemption challenged on this matter and relented. Steinbrenner got to keep his deal and was reinstated on the council.[38]

The fact that MLB was unprepared in this matter points to another important deficiency that Selig had to confront. Baseball's central marketing effort had been moribund for decades. The game's status as the national pastime, its unchallenged position on the cultural pedestal by any other sport until the late 1950s, its antitrust exemption from 1922 onward, and the ambiguous role of the commissioner outside of integrity issues all conspired to induce a soporific arrogance and laxity. Happy Chandler and Bowie Kuhn talked about the need for marketing. The advent of free agency and skyrocketing salaries after 1976 put plain pressure on the industry to generate new revenue sources, and Peter Ueberroth nudged baseball in the right direction with new sponsorship deals. Fay Vincent, experienced at the marketing giant Coca-Cola, was committed to developing a comprehensive marketing plan, and he hired Len Coleman to assist in the development of new markets. But Coleman's efforts primarily concentrated on expanding the opportunities for black youths to play baseball, and Vincent wasn't around long enough to set much else in motion.

Thus, by the time Selig became the acting commissioner in September 1992, MLB had no director of marketing and no central marketing operation.[39] Finally, in June 1996, baseball hired its first director of marketing. At the time, Selig commented, "My biggest shock when I became chairman of the executive council in September 1992 was to find that baseball never had a central marketing operation."[40] One might reasonably ask why Selig, the most active owner in baseball's governance before 1992, did not know this. And if Selig was shocked in 1992, why did it take him almost four years to fill the void? Nonetheless, MLB's marketing efforts have grown steadily and successfully since 1996.

The day after hiring a marketing chief, Selig gave his sanction to the Minnesota Twins to explore selling the team to buyers who would move the franchise to another city. Selig was thereby putting Minneapolis on notice that baseball expected public funds to build a new ballpark. This was one of many such notices that Selig was to give to American cities.

Also in June 1996, the restructuring report from John Harrington's committee was finally finished. Harrington's plan was radical, and Selig supported it. The plan would have fifteen teams switching leagues, with all Western and Eastern clubs in separate leagues. It was too radical, however, for most owners. After several vitiations, on October 15, the owners voted to have one team move from the AL to the NL, stipulating only that the team would be chosen from the Royals, the Twins, and the Brewers. On November 5, the Brewers, looking to benefit from a rivalry with the Cubs and bring the NL back to Milwaukee, volunteered to move.

In late October, Pete Rose applied for reinstatement. Selig was reportedly against it, or, at least, he didn't act on it. Nor has he since. Baseball fans love to debate this issue, and, despite the inanity of keeping baseball's all-time hit leader out of the Hall of Fame on moral grounds, Rose's exclusion may be justified on the grounds that it brings the game more press.

In November, Selig approved the trade of Chuck Knoblauch from the Twins to the Yankees, even though it included a $3 million payment to the Twins. Earlier in 1996, Selig had approved the trades of John Olerud and Kenny Rogers, even though they each involved $5 million trading hands. In each case, the $1 million cash limit on trades, originally set by Bowie Kuhn in 1976 as $400,000, was surpassed. Clearly, the threshold was arbitrary, and the commissioner wielded total discretion in approving or vetoing these trades. And Selig was about to witness probably the greatest player sell-off in baseball's history. After winning the 1997 World Series and failing to get public funds for a new stadium from Dade County or Miami, Wayne Huizenga traded away Moises Alou, Kevin Brown, Devon White, Jeff Conine, Al Leiter, Robb Nen, Gary Sheffield, Bobby Bonilla, and Charles Johnson, all integral parts of the champion Florida Marlins. Huizenga thus lowered the Marlins' payroll from $53 million in 1997 to $19 million in 1998 and to $16 million in 1999.

Selig sat by and did nothing. This passivity was in sharp contrast to Kuhn's prohibiting the A's 1976 sale of Vida Blue to the Yankees for $1.5 million and of Joe Rudi and Rollie Fingers to the Red Sox for $1 million each. Both Selig and Kuhn could not be acting in the best interests of preserving baseball's competitive integrity.

An even larger money issue was about to fall on Selig's desk. Peter O'Malley wanted to sell his Dodgers for a record $311 million to the News Corporation's Rupert Murdoch. At the time, the News Corp's Fox subsidiary owned the national contract for MLB broadcasting and the local cable contracts for twenty-two of baseball's thirty teams. If Murdoch became an owner, he would have access to the financial statements of the teams he negotiated with over local rights fees. He would have the resources of a company with more than $11 billion in revenues and could possibly use them to push player salaries further into the stratosphere. And Ted Turner had a visceral dislike for the man. Turner even showed up at his first owners' meeting in nine years to counsel against allowing the team sale. Many feared that Murdoch would become the most powerful man in baseball. Nonetheless, the owners liked the idea of Murdoch boosting franchise values and bringing along his media clout. They approved the transaction, and Murdoch bought the team in March 1998. Luckily for baseball, Murdoch had little interest in controlling the industry. He mostly wanted to control the regional sports channel market in Los Angeles.

By the summer of 1998, baseball seemed to be recovering from the devastation of the 1994–1995 strike. The industry had revenue sharing, a luxury tax, interleague play, three divisions per league, and a wild card—and it had all come under Selig's leadership. It finally had a leader who unequivocally represented the owners' interests and was able to bring them closer together. Astros owner Drayton McLane said, "Bud knows how to get things done." Twins owner Carl Pohlad added, "He is the most effective political leader I have met. Every owner trusts him."[41]

So, the owners were ready to prevail on Bud Selig to stop dis- avowing interest in the job and to make him the permanent com- missioner of baseball. On July 8, 1998, they voted to offer him a five-year term at a reported initial salary of at least $3 million (still less than half what was being paid to the NBA's David Stern and the NFL's Paul Tagliabue). Few were surprised when the man who didn't want to be commissioner, or so he said, accepted.[42] On August 1, 1998, Bud Selig formally became baseball's ninth com- missioner.

8

Baseball's Permanent
Commissioner, 1998-

Baseball was catching some good bounces. The new iron man Cal
Ripken passed Lou Gehrig's consecutive game streak in September 1995 and kept extending the record until the Orioles' last home
game of 1998. That's when Mark McGwire and Sammy Sosa were
taking over the headlines with their successful and scintillating assault on baseball's most cherished single-season-home-run record.
All the while, the passion-provoking Yankees had serendipitously
started a new dynasty, and baseball's average game attendance was
climbing back toward its 1994 record. The recovery from the devastation of the 1994–1995 strike continued with Barry Bonds's heroics, establishing 73 as the new single-season home run milestone
in 2001. In 2003, the Cubs, with a world championship drought of
ninety-five years, and the Red Sox, with a drought of eighty-five
years, were each within one pitch of meeting each other in the
World Series. Then the Sox reversed the curse in 2004, and in 2005,
the Expos became the Nationals. Presiding over all these miracles
was Bud Selig.

But if Selig were a rainmaker, the national media didn't seem
to get it. Many never forgave him for being the messenger who
canceled the 1994 World Series. Selig himself had other worries
when he took over as the permanent commissioner on August 1,

1998. During his acceptance speech to the owners, Selig singled out one issue: "To me, it's the most important thing I have ahead of me: reducing acrimony. That also includes within ownership. My father was a great peacemaker, and obviously I've inherited that. I don't like to waste a lot of energy fighting."[1] Selig admired the "league think" mentality built in the NFL by Bert Bell and Pete Rozelle and the league's labor peace built by Paul Tagliabue and Gene Upshaw. Above all else, that's what he wanted for baseball: a partnership with the players and among the owners. Neither would be easy, but if either was to happen, Selig seemed as likely as anyone to do it.

The owners were so convinced that Selig was the right man that they strengthened the office with baseball's new constitution, adopted on January 19, 2000. In addition to merging the AL and the NL for most governance purposes, the 2000 constitution adds two crucial sentences to Article II, Section 4, that define the commissioner's "best interests" powers as they apply to integrity:

> Integrity shall include without limitation, as determined by the Commissioner, the ability of, and the public perception that, players and Clubs perform and compete at all times to the best of their abilities. Public confidence shall include without limitation the public perception, as determined by the Commissioner, that there is an appropriate level of long-term competitive balance among Clubs.

That is, competitive balance and hence revenue-sharing procedures, except insofar as they are constrained by collective bargaining, are legitimately part of the commissioner's "best interests" powers.

While this provision undoubtedly adds to the authority of the office, it is unclear how much incremental power it actually bestows on the commissioner. Not only is it limited by the labor agreement, but it is limited by Article VI, which has been in the constitution since 1945. Article VI, Section 1, stipulates that the commissioner serves as arbitrator for all disputes between clubs except those "whose resolution is expressly provided for by another means in this Constitution [or other document]." Any changes in revenue-sharing procedures, for instance, are subject to a three-quarters vote by the owners. Nonetheless, if MLB's revenue-sharing committee, which adjudicates the interpretation of reported revenue from related party transactions (for example, when the team owner also owns the team's broadcasting station or network), decides that the revenues from YES, NESN, CSN, or MASN are, say, 20 percent greater than those reported, and the team contests the committee's judgment, then the commissioner in theory has the final say.

The actual procedure provides for a designated accounting firm (PricewaterhouseCoopers in 2005) to estimate the fair market value of items subject to related party transactions. This value, particularly if it involves media rights, may be in the tens of millions of dollars and may even exceed $100 million. If a team objects to the accounting firm's valuation, then it can appeal the decision to the owners on the revenue-sharing committee. The three members on this committee are appointed by the commissioner.[2]

Furthermore, Article VI, Section 2, stipulates that the clubs "agree to be finally and unappealably bound by actions of the Commissioner." Courts in the past have required due process and adherence to common legal principles for this provision to stand up, providing a crack in the door for an offended team to challenge a commissioner's ruling. It is not unlikely that aggrieved owners will attempt to exploit this crack in the future.

The 2000 constitution makes one further change that strengthens the commissioner's hand. The maximum fine on a club, which was raised under Ueberroth to $250,000 and stayed at that level through 1999, was raised eightfold to $2 million in 2000.

It is significant that with the formal merging of the AL and the NL, the governing document is now named the Major League Constitution, instead of the Major League Agreement. The term *agreement* dates back to 1903 when the two separate leagues and business organizations, the AL and the NL, agreed to work together. Now, for the first time, they were formally acknowledging that they were in the same boat. Up through the 1990s, the owners of the AL and the NL frequently met separately, even to discuss industrywide business. When new owners entered baseball, they often expressed dismay at the parochialism of the leagues. The interleague rivalry was just one more division that impeded effective coordination and governance in baseball.

The Blue Ribbon Panel and Collective Bargaining

While Selig and others were delighted that baseball had its first (nongate) revenue-sharing agreement in the 1996 CBA, they also believed that baseball's economic system was still too skewed.[3] Selig had a pet phrase that makes considerable sense: the fans of each team need to have "faith and hope" that their team has a chance to win at the beginning of each season. Without this faith and hope, fans will eventually lose interest, and the game will suffer. Selig traced the inability of many teams to compete to deficient financial resources. Reinforcing Selig's concern was the sharpening revenue inequality in MLB and the growing dominance of the Yankees and other high-revenue teams during the 1990s.

The facts confronting the Blue Ribbon Panel were compelling. From 1995 through 2001, only four teams from the bottom half of team payrolls reached the postseason. And those four teams did not do very well once they got there. Of the 224 postseason games played over this period, teams from the bottom half of payrolls won only 5 games. That is, teams from the top half of payrolls had a postseason winning percentage of .978! None of the four bottom-payroll teams got beyond the first round of the playoffs.

To deal with this growing problem, in early 1999, Bud Selig handpicked a panel of four prominent citizens and twelve owners to study baseball's economic system and make recommendations about how to improve it. Selig's outside experts were George Will, Paul Volcker, George Mitchell, and Richard Levin. Many people thought it was a mistake not to include representation from the Players Association. If, after all, the report was going to call for sacrifices from both owners and players, then wouldn't the study have more credibility with the players if they participated in drafting it? Furthermore, if one of the gains of the 1996 CBA was that players and owners would work together on the Industry Growth Fund and a budding partnership was in the works, wouldn't this have been a good opportunity to extend the partnership?

The panel studied baseball economics for fifteen months and issued its recommendations in July 2000. It suggested three major reforms. First, the panel recommended that baseball increase its revenue sharing by raising the tax on local revenue from 20 percent to between 40 and 50 percent. As part of this change, the panel suggested a new redistribution mechanism that put a proportionately heavier burden on the top teams and gave a greater benefit to the lower-middle relative to the lowest teams.[4] To avoid owners pocketing their transfers rather than investing them in building stronger teams, the panel also suggested that teams be required to have a minimum payroll of $40 million before they became eligible to receive revenue-sharing funds.

Next, the panel called for the reinstatement of the luxury tax, recommending that forty-man roster payrolls over $84 million be taxed at 50 percent. Last, the panel urged several changes in baseball's draft system that were geared toward restoring the advantage to weak teams. This advantage was intended when the reverse-order amateur draft was introduced in 1965.

The Blue Ribbon report eventually was to form the basis for the owners' collective-bargaining stance. It was not until six months after the report's release that Selig sent Paul Beeston and Rob Manfred to begin negotiations with the Players Association in February 2001. The two sides had twenty-three meetings between February 28, 2001, and June 20, 2001. When the June 20 meeting adjourned, the Players Association thought it had an agreement. Beeston had responded favorably to the players' last proposal and said he would get back to them in short order.[5] The PA thought it had a deal, but it never heard back from Beeston. Selig had abruptly terminated the discussions without explanation. Beeston felt that his efforts had been undermined, and he later resigned. The owners did not put their substantive demands on the bargaining table until December 2001—a month after the expiration of the old agreement and eighteen months after the Blue Ribbon Panel report was issued.

A likely explanation for these delays and missteps is the disunity among owners. The first delay was between July 2000 (when the Blue Ribbon Panel report was issued) and February 2001. The owners apparently could not agree what to put on the table. Since Selig had appointed twelve owners to the Blue Ribbon Panel, it might reasonably have been expected that the owners stood behind the report. Given that the 1996 agreement expired after the 2000 season (though it was extended for a year), it was peculiar that the owners did not begin bargaining until the end of February 2001. But even this bargaining, in hindsight, appears to have been premature. Selig was kept informed on a daily basis of the substance of the bargaining and gave feedback to Beeston. Yet when Beeston thought he had concluded a deal, Selig went back to the owners for support. It was not forthcoming. Either some owners changed their minds, or new interest groups of owners formed in opposition to the negotiated terms.[6]

The owners were not to come back to the bargaining table for serious negotiations until December 2001, and Bud Selig himself did not attend any sessions until January 2002—eighteen months after the submission of the Blue Ribbon Panel report.[7] The owners' demands at that point not only included the major proposals (in modified form) of the Blue Ribbon Panel but also contained several new points that were viewed by the PA as very onerous. The owners wanted to contract the major leagues by two to four teams, to sanction the 60/40 debt rule in the CBA, to establish a $100 million discretionary fund for the commissioner, and to give owners the right to release players if they thought an arbitration award was too high, among others things.[8]

While Selig and the owners undoubtedly did not expect the union to accept these demands, they felt it could give them some leverage to compromise on terms that both sides would find acceptable in the end. In any event, putting such harsh demands on the table complicated and slowed the bargaining process. The players had their own card to play: on August 16, they announced that they would strike on August 30 if there was no agreement in place. Negotiations intensified, and baseball accomplished what it was never before able to do. The owners and the players reached a last-minute deal, just in time for the Cardinals to play the Cubs in an afternoon game at Wrigley Field on August 30. It was the first time a new CBA had been signed in baseball without the game first suffering through a work stoppage. As Don Fehr aptly put it: "All streaks come to an end sometime, and this one was long overdue."

Baseball had its agreement, and fans were jubilant. But the agreement was the product of a rushed compromise. It represented not only a compromise between the owners and the players but also a compromise among the owners. To be sure, some of the high-revenue clubs were closer to the union position than to the position of the other owners. The result was that although the agreement yielded some important gains that supported baseball's economic health, it was also highly flawed.

The 2002–2006 Agreement

Other than raising the minimum wage from $200,000 to $300,000, increasing the players' benefit fund, and introducing drug testing for steroids, the principal planks in the new CBA came from the Blue Ribbon Panel report. On revenue sharing, the net local revenue tax was increased from 20 percent to 34 percent, and all the funds thereby collected would be distributed on a straight pool basis—a distribution scheme that relatively benefited the teams in the second and third quartiles and hurt the teams in the top quartile the most. This sum was supplemented by an additional $43.3 million in 2003, to come out of MLB's central fund (monies from national and international television, radio, the Internet, and national licensing and sponsorship), distributed on a split pool basis—a scheme that helped the bottom quartile of teams the most. The $43.3 million was set to rise gradually, up to $72.7 million in 2005 and again in 2006. In addition, each team would contribute $333,333 annually to form a $10 million fund to be disbursed at the discretion of the commissioner. In 2004, approximately $270 million was distributed from the top to the bottom teams. In 2005, this sum increased to around $300 million.

Overall, this revenue-sharing system imposes what amounts to a marginal tax rate of roughly 39 percent on the top half of teams and 47 percent on the bottom half. (For the bottom half, the rate is implicit because what actually happens is that for every incremental dollar of revenue they generate, MLB gives them 47 cents less in revenue transfers.) The expected impact here is twofold. First, player salaries will be significantly restrained. Consider the decision facing David Glass, the owner of the bottom-feeding Kansas City Royals. Suppose he faces a decision about whether to re-sign his former star centerfielder Carlos Beltran. He asks his financial people to estimate how much revenue Beltran would generate for the team by increasing attendance at the ballpark (more ticket sales, more concessions, parking and signage revenue, etc.) and via the local media. Let's say that they come back with an estimate of $20 million annually. Without baseball's revenue-sharing system, Glass would be willing to sign Beltran for any amount up to $20 million.[9] But with the current system, the extra revenue generated by Beltran would be taxed at 47 percent, leaving only $10.6 million net for Glass to keep. In this circumstance, Glass would be willing to pay Beltran only up to $10.6 million. While simplified, this illustration shows how MLB's revenue-sharing system acts as a potent restraint on salaries.

Second, the fact that effective tax rates are higher on the bottom teams (roughly 47 percent) than on the top teams (roughly 39 percent) means that the system actually tilts the incentives away from the bottom teams signing good players. Of course, the playing field is not level from the start. Teams in large markets or those that have significant synergies with related businesses are much more likely to sign or trade for the top players without the revenue-sharing system. With baseball's revenue-sharing system, they now become even more likely to do so. For instance, suppose the Mets also estimated that Beltran would generate $20 million gross for the team in revenues (though the Mets are almost certain to get more value out of Beltran than the Royals are, given the size of the New York market). Since the Mets face an effective tax rate of 39 percent, the estimated net value to the team from the signing would be $12.2 million. Thus, even if Beltran were equally valuable in Kansas City as in New York, the Mets would outbid the Royals by $1.6 million in this example.[10]

Paradoxical as it may seem, then, MLB's present revenue-sharing system is actually more likely to further imbalance the competition. Selig has made repeated claims that the system has leveled the playing field, and at first glance, it may appear that he is correct. For instance, on September 1, 2003, there were fifteen teams within four games of making it to the postseason playoffs, the highest number since 1995. On September 1, 2004, there were thirteen teams within four games of making it to the postseason. Each year, the pennant races were competitive up to the last month for roughly half of the teams.

Yet if the revenue-sharing system is to be credited with achieving greater balance, it must be because the revenues transferred to the bottom teams are being spent on increasing payroll, and the payroll disparity among teams should be narrowing. Revenue-sharing data from 2003 (the first year of the new CBA) reveal that five of the seven bottom-payroll teams actually lowered their opening day payrolls by a total of $62.6 million, despite receiving $63.1 million in revenue-sharing transfers. Furthermore, by any common measurement of inequality, team payrolls have grown more unequal since 2002. For instance, the spread from the top- to the bottom-payroll teams grew from $91.5 million in 2002 to $130.1 million in 2003 and to $155 million in 2004.[11]

The CBA did anticipate that this could be a problem, but it contains insufficient safeguards to prevent it from happening. The CBA states, "Accordingly, each Club shall use its revenue sharing receipts . . . in an effort to improve its performance on the field. The Commissioner shall enforce this obligation." But Selig seemed reluctant to do much enforcing for at least three reasons. First, until January 2005, Selig was still the owner of the Milwaukee Brewers, and his team seemed to be behaving against the spirit of this CBA clause. The Brewers' revenue-sharing transfers grew from $1.5 million in 2001 to $8.5 million in 2002 and to $16.6 million in 2003. Yet the Brewers' payroll decreased from $52.7 million in 2002 to $40.6 million in 2003 and to $27.5 million on opening day in 2004.

Second, Selig and the owners decided that a broad interpretation of this CBA exhortation was the proper one. So, if a team had $100 million in debt and it used its transfers to pay down the debt, this would make the team financially more sound and would eventually assist the team's on-field performance. The PA, of course, believes that the CBA language dictates otherwise, and this is likely to be a bone of contention in the next round of negotiations.

Third, from the standpoint of efficiency, it makes little sense to have central rules about how a team should spend its money. Don't local owners and executives best know their predicament and their needs? If they are forced to spend, say, an extra $10 million on major league players in a particular year, they might spend it by signing a player whom the team doesn't really need instead of on player development or instead of banking it for a more effective expenditure in a subsequent year.

The incentive/implementation problem with MLB's current revenue-sharing system is easy to fix—in theory. The present system penalizes success and rewards failure. Until 2004, the Philadelphia Phillies in baseball's fourth-largest media market (and largest unshared media market) were actually recipients of revenue transfers ($9 million in 2003)![12] The reason is because the Phillies' ownership mismanaged the team. On the other end of the spectrum, the Boston Red Sox, in the sixth-largest market, were paying the second most in revenue sharing ($38.7 million in 2003).[13] The Phillies should not be rewarded for managing poorly, nor should the Red Sox be penalized for managing well.

The proper way to design revenue sharing is through a tax on *forecasted*, not actual, revenue. Forecasted revenue is a function of the market's characteristics: media market population, the number of large corporations, per capita income, the size of the baseball television territory, and so on.[14] Based on these characteristics, teams should have a fixed amount they contribute to or receive from the system each year. If a team performs well on the field, promotes itself well in the local market, and engages in effective community relations projects and thereby raises its revenue, it should still pay (or receive) the fixed amount—no penalty for success. If the team performs poorly on the field, does not promote itself well in the local market, and does not engage in effective community relations projects and thereby lowers its revenue, it, too, should pay (or receive) a fixed amount—no reward for failure.

Selig lifted baseball's fortunes by convincing the owners to behave as an incipient partnership and introduce revenue sharing.

The next step for effective leadership is to design the system so that it better accomplishes its main goal: improving competitive balance.

Baseball, of course, can achieve temporary success with competitive balance—all it takes is a stroke of good luck. Team payrolls do not correlate perfectly with team performance. Indeed, in any given year, variations in team payroll account for anywhere between 15 and 50 percent of variations in team performance. Thus, between 50 and 85 percent of team performance is determined by factors other than payroll, such as team chemistry, management prowess, luck, injuries, and so on. So, it is always possible for baseball to have a good year or two. To balance the odds better and have long-term success, however, baseball would do well to align its incentives properly.

To be sure, baseball's revenue-sharing system also has the goal of reducing salaries. Early returns suggest that salary growth has been blunted. New free agent contracts fell in value by nearly 20 percent during the 2002–2003 off-season, fell by more than 20 percent the following year, and were flat the next. Average player salaries have also drifted down modestly.

The 2002 CBA has other mechanisms that have restrained player salaries, and these will have to be strengthened if the revenue-sharing system is redesigned. One such mechanism is the luxury tax.

The luxury tax was applied to teams with payrolls of more than $117 million in 2003, with the threshold rising in steps to $136.5 million in 2006. Incremental payroll over these levels is taxed at 17.5 percent for first-time transgressors, 30 percent for second-time offenders, and 40 percent for third-timers.[15] In 2005, the Yankees are expected to pay nearly $30 million in luxury taxes, in addition to more than $60 million in revenue sharing. The Red Sox have been the only other team above the luxury tax threshold since 2002, but they have surpassed it by only a few million dollars. Despite its relatively low rates (the NBA luxury tax is nominally at 100 percent but effectively rose above 300 percent during 1999–2005), baseball's luxury tax seems to have deterred teams from going over the threshold. Even the Yankees, with their massive revenues (approaching $350 million annually), seem to have hit their limit during the 2004–2005 off-season. Both Pedro Martinez and Carlos Beltran evinced interest in signing with the club, but Steinbrenner demurred. Not even George has bottomless pockets.

The 2002 CBA had still other salary-restraint provisions. Team debt limits were set at ten times team EBITDA (earnings before interest, taxes, depreciation, and amortization), with a $25 million debt exclusion.[16] Thus, a team with no earnings is allowed only $25 million of debt. The actual rule will not be enforced until 2006, but teams were expected to convince Commissioner Selig that their trajectory in earlier years would bring them to compliance in 2006. Selig, in turn, was empowered to enforce budgetary discipline if teams were deemed profligate. Since average team debt in 2001 exceeded $100 million, most teams must be under considerable pressure to bring their finances in compliance. Although the CBA stipulates that the commissioner is not allowed to use this mechanism to pressure teams to lower payrolls, it seems impossible to independently monitor what kind of pressure is applied on the clubs. This is a matter that has raised a few eyebrows at the Players Association and will likely be heatedly contested during the next round of negotiations in 2006.

Furthermore, the CBA requires teams to fully fund all deferred salaries (usually, salary payments made after a player retires) within eighteen months of the year in which the player earns the salary. This rule prevents teams from obligating themselves to future salary expenditures without securing the wherewithal to cover the obligation. Finally, a new draft rule specifies that if a team is not able to sign a draft pick, then it obtains an extra pick in the same round the next year. This provision gives the clubs some added leverage in negotiating signing bonuses with the agents of amateur players. Outside the CBA, increasing cost and decreasing coverage of player injury insurance, especially after 2002, also led the owners to be more cautious in signing large long-term contracts.

Put all these salary restraints together, and the owners appear to have scored a significant collective-bargaining victory in the 2002 accord. Indeed, Selig, for the first time, began to speak about baseball having an economic system that works. Thus, even though the competitive balance goal may remain elusive, the financial stability of the system has been strengthened.

Don Fehr's negotiating hand was weakened by the players' reluctance to go on strike. Average salaries had surpassed $2 million, and the players were unwilling to lose a year of their short playing careers. They were also leery of risking the scorn of fans if there was another work stoppage.

Selig had led the owners to what most perceived to be their first collective-bargaining victory—and he did so without a work stoppage. In the end, this was more important than the design imperfections of the system or other missteps of the commissioner's office.

Contraction

A piece of baseball's labor pains was the plan for contraction. One day after the Arizona Diamondbacks came back to beat the New York Yankees in the ninth inning of game seven of the 2001 World Series, and just a few weeks after Barry Bonds had set a new home run record of 73 in a single season, Bud Selig had some harsh news to share with the media. It wasn't a good time for bad news: the country was still reeling from the terrorist attacks two months earlier on September 11. Selig announced that the owners had decided to "contract" at least two teams for the 2002 season.

Some thought that Selig was just posturing for leverage vis-à-vis the Players Association, which didn't want to lose eighty union jobs if two teams were eliminated, and vis-à-vis cities, such as Minneapolis that was resisting the commitment of public funds to build a new stadium for the Twins. Why, after all, would baseball want to reduce the number of its teams after six years of spectacular revenue growth of nearly 15 percent per year? Most industries, even monopolies, expand output when the demand for their products grows rapidly. Indeed, even Selig's Blue Ribbon Panel report stated that "if the recommendations outlined in this report are implemented, there should be no immediate need for contraction."

But Selig insisted that he was serious. The problem for baseball was that the Metropolitan Sports Facility Commission (MSFC) of Minneapolis also thought baseball was serious and did not plan to stand idly by as the Twins were eliminated. Even the Players Association brought a grievance, but it was the MSFC case that ultimately thwarted the contraction gambit. The MSFC argued that the Twins were obligated to play during 2002 under the terms of their Metrodome lease. Jesse Ventura testified before the U.S. House Judiciary Committee that MLB was seeking to extort a new stadium from the state by threatening to shut down the Twins. He added, "Major League Baseball is really no different than OPEC; it controls the supply and it controls the price with absolutely no accountability."[17] The MSFC won at the trial and appeals court levels, and the state supreme court refused to hear the case. Legally blocked from eliminating the Twins in 2002, MLB announced that it would delay contraction until 2003.

The MSFC then brought another suit against MLB to thwart contraction for 2003. In order to develop this case, the MSFC lawyers subpoenaed a variety of MLB's financial documents. The court ruled that MLB had to release the documents; rather than do so, MLB agreed not to contract the Twins in 2003 either. Indeed, MLB thought better of the whole contraction enterprise. It agreed in the 2002 CBA that it would not attempt contraction again at least until 2007. The team that MLB was prepared to pronounce dead after the 2001 season went on to the postseason playoffs in both 2002 and 2003.

Stadiums and Public Subsidies

Baseball's flirtation with contraction was simply a more extreme form of a game that MLB and the other monopoly team sports leagues have been playing for some time. By reducing output below where it would be in a competitive market, sports leagues maintain a steady state of excess demand. There are always economically viable cities that want to host a team but don't have one. Cities are thus thrust into competition with one another to attract a team. The competition takes the form of offering teams larger public subsidies to build and more attractive terms to lease a new stadium.

Bud Selig, with Dave Winfield, San Diego mayor Dick Murphy, President
Jimmy Carter, and Padres owner John Moores, at the opening of Petco
Park on April 8, 2004.

But baseball kept running into recalcitrant cities that were reluctant to fully fund new stadiums, especially cities that already had a
team. The team threat that it would migrate to another metropolitan area seemed to be wearing thin. Coming from a team owner, a
threat also had the counterproductive effect of engendering resent-
ment, making it more difficult to muster the requisite political support. No team had moved in baseball since the second incarnation
of the Washington Senators went to Texas after the 1971 season.
Furthermore, cities were increasingly confronted with fiscal strin-
gency, and economists were turning out studies that said sports
teams and stadiums by themselves can't be expected to promote
economic development.

So, the new idea was to toss two threats at intransigent towns.
Build, or we'll either move or expunge the team. Selig explicitly
essayed the double threat strategy in an April 25, 2001, letter to
Florida state senator J. Alex Villalobos: "Unless [public stadium]

funding was secured, the Marlins would be a prime candidate for contraction or relocation. Bluntly, the Marlins cannot and will not survive in South Florida without a new stadium."[18] This threat may have done more harm than good. Many legislators saw blackmail and took offense. State senator Kendrick Meek, a Democrat from Miami, told the *Miami Herald*: "It sounds like Tony Soprano writing that letter, trying to threaten and put pressure on us."[19] Indeed, even after the Marlins and the city of Miami finally reached an agreement on public subsidies and a site for a new stadium in early 2005, in May the state legislature refused to allocate $30 million to the project in sales tax credits[20]—something it had done for most other professional sports facilities over the previous two decades.

Selig also traveled to Oakland to proclaim that the Athletics would need a new stadium if they were to remain in Oakland. So far, the strategy has not paid off for the A's. But in Seattle, San Diego, Cincinnati, Chicago, St. Louis, Denver, Phoenix, Minneapolis, Milwaukee, Tampa Bay, Pittsburgh, Philadelphia, Detroit, Atlanta, Houston, Arlington/Dallas, Baltimore, Cleveland, Toronto, and Washington, D.C., it has worked just fine.[21] More than $6 billion has been spent on constructing facilities in these cities, with approximately two-thirds of the funding coming from the public coffers.

Milwaukee's Miller Park

In each of these stadium cases, MLB has played hard ball. From the standpoint of consumer protection, it is hard to justify baseball's policies. Yet it must be acknowledged that Selig and MLB are doing what any sports league would do: they are taking advantage of their economic circumstance and political power to extract the maximum possible benefit. Although Selig might not have always played his cards to their greatest effect, he has once again gone to bat unabashedly for the owners in the stadium game. In contrast, earlier commissioners were prone to soft-pedal the issue. Fay Vincent, for instance, expressed this view: "It's hard for me to argue that local governments should be put in position to finance these facilities to help owners who themselves are enormously wealthy. That's a fairly tough way to run a business. I mean, c'mon."

Bowie Kuhn did all he could to hold up Bob Short's relocation of the Washington Senators to Texas. And Ford Frick told Congress that it was okay for a team to leave a city if it were a two-team city but not if the relocation meant the town would be bereft of Major League Baseball.

Selig is not the natural person to be making relocation threats. He did, after all, participate in the state of Wisconsin's suit against the Braves and the NL when the team moved to Atlanta. He testified eloquently before the U.S. Congress about how that relocation ripped out his heart and the heart of his community. In his words: "The people in my home state felt hostility, bitterness and a deep sense of betrayal toward Major League Baseball for allowing the Braves to abandon us."[22]

To baseball's credit, the industry has had more franchise stability than the other sports have. No team actually relocated between 1972 and 2005. Nevertheless, many teams did threaten their local communities with relocation unless a new stadium was built with public funding, and thus baseball still took advantage of its monopoly position to extract subsidies.

One threat was made by Bud Selig to his hometown of Milwaukee. *Threat* might not be precisely the right word, as was explained by James Klauser, who served as secretary of administration while Tommy Thompson was the governor of Wisconsin: "What he would say is, 'Unless we build a facility we can't economically survive here.' He never said, 'If we don't get a new stadium we'll leave.' It's the same thing, isn't it?"[23]

Back in 1987, Selig drove from Milwaukee to Madison for a meeting with Tommy Thompson. He told the governor that the Brewers were going to build a new stadium with private funds.[24] He meant it at the time, but baseball economics started to shift, as did his team's fortunes. For one, the owners had a $280 million collusion settlement with the players to pay, and the Brewers' share of it was $11 million. For another, with local cable TV revenues taking off and new stadiums coming on line, player salaries were soaring. The Brewers at first tried to compete with the big-market clubs in the players' market. Thus, as the Yankees' payroll rose from $18.4 million in 1989 to $34.9 million in 1992, the

Brewers' rose from $11.7 million in 1989 to $30.0 million in 1992. The team's on-field performance, however, did not improve with the growing payroll, and team debt began to pile up. Rising debt meant higher interest payments, which led to negative cash flows and more debt. Matters became abruptly worse with the 1994–1995 strike. In 1994, the Brewers experienced a record $14 million operating loss. The team was in a downward cycle. Team debt rose from $3 million in 1990 to $63 million in 1996. The Milwaukee market was not an easy one for baseball. It was the twenty-seventh-largest metropolitan area in the country, and, even worse, its television market was tightly circumscribed by the Cubs and the White Sox being ninety minutes to the south, the Twins being six hours to the west, and Lake Michigan being directly east. Selig finally decided that the team needed public support to build a new facility. Under pressure from his partners, Selig reluctantly went back to Governor Thompson to negotiate a public subsidy.[25]

As expected, it was a struggle all the way. Selig benefited from the support of Robert Kahlor, then the chairman of Journal Communications, Inc., which owned the *Milwaukee Journal-Sentinel*, as well as WTMJ, the local radio station that carried the Brewers' games. Thus, Kahlor was able to lend strong editorial support. But Kahlor was able to do even more when Governor Thompson appointed him as head of the stadium task force. The stadium bill that ultimately made its way to the state legislature in late 1995 called for a $250 million stadium, with $90 million coming from the Brewers. Jay Heck, the executive director of Common Cause in Wisconsin, said that the bill "was arguably the most heavily lobbied issue in the history of Wisconsin." State records indicated that at least forty-eight registered lobbyists worked on the bill. They billed a total of over forty-nine hundred hours at a cost of nearly $650,000.[26] All that effort brought passage in the state assembly, but the bill got hung up in the senate. After debating the bill in the early morning hours of October 6, 1996, the senate voted it down 16 to 15. Selig was in the halls that morning, lobbying intensely. Another vote was called, and again it went down. It was around 4:30 A.M. when the majority leader was about to gavel the session closed, but his assistant majority leader stopped him. "No, no, don't adjourn," she called out, "George is going to change his vote."[27] George Petak, a Republican from Racine, had been against the bill because it included his district in the tax catchment for the stadium. But his emotions somehow got the better of him at the last minute, and he stated that he didn't want to see Wisconsin lose its Brewers. So Selig got his publicly subsidized stadium, and Petak got the boot from his constituents when, nine months later, the citizens of Racine held a special election and Petak became the first legislator in the state to be recalled.

According to a May 2002 report by the Wisconsin Legislative Audit Bureau, as of the end of 2001, the total cost for the stadium project, including infrastructure, was $424 million—$174 million above the amount stipulated in the bill. The Brewers' share remained at $90 million. To meet this obligation, the Brewers signed a twenty-year naming rights agreement with the Miller Brewing Company for $41.1 million. Another $50 million came in low-interest loans from the local chamber of commerce, the Milwaukee Economic Development Corporation, and two Milwaukee foundations. Subsequently, the quasi-public Stadium District took over between $36 million and $41 million of these loans. In 2002, the Stadium District swapped these loans (which were debt held by the Brewers) for a reduced obligation to cover certain stadium costs. Thus, of the $50 million that the Brewers borrowed, the team ultimately was responsible for paying back only around $10 million.

In exchange for this exceptionally modest contribution, the Brewers got a hefty return. First, the chamber of commerce guaranteed that the team would sell at least ten thousand season tickets during 1995–1997 and at least twelve thousand beginning in 1998. Second, the team would have a state-of-the-art retractable-roof stadium, with more than $4 million in furnishings for the team's offices, at an annual rent of only $900,000.

Third, the team would keep all revenue generated at the stadium, including naming rights, premium seating, catering, signage, and even nonbaseball events. Fourth, the district would pay $1.75 million annually into a renovation and improvement fund for the ballpark.

Fifth, the district would pay $3.85 million per year to help defray the stadium operation and maintenance costs, and the cost of repairs, uniforms, cleaning, utilities, and insurance, as well as the salaries and the benefits for seasonal employees. These costs are almost universally defrayed by the team in other cities. This annual payment by the district, however, was ended in exchange for canceling the team's roughly $40 million debt to the district in 2002.

The new stadium that was supposed to undergird a competitive team opened in April 2001. But the Brewers only got worse in their new facility. The team descended from a lowly average of 76.5 wins per year during 1996–1999 to a woeful average of 64 wins during their first three years in Miller Park, 2001–2003. The team had not achieved a winning season since 1992 and had not made the playoffs since 1982.

After the 2003 season, the team broke some more bad news— the payroll budget for 2004 was going down again, this time to around $30 million. (It had been $52 million in 2002 and $40 million in 2003.) Furthermore, the Brewers' own projections showed that the team budget for payroll and player development would stay flat between 2004 and 2006, despite estimated increases in net revenue-sharing receipts from the rich MLB teams, from $18.35 million in 2003 to $21.45 million in 2006.[28]

Ulice Payne, the Brewers' new CEO and a respected Milwaukee businessman, expressed displeasure with the falling payroll and was shown the front door. His separation settlement with the Brewers was estimated to be worth $2.5 million.

Payne's dismissal set off the political alarms. Former governor Tommy Thompson, the U.S. secretary of the Department of Health and Human Services at the time, asserted, "The Brewers made it clear that if we built a modern, state-of-the-art stadium, it would provide them with the resources to field a winning baseball team. . . . The Brewers need to put an end to the games. They need to invest in a winning team."[29]

State senator Mike Ellis declared, "The Seligs just scammed the living dickens out of the people of this state." And Milwaukee mayor John Norquist bluntly stated, "The Brewers have an ownership problem." Fifty-four state legislators signed a letter demanding that the Brewers open their books to the Legislative Audit Bureau (LAB) for an audit.[30]

Meanwhile, the Brewers' acting president Rick Schlesinger gave an interview to the *Milwaukee Journal-Sentinel* and admitted, "I can tell you that I had a couple of meetings with Ulice, Quinn [the chief financial officer] and the commissioner."[31] Since Selig held his 30 percent ownership in a blind trust since 1998 and was supposed to have nothing to do with team management, Schlesinger's comment raised some questions about the appropriateness of his discussions with Selig. Though, of course, it would have been perfectly legitimate to talk with Selig if Bud were wearing his commissioner's hat. But how could one tell which hat Selig was wearing? At the very least, there was the appearance of a possible impropriety here. The fact that Selig's daughter, Wendy, was the team's president and CEO during 1998–2002 and the chair of the board into 2005, and his son-in-law, Laurel Prieb, was a team executive did little to diminish the appearance of possible impropriety. Further obscuring the demarcation between the commissioner's office and the Brewers' ownership, Major League Baseball took out a full-page ad in the *Journal-Sentinel* during this dispute to tell its readers that Selig had received the "Recognition of Goodness Award" from the Jewish Foundation for the Righteous.[32]

The political heat seemingly became too much for Selig. On January 16, 2004, he announced that his family was putting its share of the Brewers up for sale. His statement included the following sentiment: "It is time for me to sever my ties with the Milwaukee Brewers. [It is] in the best interests of the game."[33] One can only wonder why it took him twelve years to realize that there was a conflict between being an owner and the commissioner at the same time. Perhaps it is something in the water at that elevation: it took Garry Herrmann, the owner of the Cincinnati Reds and the chair of baseball's National Commission, seventeen years to recognize a similar conflict.

In fact, before Selig sold the Brewers, the conflict had doubled. Baseball's owners bought the Montreal Expos, and the commissioner would own part of two teams.

Bud Selig announcing the appointment of his daughter, Wendy, as the Brewers' new president and chief executive officer on August 4, 1998.

The Montreal Expos Bid Au Revoir to Quebec

The unfolding of Selig's strategy for the Expos depended significantly on baseball's antitrust exemption. The Expos' owner in the early 1990s was Claude Brochu. First Brochu and then Jeffrey Loria had been interested in moving the Expos to Washington, D.C. Who wouldn't have? It is the country's eighth-largest media market, the fifth-largest host to large corporations, and the nation's capital. The latter afforded any D.C. team the golden opportunity to cater practically daily political fund-raisers at its stadium. The antitrust exemption, though, would help baseball thwart any relocation attempt by Brochu or Loria.

The Expos became a notable problem after the 1994–1995 strike. At the time when the strike began on August 12, 1994, the Expos were thirty-four games above .500 and leading the NL East by six games. Expos' fans had victory snatched from under them. Like other owners, Brochu's Expos suffered financially from the work stoppage, and Brochu began to trade or not re-sign some of the team's key players. The Expos' performance on the field trailed, and support for the team waned. Brochu began to push for public subsidies for a new stadium. On October 4, 1998, Selig flew to Montreal to meet with Quebec's premier, Lucien Bouchard. Selig repeated the standard message: the Expos need a new stadium if they are to remain a viable entity in Montreal. Bouchard told Selig what he had been telling Brochu: "We will not make the funds available. That's final."[34]

Brochu decided that it was time to sell and move the franchise. He had talks with buyers in D.C., in northern Virginia, and in Portland, Oregon. But Selig stood in his way and counseled patience. Baseball did not want to lose one of its two franchises in Canada. Major League Baseball was, after all, trying to spread the game internationally. Brochu wearied and sold his share to the New York art dealer Jeffrey Loria.

But as Loria bought the managing-partner share of the team for $12 million, Selig and the barons were hatching another scheme: contraction, and their eyes were on the Expos and the Twins. Selig knew that to get away with contraction, it would require the complicity of Congress, so MLB began to ramp up its lobbying effort on Capitol Hill. Selig hired the powerful D.C. law firm Baker and Hostetler to coordinate this effort. Major League Baseball formed a political action committee (PAC). Between 2002 and mid-2004, baseball's PAC raised $488,295, with nearly all of it coming from team owners. Of this, $102,500 went to members of the House and the Senate Judiciary Committees. Major League Baseball also spent big lobbying bucks outside the PAC—a total of $5.05 million during 1998–2004.[35] As it happened, however, it wasn't the U.S. Congress that thwarted contraction. It was the political process in Minnesota.

So MLB needed a new strategy for the Expos. And there was a new problem—Jeffrey Loria. Loria objected to the effort to contract his team and threatened to bring an antitrust suit against MLB. Loria was also in a battle with his minority partners, who happened to represent many of the largest companies in Canada.

Based in New York City, Loria was an absentee owner. He turned management over to his thirty-one-year-old stepson, David

Samson. Samson was a former asset manager at Morgan Stanley with no experience in the sports industry. He was five-foot-five, petulant, and bossy. He earned the sobriquet "Little Napoleon" in the Expos' offices.

When Loria bought the team, he pledged to put up an additional $39 million toward a new ballpark. He hadn't done so, when on March 17, 2000, he issued a cash call to the minority partners. Nothing was going right, and the partners offered to buy Loria out. He refused and issued several cash calls over the ensuing year and a half, which he met and the minority partners did not. Loria's share of the team rose from 24 percent to 93 percent.

Loria was not advancing the cause of a new stadium, and he was not putting new money into the team. Attendance fell lower and lower. Loria wanted to move the team and again threatened MLB with antitrust action. Baseball needed a solution.

Lots of different scenarios were entertained. One had Steve Schott, the owner of the Oakland A's, moving his team to Anaheim and shutting down the A's. John Henry, who wanted out of Miami, would buy the new team in Anaheim. Major League Baseball would fold the Devil Rays, and Loria would move the Expos to Tampa Bay. The permutations were practically infinite.

The one that eventually worked involved a different team. John Harrington and the Yawkey Trust were also frustrated with their efforts to get Boston to build the Red Sox a new ballpark. Harrington had claimed that Fenway Park was structurally unsound and urgently needed to be replaced. They decided to put the Red Sox up for sale. One of the groups forming to buy the franchise was led by Tom Werner and Larry Lucchino. They were looking for capital around the time when John Henry's attempt to buy the Anaheim Angels collapsed. The three joined together, making the Marlins available for sale. The solution had presented itself: arrange for the Sox to be sold to the Henry/Werner/Lucchino group, sell the Marlins to Loria, and have MLB buy the Expos, for later relocation and sale. Many problems went away in one stroke, and Selig would now have an ally for revenue sharing and his other projects in Boston, a big-city market. Werner had previously owned the small-market San Diego Padres, Lucchino had been working for John

Moores (who bought the team from Werner) in San Diego, and John Henry's Marlins were considered small market. In any event, they were all baseball men and long-standing allies of Bud's, and if Selig cleared the way for them to buy the Red Sox, then their bond would only be strengthened.

Ultimately, the Sox, Fenway Park, and 80 percent ownership of the New England Sports Network (NESN) were sold to the Henry/Werner/Lucchino group for $700 million, plus $30 million of contributions to Yawkey Trust charities. A rival bid from Cablevision's Charles Dolan was at least as high as the Henry/Werner/Lucchino offer, but there were various questions about Dolan. One concern was a possible conflict of interest since Dolan's brother and a family trust owned the Cleveland Indians. Dolan had no experience in the baseball industry and the internal operation of Cablevision were also areas of concern. The choice of the Henry/Werner/Lucchino group was a good one for baseball.[36] The group has preserved and improved Fenway Park with more than $100 million of its own funds (new engineering studies found no structural problems that couldn't be fixed), has provided a model for all teams in developing constructive community relations, and has brought a championship team to Boston for the first time in eighty-six years.

Baseball also managed to pacify Loria—at least temporarily. His Marlins won the World Series in 2003, and, though it has hit a snag, his quest for a new publicly subsidized ballpark seems to be progressing.

The details of the tripartite trade are these. Major League Baseball (the other twenty-nine owners) bought the Montreal Expos for $120 million, with the intention to move and sell the team (for a much higher price). Major League Baseball then loaned Loria $38.5 million (he'd only have to repay $25.3 million of it if the Marlins didn't get a new park within five years), and Loria bought the team from Henry for $158.5 million. Although Henry had bought the Marlins for $150 million, he had amortized roughly 40 percent of that and had a basis (adjusted purchase price) of around $90 million. This meant that Henry would have had to pay capital gains taxes on the sale of the Marlins on nearly $70 million of gains. Would have, that is, had MLB not arranged for him to buy the Red Sox. Since he was buying a "like kind asset," he was not subject to capital gains.

The remaining piece of the deal was for MLB to move and sell the Expos, a step that became increasingly urgent with time. Once Expos fans realized that the team would be gone in a few years, their already marginal interest in baseball diminished even further. Major League Baseball decided that the team couldn't do any worse in Puerto Rico than it was doing in Montreal and arranged for twenty-plus games to be played in San Juan in both 2003 and 2004. Though attendance in San Juan was slightly better than in Montreal, the team lost an estimated $60 million under MLB ownership. Puerto Rico was hardly a long-term solution.

So Selig was anxious to sell the team. This transaction, however, ran into various obstacles. First, Loria's minority partners sued Loria and MLB for conspiring to undermine the viability of the franchise in Montreal. It took more than a year before that case was dismissed. Second, Peter Angelos, the owner of the Baltimore Orioles, did not want a team forty-five miles to the south of Camden Yards. Third, Comcast did not want a new regional sports network to emerge in the mid-Atlantic states that it did not control.

Baseball Returns to D.C.

Peter Angelos bought the Orioles in 1993 for $173 million. Angelos had made his reputation as a bold lawyer who earned millions of dollars in class action suits on behalf of asbestos workers. As a neophyte owner, Angelos's sympathy for labor and his natural aggressiveness were on full display. In 1994–1995, Angelos opposed the Selig-led labor strategy of hiring replacement players. Benefiting from the combined Baltimore/D.C. market and a new stadium, Angelos also opposed revenue sharing, calling it "the antithesis of the very essence of the country: competition."[37] But over the years, Angelos learned to appreciate Selig's skills, to understand that it was in his interest to be supportive of the commissioner, and to be a team player. When the 2002 labor negotiations came around, Selig appointed Angelos to the negotiating committee.

Angelos had developed a decent rapport with the union and was a key figure arguing for the eventual elements of the 2002 CBA.

After a three-judge arbitration panel ruled against the former Expos' limited partners in their grievance against Jeffrey Loria and MLB in November 2004, the path was now clear for MLB to sell the team. Angelos immediately reminded everyone that he was opposed to a new team in D.C. Bob DuPuy, baseball's COO, was under instructions from Selig to find a way to appease Angelos. Washington, D.C., was the best available market for baseball by a long shot, and D.C.'s mayor Anthony Williams seemed to be bidding against himself in offering a publicly funded new stadium.

While other communities (northern Virginia; Norfolk, Virginia; Las Vegas; Portland, Oregon; Monterrey, Mexico, among others) were expressing interest in attracting the Expos, none had come forward with a politically approved, concrete plan. Mayor Williams's offer was almost too good. The overall development cost of the new facility would approach $600 million. The only direct contribution from the team would be $5.5 million in yearly rent. Ticket and concessions taxes would also come partly out of the price charged, so this would represent an indirect contribution from the team of another few million per year. In return, the team would get to keep all revenues generated at the park. A reasonable reckoning had the team paying less than 20 percent of the annual debt service on the construction bonds, constituting a better-than-average deal for the team. Furthermore, D.C. agreed to put $18.4 million into refurbishing the perfectly serviceable RFK Stadium to be used until 2008 while the new facility was being built.

The offer was so good, in fact, that members of the city council rallied behind council chair Linda Cropp to pull Williams's deal off the table. Quick and skillful maneuvering, however, sidestepped the problem, and the Williams offer, with minor tweaking, was confirmed.[38]

Now, Bob DuPuy had to find a way to conciliate Angelos. Not all MLB owners were happy that Angelos was going to be "bought off." Baseball's constitution gave each team a territorial monopoly over a defined area. In the Orioles' case, the area included only counties in Maryland. Angelos's television territory was broader,

Bud Selig, with MLB's COO and Selig's right-hand man Bob DuPuy, at the Hall of Fame induction ceremony in Cooperstown, New York, July 2003.

but TV territory for each team is extended to cover the entire country and is understood to be fungible as teams move and the game expands. That is, Angelos did not seem to have any legal ground on which to stand. Baseball's constitution did not guarantee him a certain television territory in perpetuity, and Angelos's desire for an area monopoly would be indefensible in court.

Equally important, if MLB tried to buy Angelos's acquiescence, it would set a precedent for other franchises. If MLB puts a team in Portland, Oregon, in the future, will it have to pay an indemnity to the owners of the Seattle Mariners? Or if a team goes into the San Bernadino/Riverside area of California, are the owners of the Dodgers and the Angels entitled to compensation? Similar questions arise for Sacramento with the Giants and the A's, for northern New Jersey with the Yankees and the Mets, and so on. Did MLB really want to establish an indemnification principle when a new team was entering into a broader television market that was not even part of the protected territory in the MLB constitution?

Selig, then, would have had strong grounds and widespread ownership support to simply go ahead with the move of the Expos to D.C. and tell Angelos that he had to live with the outcome. Selig may be willing to play hardball with cities, but he was reluctant to do so with Angelos. For one, Angelos was threatening legal action. However dubious his legal case may have been, Angelos would have filed it locally and probably received a sympathetic hearing, at least initially. Any legal action would also have brought document discovery. Discovery in this case could potentially involve any documents related to team ownership, MLB's relations with host cities, owner relations with the central office, or team finances. Some of these documents may be particularly sensitive, embarrassing, or even indicting. Major League Baseball capitulated in the Minnesota case so as to avoid discovery. It is reasonable to assume that Selig was not anxious to go through discovery on this matter, either.

Perhaps even more important to Selig, the case would have created a new division and bitterness among the owners. Selig's central project since entering the game in 1970 had been to build a partnership among the owners. Anything that threatened the tenuous, inchoate partnership that Selig had been able to forge was to be avoided at all costs.

When asked why he was bending over backward to gain Angelos's cooperation, Selig expressed strong feelings:

> I really believe in the partnership concept, which is a thing I've tried to sell. As [former Tigers owner] Mr. Fetzer used to tell me: "We want to beat each other's brains on the field but Buddy, off the field we're partners." I know it sounds trite, but it is true. Look, Art Rooney [the former owner of the NFL's Steelers] understood it, George Halas [the former owner of the NFL's Bears] understood it, Wellington Mara [the former owner of the NFL's Giants] understood it, and so on and so forth. John Fetzer understood it, but there are very few who really understand. So now I see about Peter Angelos. Well, this is . . . they're dumping a team twenty [sic] miles away; you can make all the compelling arguments; I've heard them all, on all sides, and I know that some people think I'm bending over backwards. But I think we are partners off the field and I do think that in unusual circumstances where it becomes obvious there will be some economic damage that we ought to think about something that at least is fair.

Fair—three people might have three different ideas about what is fair, but that's my feeling on the subject. And that's why I believe that, and I also believe that to do, to do something to move ahead where you know that you're hurting a partner, and not doing anything about it, is wrong—it's just not right. And so, the question of what to do, the question is very complex, and we've spent thousands of hours trying to do it. But that's my philosophy, and it's just as simple as that. And I've told Peter Angelos that, over and over again. There are some commissioners, I'm sure, who would just say "Hey, listen, tough luck, but Washington's not part of your territory and you've got to go do what you have to do but . . ." If we're going to avoid the owners' wars of the thirties, forties, fifties, sixties, seventies, eighties, nineties, for good or bad, I'm a little reluctant to say this but I'm going to say it anyway: I think these people all, at every level, trust me because they know in the end I'm going to bend over to try to be fair. And I do.[39]

So, Selig weighed the pros and the cons and decided that baseball was better off making a deal with Angelos. But that was more easily said than done. Angelos drives a tough bargain.

Bob DuPuy spent months in active negotiations with Angelos before they came to an agreement. Indeed, MLB could not abide another season for the Expos in Montreal and San Juan, and so it decided in December that the team would be moved to D.C. for the 2005 season. This decision was made before an accord was reached with Angelos. Finally, in late March 2005, a deal was reached with Angelos that provided for him to receive a guaranteed price of $365 million when he sold his franchise. This price would include Angelos's share in the new regional sports network MASN (Mid-Atlantic Sports Network) that was being created. Angelos would initially own 90 percent of MASN, but this share would fall to 67 percent over thirty years. The remaining share would be owned by the group that purchases the Washington Nationals. The Orioles would have the same television market but would now share it with the Nationals. Major League Baseball would also pay Angelos $75 million for the rising share of MASN that would go to the owners of the Nationals.[40] Furthermore, MASN would pay the Nationals a yearly rights fee equal to its fair market value, with the latter to be determined by a third party. For the Nationals' first year, the rights fee payment would be between $20 million and $25 million.

Overall, it was a good deal for Angelos, but MLB did not give away the store. Baseball, after all, still had to sell the Nationals, and the more of the team's potential revenues that were given to Angelos, the less MLB would be able to get for the team. In this case, it seems likely that Angelos could sell his team today for $365 million, even without the majority ownership of the regional sports network. Adding another $75 million for a majority ownership of MASN is a bargain. So, Angelos got some bottom-line guarantees, but he did not get a giveaway.

A trickier problem presented itself when Comcast and Brian Roberts sued the Orioles. Comcast has the existing contract to televise Orioles games, and it is also a major cable distributor in the mid-Atlantic area. The existing contract gave Comcast the right of first refusal to bid on renewing its rights to televise the Orioles. Angelos apparently ignored that contract clause when he set up MASN. Comcast is now using the clause to insinuate its way into the ownership of MASN. Comcast, moreover, is a major player in MLB. It is a part-owner of the Phillies, but, more important, it is about to launch a new regional sports network (RSN) with the New York Mets, is a joint owner of other RSNs telecasting baseball, and is a major cable distribution company around the country that carries sports channels. Comcast must be accommodated, and this must be done expeditiously. As of mid-2005, it is unclear how the matter will be resolved, but for the time being it has gummed up the sale of the Nationals. Until the Nationals' television situation is clarified, the value of the team is up in the air. There are many strong groups wanting to buy the team, but until it is known what assets the team includes, it is difficult to put a price on it.[41]

Stadiums: A Final Word

Commissioner Selig's record on stadiums would not be complete without acknowledging a very significant financial element in the 2002 CBA. Baseball's revenue sharing is based on each team's "net local revenue," defined as local revenue minus stadium costs. Stadium costs include not only operating expenses but also capital expenses. Capital expenses can either be the upfront financial contribution of a team to stadium renovation or construction amortized over a ten-year period, or it can be the principal portion of annual debt service payments on a construction bond. This definition means that teams' contributions to stadium construction lower their revenue-sharing burden to (or increase their revenue-sharing receipts from) other teams. Put differently, MLB as a whole is indirectly subsidizing the construction of stadiums.

Consider an example. The Yankees are proposing a new $800 million stadium that they would finance privately. If the Yankees were to amortize this sum over ten years, it would mean that they would be deducting an additional $80 million a year in stadium-construction expenditures. Since the Yankees face an estimated 39 percent marginal tax in baseball's revenue-sharing system, reducing net revenues by $80 million will save the team $31.2 million a year for ten years in revenue transfers. Using a 6 percent discount rate, this translates into a present value of roughly $230 million. That is, MLB would be indirectly contributing $230 million to the construction of the new Yankee Stadium.

While the NFL's G-3 program has been widely heralded (and with good reason), MLB's stadium policy may actually be more generous. The NFL's G-3 program has provided a maximum of a $150 million loan to a team for building a new facility. The "loan" is paid back out of sharing 34 percent of club seat premium revenues at the new stadium. Because the team would be obligated to share this 34 percent anyway, the loan is really a grant. The NFL, then, has been subsidizing team stadium construction and thereby helping to lower the public burden. As the Yankees' example illustrates, however, MLB's program can actually provide more league financing than the NFL's can.

(Of course, in both the MLB and the NFL programs, the new stadiums help to generate new revenues that are subject to sharing. It is therefore likely that the team will end up contributing more in absolute terms, despite the league's stadium subsidy. Nevertheless, to ascertain the size of the subsidy, the proper comparison is between the amount of the revenue-sharing obligation with the program and without the program.)

Marketing and Commercializing the Game

Despite earlier, isolated efforts, MLB did not have its first proper director of marketing before 1996. Selig appointed a director, and a full marketing operation was spawned.[42] Initial financing for the promotional effort came from the new television contract and the Industry Growth Fund that was set up in the 1996 CBA and has continued forward from that point. Major League Baseball currently commits more than $20 million per year to its national marketing; club marketing budgets—often several million dollars each—are on top of that.

In one of the most innovative and successful investments in any U.S. sports league, in 2001, MLB launched Major League Baseball Advanced Media (MLBAM).[43] It is a separate entity, owned by the thirty clubs, with its own offices in the Chelsea section of New York City. When the owners voted in 2000 to centralize all of baseball's Internet operations and revenues, it opened the door for MLBAM's operations.[44] Without the commissioner working the phones and advocating for partnership and sharing, MLBAM would not have been possible. MLBAM established the mlb.com Web site. Mlb.com provides comprehensive data about the game: the players, the teams (major and minor league affiliates), news, analysis, and history. But more important, it provides access to live radio and television coverage (via Internet streaming for high-speed connections) to all the games. It also provides packages that contain short and extended game highlights. These packages, which are available on a game, a monthly, or a seasonal basis, are especially attractive to so-called out-of-market fans. Thus, a Red Sox fan living, say, in Florida or Indiana, outside the NESN territory, can watch every Red Sox game at mlb.com.

From this foundation, MLBAM has expanded its operations to offer a multitude of services. It sells highlights, live radio, and video to fans on their cell phones. It runs simultaneous "game day" descriptions of each game, describing the action pitch-by-pitch (provided at no cost). Also at no cost, it carries a hosted video broadcast with game highlights from the same day. It acquired the Internet ticket vendor Tickets.com and now sells tickets not only for baseball games but for all forms of entertainment. It sells all MLB-licensed products. It runs the Web sites for Major League Soccer and for ten individual soccer teams, as well as for minor league baseball and minor league teams.

In short, MLBAM has become the sports industry leader in Internet services and sales. Mlb.com had 190 million visitors and 1 billion page views in 2001; it had 1 billion visitors and 10 billion page views in 2004. In 2001, it had 125,000 subscribers; in 2004, it had 840,000. Online ticket sales have grown from 1.8 million in 2001 to an estimated 15 million in 2005. Revenues have multiplied from $36 million in 2001 to an estimated $235 million in 2005 (with a cash flow of more than $75 million). With cash flow growth rates of over 40 percent annually, major league teams are beginning to reap significant dividends from MLBAM, and, just as important, these revenues are equally distributed to all teams.

Over the last ten years, baseball has also made important gains in internationalizing the game. One of the more significant steps came in December 1998 when MLB signed an agreement with Japanese baseball to establish the so-called posting system. This system provides for the transfer of Japanese players to MLB. A Japanese team posts the names of any of its players that it is willing to transfer (for a fee) to MLB. The team that bids the highest transfer fee is then given the rights to negotiate with the player. If the team and the player come to terms, the Japanese team is paid the bid, and the player moves to the United States. One of the greatest gains from this system is that MLB has attracted some of the top stars from Japan, such as the Seattle Mariners' right fielder extraordinaire, Ichiro Suzuki. Not only has this made the U.S. game more exciting, it has attracted enormous press and fan interest in Japan. Dozens of photographers and journalists follow the Japanese stars on a day-to-day basis, and millions of Japanese watch the live MLB games broadcast daily on Japanese television. In fact, the U.S. game has become so popular in Japan that the Japanese league has seen its own popularity diminish in recent years.

Major League Baseball is reaping a huge financial windfall as well. Not only have licensed products in Japan had skyrocketing sales, but the new six-year MLB television agreement (2004–2009) with Dentsu in Japan provides for $276 million, or $46 million per year.[45]

Capitalizing on the game's popularity in the Caribbean, Japan, Taiwan, and South Korea and its incipient growth in China, MLB has organized the World Baseball Classic to begin in March 2006. Inspired by the soccer World Cup, the competition will be organized regionally, with winners rising to the final round. Because it will take place before MLB's regular season, the expectation is that major leaguers from each country will be able to participate for their homelands. After months of difficult negotiations, in mid-September 2005, Japanese baseball agreed to participate in the first World Baseball Classic.[46] It is too early to predict what impact this new competition will have on spreading the game internationally. The real point here is that MLB is continuing to innovate and push the envelope—something that it did not do for its first nine decades.

To be sure, sometimes it seems that MLB pushes the envelope too fast. The allure of the short-term buck is often too great. So it appeared when MLB signed a deal for a paltry sum to put *Spider-man II* movie logos on its bases. This was crass commercialism and showed no sensitivity to the game's historical traditions. The NASCAR culture might welcome advertising all over a driver's uniform, but it has never happened in MLB. Major League Baseball at least had the good sense to cancel the deal in the face of widespread public ridicule. If this type of advertising is to happen in the future, it will have to be done cautiously and thoughtfully.

To many fans and analysts, baseball also erred in its project to reverse the decline in All-Star Game ratings. In announcing a new January 2003 plan to give the home-field advantage in the World Series to the league that won the All-Star Game that year, Selig explained that the game had devolved into a mere exhibition. In fact, it has always been an exhibition, but what has happened in recent years is that it has spawned a series of collateral media events, such as the home run derby and the Old-Timers Day Game, and has given the All-Star Game itself more of a frivolous aura. Selig asserted that the game needed something at stake. The consequence would be home-field advantage in the World Series. Now fans were supposed to care again about the game, and ratings were supposed to rise.

Lots of fans were left scratching their heads. Does an all-star player from, say, the Rockies really care if the Cardinals have home-field advantage over the Red Sox in October? And if the players don't care, why should the fans? The consequence seems totally artificial. And sure enough, it seems that the fans didn't care. The All-Star Game ratings in 2003 were 9.5, exactly the same as in 2002. In 2004, the ratings resumed their downward drift to 8.8.[47] The ratings fell again in 2005 to 8.1.

Some players and fans are also skeptical about the 1997 introduction of interleague play. Their problem is not so much that it disrupts tradition but that it undermines the legitimacy of competition. Within a division, teams play one another with the same frequency, so there is no imbalance.[48] With interleague play, however, in any given year, some teams face weak teams from the other league, while other teams face strong teams. Obviously, the former group benefits from this imbalance. The critics argue that this undermines fair play and the integrity of the pennant races.[49] Their point is not unreasonable. An important question, though, is the magnitude of the imbalancing effect and whether it is compensated by the possible excitement from interleague competition. Depending on the year, the attendance at interleague games tends to run roughly 10 to 20 percent higher on average than for intraleague games. Thus, interleague games appear to be a commercial success, though some econometric work suggests that most of this success is illusory because it is attributable to factors other than the interleague competition itself. For instance, interleague play does not begin until late spring when the weather is warmer and less rainy in most host cities. The improved weather may account for a good portion of the attendance uptick. In addition, interleague games have tended to be played on the weekends, also contributing to higher attendance.[50] Nonetheless, most fans seem to enjoy this new dimension of competition, and MLB's owners seem to have embraced it as well.

The groveling for ratings is also evident in the World Series' television strategy. Since the mid-1980s, all World Series games have been played after 8 P.M. (Eastern time). Ratings are higher in prime time, and higher ratings mean higher rights fees in the short term, or so the logic goes. In fact, World Series ratings have fallen steadily from the mid-20s to the low teens over the last twenty-five years. If the games are on too late for children to watch, then they cease to be a family event, and fewer adults are likely to watch as well. But more important, if a kid cannot stay up to watch the culmination of the season, the jewel of the year, he or she will lose some interest in watching the long season leading up to the championship series. It is not surprising that television ratings for baseball have fallen most rapidly for the young demographic. Children are the paying fans of tomorrow, and baseball cannot afford to treat their waning interest with indifference.[51]

To its credit, however, MLB has been making other important efforts to entice the interest of children. The commissioner's Initiative for Kids, launched by Selig in 2004, includes a program to give away over a million tickets per year to disadvantaged children across the country. Conveniently, Ameriquest signed on as the corporate sponsor for the program and buys each ticket from MLB teams for $1 each. Because the tickets are "purchased," they are counted in the official attendance figures and help to create the sense of an increased popularity of the game.[52]

Also problematic, baseball has been losing its African American fan base. The share of major leaguers who are African American decreased from 27 percent in 1975 to 10 percent in 2004. Many factors have contributed to the drop: lack of space in urban areas, greater expense of equipment, and fewer college scholarships in baseball than in basketball or football, among others. But just as it did when Jackie Robinson entered the major leagues in 1947, MLB needs to reclaim its hold on the African American population. As it has with the youth, MLB has started various programs, but it needs to make a substantially larger commitment if it is to reverse the tide for both groups.[53]

Steroids

Following the publication of Jose Canseco's book *Juiced*, in March 2005, steroid use, first in baseball and then in other professional sports, somehow seemed to become the most urgent issue confronting the U.S. Congress. Selig and the owners, along with the Players Association, took a lot of heat, and some people even suggested that Selig and his lieutenants were snickering behind the curtain as home run records were being serially shattered.

Reality is otherwise. Selig and the owners were constrained by the posture of the Players Association, whose leaders believed that steroid testing without cause was an intrusion on the civil liberties of the players. Public opinion came to embrace a different view; namely, the use of performance-enhancing drugs created an imbalanced playing field, encouraged clean players to become users, and set a horrible example for America's youth. This view was not always held, much less always articulated. Indeed, the media never clearly correlated player performance with substance abuse. Nor was it ever clarified what share of a player's power was attributable to his willingness to spend hours in the weight room and what share was attributable to steroids. After all, the same people who were using steroids were committed to body building and a rigorous training regimen. Finally, the state of the science on what substances were harmful and/or performance enhancing, as well as the ability to detect the presence of such substances in the body, was and is far from perfect.

In this evolving and confused environment, Selig and MLB proceeded ahead to learn what they could and to move policy forward, given the political constraints. Before the mid-1990s, the substances of choice in the clubhouse were amphetamines and recreational drugs. The prevailing view was that top offensive performance in baseball demanded quick reflexes, good hand-eye coordination, quick feet, flexibility, and strong wrists—not bulky muscles.

An FBI special agent, Greg Stejskal, told the news media in March 2005 that he had notified Major League Baseball about ten years earlier that steroid use was a developing problem in baseball.

Indeed, it was probably in the mid-1990s that people in baseball became generally aware that anabolic steroids were being used by some players. At the time, many anabolic steroids were illegal if purchased without a prescription.

But as baseball became more aware of this as a growing issue, the commissioner's office did, in fact, act. In 1998, Selig convened a group at his Milwaukee office, including team physicians, trainers, and outside medical experts. It was decided to begin an investigation and to gather as much information about steroid use and its effects as possible.

The next year, together with the players union, Major League Baseball helped to finance a study on androstenedione, or andro. It turned out to be a seminal study on the substance and was subsequently published in a leading medical journal.

In June 2001, MLB published a pamphlet in English and in Spanish that was distributed to major league and minor league players. It laid out in considerable detail the known effects of various classes of performance-enhancing drugs. Major League Baseball also hired a new medical staff to advise it on drug policy.

Baseball reasoned that if it could get players to the majors clean, then it had won half the battle. So in 2001, MLB decided to put a drug-testing and penalty program into effect for the minor leagues. It wasn't until May 2002 that Ken Caminiti gave his interview to *Sports Illustrated*, estimating that half of major leaguers were using steroids.

In 2002, MLB and the union agreed to their first steroid-testing and penalty program. In 2004, it was agreed—in the middle of a collective-bargaining agreement—to significantly extend that program.

It would be easy to go back and identify instances when MLB might have gotten the message sooner. It would be equally easy to argue that baseball might have acted more quickly or punitively. It is a safe bet that today Selig and others wish they had done more earlier. But it is also proper to remember that baseball was hampered by the confidentiality of doctor-patient relationships, the sanctity of the clubhouse culture, and union concerns about Fourth Amendment privacy rights.

The dimensions and the implications of the drug issue in professional sports are just beginning to be understood. One must understand the scope of the problem before one can devise effective policy. Eradicating drug abuse is no simple matter. New chemical compounds, new delivery methods, and new masking agents are being developed every day.

Underscoring the intractability of the problem is the fact that the bulk of athletes under investigation in the BALCO scandal are Olympians, and the International Olympic Committee is reputed to have the gold standard in antidoping policies. Three to seven years down the road, gene modification therapy will further complicate the landscape.

Selig was mocked in some quarters when in mid-May 2005 he first called for a three-strikes-and-you're-out penalty and then embraced a legislative effort to fight performance-enhancing drugs in all sports. Why had he all of a sudden become a proponent of standardized testing and stricter penalties, when he had just a month earlier said that baseball's program was working?

Selig, of course, has to work with the political hand he is dealt. While he thought the new 2004 program was moving baseball in the right direction, he never thought or said he thought that it was ideal. With Congress pushing the issue and the media playing it up, Selig saw an opportunity to put pressure on the Players Association. By stepping out and taking the lead on the issue, he also had an opportunity to improve the perception of integrity in baseball.

Even though he called for stiffer penalties (fifty days for a first offense, a hundred for a second, and lifetime for a third) and for turning the program's administration over to an independent body, Selig did not call for blood testing. Each of the major team sports leagues today (MLB, NBA, NFL, and NHL) depends solely on a urine sample to detect a player's use of drugs. Currently, there is no urine test for human growth hormone (HGH), an important performance enhancer.

Baseball is funding an effort to develop a urine test for HGH. But at present none exists, and it may be years before one is developed . . . if ever. Without blood testing, any player can migrate from identified steroids to HGH with impunity. This is hardly an assurance the game is clean.

Thus, as in other areas, Selig might have acted more aggressively, more consistently, and more persuasively than he did. However, arguing that his actions were short of ideal is different from arguing that his actions were wrong or devious.[54] In fact, Selig has tried to move baseball in the right direction since the mid-1990s on the issue of performance-enhancing drugs. He and subsequent commissioners will have an ongoing challenge to deal with the doping dilemma. Even with the support of the U.S. Congress, the problem will only grow more complex.

Conflicts of Interest and Self-Interest

When William Hulbert was named as president of the National League in 1877, he was the owner of the Chicago White Sox. He remained in both capacities until his death in 1882. When the National Commission was formed in 1903 as part of the agreement between the American and the National leagues, the chair of the three-member board was Garry Herrmann, the owner of the Cincinnati Reds. With this pedigree, one might be tempted to argue that there was no conflict of interest for Bud Selig to be baseball's commissioner and the principal owner of the Milwaukee Brewers at the same time during 1992–2005.

There is another lineage, however, that might lead to a different conclusion. The original NL constitution of 1876 stipulated that the league's secretary-treasurer, who was the only operating officer in the league, could not be associated with any team. When Bert Bell was asked in 1946 to become the commissioner of the National Football League, he owned a part of the Pittsburgh Steelers. Bell sold his interest in the team before he became the commissioner. Today, the NFL and the NBA constitutions (rules 8.2 and 24.b, respectively) identically stipulate that "the commissioner shall have no financial interest, direct or indirect, in any professional sport." That is, the commissioner cannot own a team or even a piece of a team in his own league or in any other league.[55]

Since one of the commissioner's duties is to adjudicate conflicts between teams and another is to look after the overall interests of the game, it seems that whatever heritage one embraces, there is a solid conceptual basis for the position that the commissioner should not also be a team owner. Indeed, Bud Selig now says that he always recognized that to be the case.[56]

Selig maintains that he was just waiting for the right time to sell the team. In his case, the right time was after his team had a new stadium and was receiving $18 million–plus a year in revenue sharing. That is, the right time was when the team was worth a lot. He sold the Brewers for some $220 million to Los Angeles financier Mark Attanasio in January 2005.

Even if in theory it was inappropriate for Selig to own the Brewers while he was commissioner, did it matter in practice? There are not many instances of direct conflict that one can point to, but there are some.

First, in the mid-1990s, Selig was getting paid as CEO of the Brewers at the same time that he was getting paid as acting commissioner of MLB. The Brewers did not thrive as a team in the 1990s, and some people wonder whether it suffered from neglect. Michael Megna, for instance, who appraises sports franchises and worked in the past for the Brewers, opined, "Selig was trying to wear too many hats and was too ambitious."[57]

Second, in 1995, Selig obtained a $3 million loan for the Brewers from Twins owner Carl Pohlad. Baseball rule 20c, however, states that owners cannot loan one another money without first receiving permission from the commissioner and all the other owners. The main purpose of this rule is to avoid the mere appearance of a conflict of interest. Selig did not go to the other owners for approval.[58]

Third, when Selig announced MLB's contraction plan in November 2001, it was widely believed that the Twins was one of the targeted teams. Many accused Selig of having a conflict of interest. Without the Twins, the Brewers would recapture fans in western Wisconsin and parts of Minnesota, and its television market would expand considerably. In fact, Selig himself had done a study back in 1965 on the impact of the Twins on the old Milwaukee Braves after the Senators moved to Minneapolis in 1961.[59] His conclusion at the time was that it lowered the Braves' attendance by less than 5 percent. Hence, it is possible that Selig's Brewers would have benefited a bit from contracting the Twins, but it is likely that the benefit would have been quite modest. In any event, Selig's buddy Carl Pohlad was interested in being bought out by MLB, and that, rather than the Brewers' gain, may have been Selig's main motivation in targeting the Twins for contraction. Nonetheless, here and elsewhere, whether and by how much Selig would have benefited may be beside the point. The larger point is that the perception of a conflict of interest weakened the perception of the integrity of the office.

Fourth, under baseball's revenue-sharing system, Commissioner Selig is in charge of making sure that each team receiving transfers spends the money "in an effort to improve its performance on the field."[60] If Selig enforced this provision on other teams receiving transfers, then he would also have to enforce it on his Brewers—thereby raising the Brewers' payroll. Instead, as the Brewers' revenue-sharing receipts rose from $1.5 million in 2001 to $9.1 million in 2002 and to $18.35 million in 2003, the team's opening day payroll moved in the opposite direction: falling from $52.7 million in 2002 to $40.6 million in 2003 and to an opening day payroll of $27.5 million in 2004, the lowest of baseball's thirty teams. Accordingly, other revenue-receiving teams also found slack enforcement of this CBA provision. During 2003, five of the seven bottom-payroll teams actually lowered their opening day salaries by a total of $62.6 million, despite receiving $63.1 million in revenue-sharing transfers.

Selig can respond, of course, that allowing these teams to use their revenue transfers to pay down debt or hire new staff would eventually improve team performance. He can also argue that it is inappropriate to straitjacket each team with a fixed payroll obligation. The latter argument in particular makes good economic sense. Each franchise has different needs and different strategies for building a winning team. Here, too, then, there is some ambiguity about whether Selig's behavior was conflicted, although the Players Association is likely to argue that the language in the CBA provision is perfectly clear and that it has not been implemented. This is a drama that will play out in 2006 when the next CBA is negotiated.

Finally, some people claim that baseball has been too good to Bud Selig. Major League Baseball opened up handsome new offices for Selig in Milwaukee where he conducts most of his business. The New York staff and the team owners often have to make special trips to Milwaukee to meet with him. In 2005, MLB also opened up its Western office in Scottsdale, Arizona. When Bud sold the Brewers in January 2005, his son-in-law, Laurel Prieb, who had been working as a Brewers executive, was without a job. Major League Baseball announced the opening of its new office and that Laurel Prieb would run it. The Western office may have been needed and Laurel Prieb may have been the perfect person to fill the job, but for outsiders, at least, this move evoked some skepticism.

Six More Years

While some owners would have preferred that Selig dealt with his conflicts of interest more forthrightly and other owners believed that Selig was too often manipulative in dealing with the owners,[61] the overwhelming sentiment among the barons was that Selig was doing a good job—especially compared to those who came before him. His imperfections notwithstanding, he held the owners together and was moving the industry forward. His leadership brought the owners what they perceived to be their first collective-bargaining victory and did so without causing a work stoppage. Furthermore, under Selig's watch, baseball had introduced revenue sharing, expanded playoffs, the wild card, interleague play, MLBAM, and other marketing initiatives.

For his contributions, in October 2003, the owners rewarded Bud Selig with another six-year contract. This time his compensation was in the same league as commissioners David Stern in the

NBA and Paul Tagliabue in the NFL. Selig would earn a base salary of $6 million annually, with bonuses raising his total yearly compensation to between $10.2 million and $12 million. A lot of money, yes, but a mere fraction of what Kenneth Lay was earning while he drove Enron into the ground and approximately two-thirds of what the Yankees were paying Kevin Brown in 2005.

9

Governing Baseball
Assessing the Past
and Anticipating the Future

Back in 1920–1921, when baseball created the institution of the commissionership, the circumstances were special. The existing governance structure had become dysfunctional; the relations between the major and the minor leagues, between the owners and the players, and among the owners were unsettled; and the game had just suffered through one of its worst gambling scandals. In 1918, with the country disrupted by World War I, interest in baseball had fallen to an all-time low.

The 1919 World Series was the first after the war, and the burst of fan enthusiasm took everyone by surprise. Baseball needed the 1919 World Series to go well to continue its recovery, but the *Chicago Herald and Examiner* reported rumors of a fix as the series began and then followed the story closely. In the end, the paper gave credibility to the notion that the series had been bought and urged club owners to do something about gamblers' involvement in baseball. The barons were afraid the public would turn its back on baseball if they admitted any wrongdoing, and they refused to acknowledge a problem. The entire controversy might have blown over if the problem had not continued to grow. During the 1920 season, players on other teams began to take advantage of gamblers' offers. Widespread rumors surfaced about games being thrown by players from the New York Giants, the New York Yankees, the Boston Braves, and the Cleveland Indians.

In September 1920, a Cook County, Illinois, grand jury was convened to look into allegations that the Chicago Cubs had thrown games against the Philadelphia Phillies. The investigation soon extended back to the 1919 World Series and to baseball gambling in general. The White Sox were enjoying another good summer in 1920 when the grand jury began calling players, owners, managers, writers, and gamblers to testify about what had happened the previous year. At the urging of Sox owner Charles Comiskey, who allegedly was trying to cover up his own knowledge of the conspiracy, Shoeless Joe Jackson and Eddie Cicotte were the first to confess their involvement in the fix. The grand jury indicted eight White Sox players. The actual trial (and the subsequent acquittal) of the eight players did not begin until June 1921.

With the grand jury indictment, baseball was facing a profound integrity crisis—and had no viable governance structure to deal with it. Riding a tenuous recovery from the nadir of the war years, the barons were desperate. Judge Kenesaw Mountain Landis latched on to this desperation and insisted upon being granted extraordinary, unilateral powers to rule over the game. The result was the 1921 Major League Agreement and the institution of the commissionership. It would have been unlikely in the extreme had this institution, hatched hastily and imperfectly during a peculiar and precarious period, continued to serve baseball well without modification throughout the years.

Indeed, even with modification, it seems to have created more harm than good. The institution spawned a mythology that one man could stand above the game. This man, hired and reappointed by the owners, was given plenary powers to represent the "best interests" of baseball and protect the fans, the host cities, and the players, as well as the owners. With full authority to judge all disputes within the game, it was inevitable that the commissioner would be abridging the free market rights of some individuals or groups. Thus, it came in extremely handy that thirty-seven days before the office of the commissioner was created on January 12, 1921, the U.S. Court of Appeals for the District of Columbia ruled that baseball was exempt from the nation's antitrust laws. This ruling was upheld sixteen months later by the U.S. Supreme Court.

However, the entanglement of the antitrust exemption with the commissionership was unfortunate for baseball in the long run. While it was true that baseball's exemption protected certain actions of the commissioner, the proposition that the exemption itself was justified because the commissioner would ensure that baseball did not abuse its monopoly privileges was problematic. This notion served only to underscore the myth of a benevolent, omnipotent individual who at once looked out for the welfare of all constituencies of the game.

As it turned out, somewhat serendipitously, the marriage of the commissionership and Judge Landis provided the strong medicine that the sick industry needed in 1921. Landis looked out at the owners and saw helplessness. When he accepted the job, he told the barons, "The time had come where somebody would be given authority, if I may put it brutally, to save you from yourselves." And to his credit, he did just that—for a while, at least. His heavy, if not capricious, hand restored the perception of integrity in the national pastime.

When Landis tried to insert himself into the resolution of the game's business problems, however, he was considerably less effective. Yet his lack of productivity in the realm of business was less of a concern. Aside from its relations to the minor leagues and, of course, the Great Depression and World War II, which, alas, Landis could do little about in any event, MLB did not have many serious economic problems between 1921 and 1944.[1] Major League Baseball had a player reserve clause, no rival leagues in baseball, an antitrust exemption just in case, and no real competition from other team sports. So baseball under Landis did not have many financial challenges to confront, yet it was during this era that baseball developed its patterns and practices of governance.

These patterns and practices were born out of an industry that sat alone on a national sports pedestal. And if that wasn't enough privilege, baseball was the only industry in the country that was both a legal monopoly and not subject to government regulation. Baseball's anomalous exemption became even more so when, in 1957, the U.S. Supreme Court declared that football was subject to the nation's antitrust statutes and asserted that baseball's exempt status was "unreasonable, illogical and inconsistent."[2] Even so, baseball got to keep its exemption. Only now it would spend appreciable energy trying to persuade politicians and the courts that it merited its special status.

Baseball maintained that its all-powerful commissioner would prevent monopoly abuses and would protect the fans. Even had the owners actually intended such a role, this was an impossible burden to put on the commissioner's shoulders. Whenever a commissioner attempted to abridge the owners' economic powers, his lifeline was cut short, and the owners would change the constitution to ensure that no commissioner would do so again.

There was an inherent contradiction in the underlying premise of the office: the commissioner was supposed to discipline the very owners who elected and would vote on reelecting him. As Fay Vincent pointed out prior to his 1992 resignation, this contradiction would only be aggravated if the commissioner could be fired by the owners before the expiration of his term. Baseball's constitution remains ambiguous on the question of whether a commissioner can be dismissed by a vote of the owners. Vincent asserted that since the constitution stipulates that a commissioner's authority cannot be diminished while he is in office and dismissal is the ultimate diminution of power, that dismissal itself is prohibited. When the constitution was rewritten to clarify the commissioner's role in 1994, however, the owners chose to leave this issue unresolved. Without resolution of the right-to-dismiss question, which stands at the heart of the commissioner's ability to act independently of the owners' wishes, it is difficult to accept the premise that the commissioner was ever able to protect the fans' interests in any fundamental way.

However, if the commissioner took the mythology of his office seriously, as did Landis, Chandler, Kuhn, Ueberroth, Giamatti, and Vincent to varying degrees, then he would inevitably bump up against the owners' desire to maximize profits. In contrast, if the commissioner had the idea that the industry belonged to the owners, as did Frick and Eckert, then he would be too weak to effect any useful change. There seemed to be no happy medium. Ueberroth may have proven to be the exception to this generalization had he not choreographed collusion in the players' market. Giamatti, too, might have become an exception, but he lasted only five months in the job before his sudden death. Baseball's barons were caught in a continual conflict: the commissioner needed to have nominal plenary powers to justify the antitrust exemption, but the industry needed a commissioner who guided the game as would a CEO. It got neither.

The end result of a self-governing, protected monopoly, depending on a nominally omnipotent but in practice closely circumscribed commissioner, was that the baseball industry was lulled into an administrative stupor. Baseball got away with its managerial arrogance, lassitude, and inefficiency for decades because no other sport rose to challenge it. However, following the NFL's championship game between the New York Giants and the Baltimore Colts on December 28, 1958, that ended with a Colts victory in overtime, football began to find its way into the soul of American sports and television culture. Basketball's booming popularity ensued in the 1980s, and the explosion of entertainment options occasioned by the telecommunications revolution followed in the 1990s.

In the post-1950 era of television and mass communications, baseball had to learn how to market itself. It never did. In the post-1976 era of free agency, baseball needed to learn how to husband its resources. It never did. In the post-1990 era of rapidly growing revenue imbalances across its teams, baseball needed to design a rational revenue-sharing program. It never did.

The NFL, for all its problems, was ably governed by commissioners Bert Bell, Pete Rozelle, and Paul Tagliablue. In football, there was no antitrust exemption and no mythology that the commissioner was protecting the public. The commissioner's job was to grow the industry. The same holds true for the NBA and David

Stern after 1983. Fans are protected from these monopoly sports leagues only insofar as it behooves even a monopoly to be responsive to its customers. Still, because of the absence of competition and their consequent economic power, monopoly sports leagues are able to garner higher television rights fees and charge higher prices for their tickets, concessions, and sponsorship deals. Their teams are also able to extract massive stadium subsidies from their host cities. Unlike MLB, the NFL and the NBA benefit as well because they have commissioners who unabashedly have sought to promote the profitability of their franchises.

But not baseball. There's something about the business culture in an environment where not much gets done. When executives are actively engaged in constructive projects and when executives work together productively, they tend to develop effective, supportive relationships with each other. Absent such engagement, with abundant idle time and no sense of fulfillment, executives often resort to sniping and infighting. When the individuals also happen to be the wealthy owners of major league baseball teams, their sense of entitlement and self-importance can blow this negative behavior out of any sense of proportion.

It is, after all, for this reason that Judge Landis spoke of saving the owners from themselves and that Happy Chandler called the owners "skunks." It is also for this reason that an owners' committee report on the state of the baseball industry in August 1955 concluded,

> Lack of cooperation between [sic] clubs. . . . A lack of planning and a failure to measure tomorrow's effect of today's hasty statement is responsible for most errors in public relations judgment. . . . A principal reason for this lack of anticipation is the almost complete absence of cooperation between [sic] the member clubs. . . . From time to time it appears that half of the club owners or officials are public dissenters on one or more matters of overall policy. . . . This disunity has been one of the blacker spots of present public policy methods.[3]

And it is why the docile Ford Frick observed in his farewell message in 1964 to the owners,

So long as the owners and operators refuse to look beyond the day and the hour; so long as clubs and individuals persist in gaining personal headlines through public criticism of their associates; so long as baseball people are unwilling to abide by the rules they themselves make; so long as expediency is permitted to replace sound judgment, there can be no satisfactory solution.[4]

It is why Bud Selig, in 2005, recalled his first owners' meeting in 1970 in these unflattering terms:

I thought at one point I was going to get caned by Gussie Bush. But I was stunned when I left there, because of the hatred and the anger. And I've often said to people that it never got better until two or three years ago. There's no question about it. The anger and the mistrust—it was really quite sad, and the sport itself suffered.[5]

It is why Fay Vincent was prompted to issue this admonition to the owners in June 1991:

I am disturbed by the apparent unwillingness of some within baseball to rise above parochial interest and to think in terms of the greater good of the game. The squabbling within baseball, the finger-pointing, the tendency to see economic issues as moral ones . . . all of these are contributing to our joint fall from grace.[6]

It is why Selig described the atmosphere at the August 1993 owners' meeting in Kohler, Wisconsin, so starkly: "I've never seen anger like that. It wasn't just bad. It was vile." And why former baseball COO Paul Beeston stated that *acrimony* was too weak a word to depict the feelings among owners at the Kohler meeting—the proper word, he said, was *hatred*.

Meanwhile, the arrogant, feuding barons did not know what to do. They perceived that they had created a potential monster in the commissionership, so they tinkered with the definition of the office. After Landis died in 1944, the owners (1) removed the provision stating that a commissioner's decisions couldn't be appealed in the courts, (2) added a clause stipulating that the commissioner could not use his "best interests" authority to contravene owner votes taken in accordance with the Major League Agreement, and (3) increased the support from one-half to three-quarters vote needed to elect a commissioner. The provision not allowing judicial appeals of the commissioner's decisions was then restored under Frick. The next major changes came under Ueberroth: the maximum fine that the commissioner could impose was increased from $5,000 (the level it had been set at in 1921) to $250,000 and the requirement for reelecting the commissioner was reduced from a three-quarters to a one-half vote of the owners (with at least five votes coming from each league).

Then, as a result of the dispute with Vincent over his alleged interference in collective bargaining, in 1994 it was decided that the commissioner would always chair the Player Relations Committee but that he could never use his "best interests" powers to affect collective bargaining. The latter was crucial to the owners, because they felt that their collective-bargaining leverage had been undermined by Kuhn in 1976, by Ueberroth in 1985, and by Vincent in 1990. The owners' position here was perfectly logical: the commissioner nominally had the ability to end an owners' lockout or alter the owners' collective-bargaining demands but had no ability to end a players' strike or modify the players' demands. The outcome was that the commissioner's power applied asymmetrically in labor negotiations and ended up giving the players more bargaining leverage.

But even with the tweaking of the commissioner's duties, the owners never found the right balance. Eventually, their dissatisfaction with what they had wrought led to rapid turnover at the top. And this turnover came just at the wrong time. As the game's economics grew more complicated and challenging after 1976, baseball needed effective leadership more than ever. The commissionership, however, was really designed to deal with integrity, not economic, issues. Placed in the wrong straitjacket, no commissioner could please the owners.

During the eight-year period between 1984 and 1992, baseball had five different commissioners. With each commissioner came at least one new head of the Player Relations Committee. While the central management of the game was in flux, the Players Association made only one switch in leaders. Marvin Miller gave way to his protégé Don Fehr in 1984, but this was a mere passing of the baton, not a changing of course. Over the last thirty-six years, the Players Association has had only two directors.[7]

Leadership continuity is vital for any organization. It facilitates good communications, consistency, and planning. It is particularly important when the organization has two dozen–plus owners, each with a different view about what the industry should do, and when it faces a strong, militant union. Matters were only made worse by the rapid turnover among owners themselves after 1976.

So, despite an auspicious beginning in the early 1920s, in the long run the institution of the commissionership of baseball did the sport little good. It was not until the owners, in a pinch, did the unthinkable and chose one of their own to be (acting) commissioner that things began to straighten themselves out.

In fact, a movement to draft Bud Selig as the next commissioner had begun among the owners as early as 1984. Selig was involved on practically all the owners' committees and was a favorite of Bowie Kuhn's, so he was frequently consulted on the commissioner's policies. Moreover, Selig was a consummate politician. He was constantly on the phone to his partners in the industry, mending fences and lobbying for action.

During the reigns of Ueberroth, Giamatti, and Vincent, Selig's role in baseball governance continued to grow. In fact, his centrality advanced to the point where he was the only logical choice to step in temporarily after Vincent resigned under pressure in September 1992.[8] Public representations to the contrary, the owners quickly became convinced that they did not want to risk another outside commissioner until after the new labor negotiations were settled and the commissioner's office was restructured. Then, of course, it turned out that the owners liked the absence of ambiguity in the commissioner's mission. They also liked having one of their own as their leader—or, as Selig became, their CEO. If it meant that baseball had to abandon its commissioner-mythology defense for its antitrust exemption, then so be it. Congress had shown that it had no stomach for actually lifting the exemption. If it did lift the exemption, Congress would no longer have a cudgel with which to threaten baseball every three or four years. The cudgel, after all, was useful because it gave members an opportunity for a C-SPAN charade to demonstrate to their constituents on national television how they were looking after their constituents' interests. Moreover, the other sports had gotten along fine without the exemption. So even if Congress were to change its attitude some day, baseball, too, could get along.[9]

Thus, even though there were potential conflicts of interest in having a fellow owner as commissioner, the far more important development was that baseball had finally taken a decisive step toward undoing the ambiguity and the stultifying effects of its governance structure. The owners deserved the right to plot their own course and to have continuity in leadership. They finally buried the mythology of the commissionership and implicitly declared: baseball is a business, just like football and basketball, and henceforth will act like one.

Selig, despite his shortcomings, was the right person to shepherd this transformation. He had committed his life to the game. He was able to talk and listen to all the owners. He had the uncanny ability of being able to convince just about anyone that he was on their side. He was, in short, able to begin to bring the owners together as partners in a way that had never been done before in baseball.

When Selig began his term as acting commissioner, he ruled by consensus. He did so both because the circumstances necessitated it (his formal role was as chair of the ten-person executive council) and because it was his natural style. As time progressed and especially after he was elected formally as commissioner in 1998, he began to be more directive. When the new baseball constitution was passed in 2000, his authority was extended, and he became still more willful and independent.

Selig's new authority includes the ability to fine miscreant owners up to $2 million (increased from the $250,000 maximum set in 1984), to arbitrate disputes emanating from the decisions of the owners' revenue-sharing committee, to distribute monies from his discretionary fund, to certify proper use of revenue-sharing transfers, and to assure compliance with baseball's new debt rules. His authority also includes the more traditional powers of the office, inter alia: to approve player trades, to adjudicate disputes between owners, to select the host city for the All-Star Game, to appoint owners to management committees (including the executive council and the revenue-sharing committee), to approve team relocations and franchise sales, to sanction the selection of teams' managing partners, to lobby for public stadium funding, to fine and suspend players and owners, and to chair the Player Relations Committee, among other things. The commissioner, of course, also has ready access to the national media if he should want to mold public opinion.

To the extent, then, that Selig is unable to gain owner support for his policies through his powerful powers of persuasion, he is able to use the authority of his office to induce cooperation. For his or her team to be successful, almost every owner has come to depend on the cooperation of the commissioner at one time or another. One baseball official explained how Selig sometimes wields his control:

> Some of his preferred tools are off-the-record character assassination made to the media and other owners, and minimizing [owners'] participation in high-profile committees. Remember that the majority of owners are egocentric and want to be respected and admired by their peers. Most have paid a significant price to become a member of this exclusive club and hate the thought of being publicly or privately shunned or minimized by other members.[10]

Since 1992, Selig has presided over several significant changes in the game. He has always defined his main goal as forging a partnership out of the disparate thirty owners. To do so, he had to overcome ownership divisions defined by league, revenue, politics, personality, religion, and history.[11] Perhaps most significantly, he led the owners out of the abyss of Kohler, Wisconsin, in 1993 into an agreement to share local revenues with one another. Originally, this agreement was contingent on the players' accepting a salary cap. High-revenue teams thought they would recoup in lower salaries what they gave up in revenue transfers. When the Players Association resisted the salary cap, however, Selig was able to persuade high-revenue owners to stay the course on revenue sharing anyway. Indeed, the system that ultimately took hold involved some high-revenue teams paying still more into the central fund via a luxury tax on high-revenue team payrolls. That is, these teams got hit twice: once by the new revenue-sharing tax and once by the new luxury tax. That this transformation transpired without a resurfacing of old tensions and animosities is testimony to Selig's strong leadership on this issue.

Selig, of course, did not accomplish this change alone. Small-market NL teams threatened to end the local television agreement among owners that enabled visiting teams to telecast away games back to their home markets. Other team owners and baseball executives lobbied along with Selig to bring about revenue sharing. But Selig orchestrated the process and guided the outcome.

The revenue-sharing system that has been introduced is far from perfect, but the underlying political accomplishment of getting the owners to think about the good of the industry at the same time that they think about the good of their teams is monumental. With the first step taken toward "league think," the other reforms since 1992 came with relative ease: divisional realignment, expansion of the playoffs, wild card teams, and interleague play. As described in chapter 8, Selig has also begun to advance the marketing of the game.

To be sure, there are still important divisions among the owners. Selig, though, has managed so far to keep most of them latent. Nonetheless, it was largely these divisions that delayed the collective-bargaining process for a year and a half during 1992–1994 and again during 2000–2002. These delays complicate labor relations and make a rational design of the CBA more elusive.[12] Selig himself has made some missteps in the bargaining process that imperiled its outcome and served to preserve much of the distrust between the two sides. As long as this distrust persists and as long as divisions prevail among the owners, it will be difficult for baseball to get beyond the crisis mode and to operate effectively with consistency.

A major battleground still existing today is MLB's revenue-sharing system. In 2005, approximately $300 million went from the top to the bottom teams. However, the burden is not equally shared at the top. In 2005, the Yankees' revenue-sharing and luxury tax payments to baseball, combined, approached $100 million, while those of the Red Sox, the second-largest payors, neared $50 million.[13] The current system irrationally penalizes success and appears to target the Yankees. By what logic, for instance, does it make sense for the Yankees to be paying approximately three times as much revenue into the system as the Mets do? The two teams occupy the same market. The principal difference between them is that to date, George Steinbrenner has invested more in his team than Fred Wilpon has in his. Should the Yankees be penalized for their success?

Similarly, the San Francisco Giants and the Oakland A's occupy roughly the same market, yet the Giants pay $10 million plus into baseball's revenue-sharing system, and the A's receive $10 million plus. The Giants paid for their own stadium on the bay and have fielded a competitive and exciting team every year since 1997. Should they be penalized?

Taxing the Yankees, though, is one policy that seems to unite practically all the other twenty-nine owners. But singling out one team is a tenuous basis upon which to engender unity. Steinbrenner had the renowned antitrust lawyer David Boies prepare a suit against MLB in the late 1990s, claiming that the game's tax system was confiscatory. He later withdrew the suit, but if the owners' revenue-sharing committee pushes too hard on the definition of the Yankees' revenues from its YES network, if Kevin McClatchy (the Pirates' owner) successfully pushes for substantial increases in revenue sharing, or if low-revenue teams fail to use their transfers to improve on-field performance, the Yankees may make more legal noise. Other disgruntled team owners may follow.

Before that would happen, however, it is likely that the Yankees and other high-revenue teams would try to promote a redesign of baseball's system. The Red Sox don't like that they are the second-largest payors in the system, despite the facts that they are in the sixth-largest media market and their television territory, as defined by baseball, is twentieth among the thirty teams. The Red Sox owners have been remarkably effective in managing their team, their stadium, and their community relations, and they, too, are being penalized for their success.

One characteristic that the Yankees and the Red Sox share is that they are both in large markets and have successfully developed their own regional sports networks. The lesson that Ted Turner and TBS (Turner Broadcasting System) taught baseball in the 1980s, and that the Yankees, the Red Sox, the Mets, the Nationals, and others are taking advantage of, is that there is a massive potential synergy in controlling both a baseball team and a television station. This synergy grows exponentially in the larger markets. In Turner's case, he used superstation technology to appropriate the entire country as his market and then underpaid baseball for its value.[14] There is synergy available, however, for all team owners if the investment in an RSN (regional sports network) is made, good relations with cable distribution companies are established, and the team and the RSN are managed properly.

The teams on the top of the revenue heap, at least, and the Players Association want to see a revenue-sharing system that promotes competitive balance on the playing field—which is, after all, the main stated purpose for which revenue sharing was introduced. The present system rewards failure and encourages teams to take a free ride. Such behavior does not promote a sense of partnership among the owners.

Arguments that the current revenue-sharing system does not redistribute enough money to the low-revenue teams are dubious. The magnitude of sharing in 2005 will reach roughly $300 million. Before it can be legitimately claimed that this sum is insufficient, as the Pirates' owner Kevin McClatchy has done, the revenue-sharing system needs to embody the proper incentives. With higher marginal tax rates on the bottom teams and with the commissioner not enforcing the CBA provision requiring revenue transfers to be spent on improving team quality, the current scheme does not promote competitive balance. Increasing the magnitude of sharing will not improve the balance unless the incentives are restructured or the implementation is improved.

Furthermore, centralized revenues are increasing rapidly, primarily from the growth of MLBAM and international television but also from national television, satellite radio, sponsorships, and licensing. Not only are these funds distributed equally, but they threaten to cut into locally generated revenues. The consequent leveling in the distribution of revenue also suggests that this is not the right time to increase the quantity of revenue sharing.

Part of the implementation of the present system involves the owners' revenue-sharing committee, whose three members are appointed by the commissioner. The committee in mid-2005 included former Padres president Dick Freeman, Paul Dolan (the president of the Indians and the son of owner Lawrence Dolan), and Mariners president Chuck Armstrong. The committee of three adjudicates disputes about the value of related party transactions (when the team owner also owns another entity with which the team does business). Such a dispute, for instance, was heard in 2005 in the case of the Red Sox and NESN. Will the Red Sox feel fairly treated by a group of owners, two of whom are from small markets and the third from a medium market that does not own a regional sports network? Moreover, Paul Dolan is the nephew of Charles Dolan, whose bid to buy the Red Sox in 2001 lost out to the Henry/Werner/Lucchino group. The same question of the perception of fairness can be asked for the Yankees and down the road for other teams.[15] Indeed, it might be plausibly argued that whatever happens to the Sox regarding NESN will set a precedent for a much larger result regarding the Yankees and YES.

Thus, baseball's current revenue-sharing system not only promotes perverse incentives, it is also heavily politicized. This is a surefire formula for creating dissension. The same system that may hit the Red Sox and the Yankees in 2005 will also affect the Mets, the Orioles, the Dodgers, the Cubs, the White Sox, the Phillies, and other teams in the years to come.

The commissioner has a key role to play in pushing for an effective redesign of the system and, in the meantime, in promoting a proper implementation of the terms of the collective-bargaining agreement with the players. Baseball's incipient dual partnership (among the owners and with the players) is a key ingredient to overcoming its historical myopia and crisis-management mentality. Like any industry, to have enduring success, baseball needs a long-term vision and a strategic plan. Without a solid sense of collegiality and partnership, it will be very difficult for the owners to set aside their differences long enough to plan for the future. Selig has helped MLB take the initial steps toward building the necessary cohesion among the owners, but this emerging unity is still frail and vulnerable. Absent intelligent policies and fair implementation, the initial gains can be undone in short order.

The owners also need the courage and the conviction to make the necessary financial investments in the game's future—even if it means less profit in the short run. If, for instance, the networks crunch the numbers and conclude that World Series ratings will fall by, say, 10 percent if the games begin at 6 P.M. Eastern time instead of at 8 or 9 P.M., it may still be in the industry's long-term interest to begin at 6 P.M., as does the NFL's Super Bowl. A game at 6 P.M. is an invitation to the American family, not just to baseball-crazed males, to participate in the national pastime. It is a call for World Series neighborhood parties in October, just like the Super Bowl parties in February. It is a message that baseball is for all Americans. In the end, it is difficult to believe that MLB's rights fees would fall if it insisted on such a policy, but even if they did, it would be a worthwhile investment in the game's future.

To keep the owners and the players focused on their common interests, to spurn the allure of crass commercialism and short-term profit, and to fashion a unity of purpose, all demand strong, visionary leadership. Baseball has redefined the commissionership in a way that makes this leadership possible, and Bud Selig has taken advantage of the restructured office to lead the game through a difficult transitional period and into the twenty-first century on an optimistic note. Baseball and Selig, however, cannot rest on their laurels.

With Bud Selig and the newly conceived commissionership, MLB has created the necessary conditions for the game's progress; the sufficient conditions remain to be fulfilled. The tasks that lie ahead are as challenging as those that came before.

EPILOGUE

If Bud Selig seemed like a successful commissioner in 2005 (when the first edition of this book was written), he may seem like a magician now. Major League Baseball has extended its unexpected labor peace through at least 2017, weathered the worst recession in seventy years with no more than a few scratches and bruises, benefitted from new stadium construction, witnessed an explosion of value in its franchises, and continued to innovate productively in an era of rapid technological change. Many would say that the Selig era of the last twenty years has been a second golden age for baseball.

Labor Peace and Revenue Sharing

A significant factor in MLB's labor peace has been the owners' willingness to give up their fight for a salary cap. The salary cap was to control labor costs as well as help promote competitive balance across rich and poor teams. In its stead, MLB has employed an extensive system of revenue sharing, a luxury tax, team debt limits, and, more recently, constraints on spending for signing drafted amateurs and international players.

Major League Baseball's revenue sharing has grown from some $20 million in 1995 to approximately $400 million today. The system's general structure is to tax teams' local revenue (net of stadium expenses) a certain percentage (34 percent in the 2012–16 Collective Bargaining Agreement [CBA]), then distribute the money equally across all teams. Since high-revenue teams pay more into the system and get the same amount out as all other teams, they end up making a net contribution. The opposite is true for the low-revenue teams. The highest revenue team, the Yankees, has contributed around $100 million or more in recent years, while several low-revenue teams have received upwards of $40 million from this system.

The first thing to note is that this system, although capless, provides a significant break on player salaries. Teams pay a net revenue tax of approximately 33 percent. So, if the Texas Rangers estimate that Josh Hamilton raises the team's revenue by $30 million a year, they might offer him a salary of, say, $29 million and still make an expected $1 million in profit—if there were no revenue sharing. With revenue sharing, of the $30 million that Hamilton might generate, the Rangers have to share 33 percent, or $10 million, with MLB; Hamilton's net value to the team is now only $20 million. In this case, the team might offer him only $19 million. Of course, in the real negotiations there is uncertainty and risk involved, so the result may not play out so cleanly, but the basic dynamic that lowers salaries by approximately one-third is still in play.

One of the problems with MLB's revenue sharing system as it existed between 1996 and 2006 is that the revenue sharing formula was divided into two parts, which worked at cross purposes with the goal of enhancing competitive balance. High-revenue teams actually experienced lower marginal tax rates than the low-revenue teams. This meant that the high-revenue teams, in relative terms, had a lower disincentive to improve the talent base of their rosters and, thereby, to generate more revenue. As a consequence, payroll disparity did not narrow, and by virtually all relevant measures—the inequality in the distribution of team payrolls, or the standard deviation or decile ratios of team win percentages, among others—competitive balance in MLB did not improve (and by some metrics may have deteriorated slightly) during the first ten years of the revenue sharing program.

Beginning with the 2006 CBA, the inverted incentives have been stripped away by using a new design in the revenue sharing formula. The marginal tax rates in the system are now basically flat rather than regressive, and the different measurements of competitive balance have shown some improvement. The adjusted tax rates have been complemented by some other new features.

Between 2006 and 2011, spending on the top amateur picks accelerated. Small-market clubs often skipped the top-rated players for fear that they wouldn't be able to sign them. These players were then drafted later by large-market teams and signed for big bonuses. This pushed up the value of the higher picks. If the growth of amateur signing bonuses continued at the 10 percent annual rate found during this period, the small-market clubs would not have been able to remain competitive in the market. The 2012–16 CBA introduced a cap and tax plan for the amateur player draft that is based upon a progressive structure of different caps for each team. The team with the lowest win percentage the prior year is allocated the highest cap, while the team with the highest win percentage is given the lowest cap. For 2012 the per team caps ran from $4.47 million to $11.49 million. These levels will increase annually at the rate of growth of aggregate industry revenue. Among other things, this new system will diminish the probability that small-market teams won't be able to sign their top picks, a problem that has weakened the balancing intent of MLB's amateur draft.

With the 2012–16 CBA, for the first time, baseball has added a competitive balance lottery for six extra picks between the first and second rounds and six extra picks between the second and third rounds. These picks will be allocated via lottery among the ten teams with the lowest local revenues and the ten teams in the smallest markets. And, for the first time, these picks will be tradable (for players, not cash).

Similar changes are being made with the international signing of players wherein each team will have a restricted signing bonus pool. Teams will have different pool allotments, inversely related to win percentage and varying between $1.7 million and $4.6 million in 2013. These allotments will also be tradable.

It is also noteworthy that the cap and tax system is being instituted instead of a rigid slotting system. The former allows for more flexibility in allocating signing bonuses. Together with the new provisions for trading, the new system rewards managerial intelligence and ingenuity.

Another significant change in the 2012–16 CBA is an upward revision in the luxury tax. While the top nominal rate will rise from 40 to 50 percent, the real impact emerges elsewhere. Under the new revenue sharing system, the teams with market size between the mean and the median will no longer receive revenue sharing. The amount saved among top teams from eliminating these transfers will be around $60 million when the plan is fully implemented in 2016 (with the saving phased in between 2013 and 2016).

At current levels, this policy would save the Yankees around $20 million by 2016. However, the Yankees are only entitled to receive this rebate if they stay under the luxury (or competitive balance) tax threshold of $189 million in payroll that year. If they go over the threshold, they lose all $20 million. Imagine that the Yankees' payroll for 2016 stands at $185 million in March and they are contemplating signing a free agent pitcher who would cost an estimated $10 million. If they signed this pitcher, it would put them $6 million over the threshold, and they would pay a 50 percent (or $3 million) tax. Further, they would lose the $20 million rebate, and the total cost to them of signing the pitcher would be $33 million (the pitcher's $10 million salary plus $23 million in penalties). The implied marginal tax rate of this signing would be 230 percent—a rather powerful incentive for the Yankees *not* to go over the threshold!

It is also relevant to note that the luxury tax threshold grew from $148 million in 2007 to $178 million in 2011 (an increase of $30 million, or 20.3 percent, over the course of the last CBA). During the new agreement, the threshold will grow from $178 million to $189 million (an increase of only $11 million, or 6.2 percent). The slower growth of the threshold and the higher tax rates signal significant payroll compression across the teams.

And, of course, the introductions of the wild card in 1996 and then the double wild card in 2012 have increased the number of teams within reach of a postseason berth. These changes have enhanced the excitement of regular season competition and given more fans hope and faith that their team has a chance to go all the way.

Revenue and Franchise Value Growth

Despite the worst U.S. economic performance since the 1930s, MLB has had an impressive run on the revenue side. Since 2006, six new stadiums have been built. Major League Baseball Advanced Media

(MLBAM) has continued to grow, and the MLB Network made its debut. Accordingly, the fan experience has steadily improved and become democratized as fans in different cities benefit from state-of-the-art ballparks, access to mlb.com, and the MLB Network.

When MLBAM launched in 2001, it generated $36 million in revenue, with an EBITDA (earnings before interest, taxes, depreciation, and amortization) of negative $12 million. In 2012 MLBAM's revenue surpassed $540 million with a positive EBITDA of over $200 million, representing an annual growth rate of 28 percent in revenue and 34 percent in EBITDA. Major League Baseball Advanced Media's live streaming of games (mlb.tv) in 2012 had some 3 million subscribers, 1 million of whom subscribed via MLB AT BAT on smart phones. The mlb.com website receives over 10 million visitors on an average day, with over 110 million page views. Nearly half of this traffic is via smart phones, and a modest—but growing—share comes through other sites, such as Facebook or Google.

The MLB Network was launched in January 2009. Major League Baseball owns 67 percent of the network, with DirecTV, NBC Universal, Time Warner, and Cox Communications owning the balance. This broad partnership with cable and satellite distributors enabled the MLB Network in its first year to reach more households (approximately 50 million) than the networks of the other major sports leagues, even though the latter had already been in existence for six to ten years. The network experienced thirty-six consecutive weeks of ratings growth during 2011. It has also received twenty-eight Sports Emmy Award nominations. By June 2012, its distribution had reached 69 million U.S. households, still exceeding the reach of any other league network by more than 9 million homes.

Teams' local television revenue has also exploded. In August 2010 the Texas Rangers, emerging out of bankruptcy, signed a twenty-year deal worth an estimated $3 billion. In April 2011 the Los Angeles Angels signed a similar deal, perhaps worth a bit more. The small-market San Diego Padres are poised to also sign a twenty-year deal, reportedly valued at $1.5 billion. Each deal includes an ownership stake for the team in the local regional sports network (RSN).

What lies behind these swiftly rising rights fees? First, the introduction and accelerated development of the digital video recorder (DVR) has transformed the value of television advertising. Whereas some 13 percent of U.S. households had DVRs in January 2007, in July 2012 some 45 percent did. These households, with a push of a button, record any television show they want and then watch it whenever they want, skipping over commercials. Corporate advertisers see a diminishing value in programming that is not time sensitive. There is little reason why viewers need to watch *The Mentalist* on Sunday nights at 10 p.m. if the time is inconvenient. They can record it and watch it on Mondays at 8 p.m., or Tuesdays at 9 p.m., or whenever—in forty minutes, skipping twenty minutes of commercials. Few fans of baseball teams, however, will want to watch Sunday's game on Monday or Tuesday. The game is time sensitive. When watching live, baseball game commercials can't be skipped by pressing a button. This dynamic that the DVR has fostered has led advertisers to put a premium on baseball (and other team sports) programming. Greater demand for ad spots leads to higher prices and, ultimately, to higher rights fees for the teams, as well as higher asset values for their affiliated RSNs.

Second, there is growing competition in the distribution of video programming. Telcos, after a lengthy gestation period of infrastructural investments, are beginning to compete with traditional cable companies. Satellite distributor DirecTV is doing the same. There is also the emergence of what are known as OTT (over the top) distributors, including Netflix, Hulu, I-Tunes, YouTube, and set-top boxes such as ROKU, which use the Internet to distribute programming. As a consequence, there are more companies bidding for the rights to baseball game programming, enabling RSNs to raise their fees and increase their distribution.

Third, the struggle by RSNs to be carried on expanded basic programming, rather than on a specialized sports tier or à la carte, has led to joint ventures between teams and cable distributors. In 2002 FOX owned twenty-four RSNs and had local rights to seventy pro teams. This was reflected in Ruppert Murdoch's purchase of the Dodgers in 1998, which he sold to Frank McCourt in 2004, once he had succeeded in preventing Disney from establishing an RSN in LA. The value of RSNs, however, has been exploding, in part due to the DVR transformation already discussed, and cable distributors have seen an opportunity to jump in. So, in 2011, Time Warner outbid FOX for rights to the NBA's Lakers, paying an estimated $3 billion for a twenty-year deal and creating two Los Angeles RSNs, one in English and one in Spanish. Meanwhile, FOX outbid Comcast in 2011, offering a twenty-year deal for local broadcast rights to the Texas Rangers, also at an estimated $3 billion. Comcast now owns nine RSNs, DirectTV owns three, Cablevision owns two, and Cox owns two (one in San Diego).

Fourth, there is uncertainty about how video will be distributed in the future. If most households will receive their video programming via the Internet instead of the television set, what will happen to the existing cable, telco, and satellite companies? Will other companies emerge to distribute sports programming on the Internet or will teams sell programming directly? Will the FCC impose constraints on how this programming is made available to consumers? This uncertainty is also driving the cable companies to buy RSNs while they have some leverage. If team sports are must-see programming, then the cable companies with ownership stakes in RSNs will have a leg up if the distribution terrain shifts from cable to the Internet. Further, baseball teams have the advantage over football, basketball, and hockey teams because baseball teams offer 162 games in the regular season and, hence, more aggregate viewership.

These factors have combined to drive up rights fees. As we shall see below, however, once these factors have played out, other forces that may halt or reverse this trend may assert themselves.

Since the publication of the first edition of this book in 2006, MLB has negotiated two new labor agreements, 2007–11 and 2012–16. Beyond the positive features described above, these agreements signify that baseball has truly turned the corner on the era of labor conflict between 1972 and 1995. Since 2000, lockouts and strikes have roiled the NHL, NBA, and NFL, and baseball has transformed itself from the sport with the most labor turmoil to that with the most labor peace. Labor peace not only pleases the fans but also facilitates corporate sponsorships, long-term television deals, multiyear premium seating contracts, season ticket sales, and industry planning.

Baseball has also made important strides in reducing the use of performance enhancing drugs. Major League Baseball's new testing and penalty policy is arguably the strongest one in U.S. professional team sports. Aside from the rare announcement of a player suspension in the Major or Minor Leagues—and the knottier problem of controlling the use of PEDs in the Caribbean—baseball's public image in this area has improved enormously. Nonetheless, it is premature to declare victory. New compounds and masking agents will require ongoing vigilance.

Major League Baseball continues to grow internationally. One driving force of this growth is the World Baseball Classic (WBC), founded in 2005. Participation in the third edition of the WBC in 2013 will increase from sixteen to twenty-eight countries. International revenue to MLB has increased from $34 million in 1998, to $104 million in 2006, and to $145 million in 2012.

The introduction of an extra wild card team in 2012, along with the use of flexible or dynamic pricing by some teams, helped to turn around attendance after it began to sag with the financial crisis in 2008. League-wide attendance grew by 0.4 percent in 2011, and as of June 26, attendance was up another 6.5 percent in 2012. Although attendance has not yet recovered to 2007 levels, ticket revenue grew from $6.097 billion in 2007 to $6.925 billion in 2011.[1]

The foregoing developments together have contributed to MLB's strong revenue growth since 2005 despite the limping economy. After growing industry-wide revenue from $1.67 billion in 1992, to $4.74 billion in 2005, and to $5.66 billion in 2007, MLB's revenue in 2012 was approximately $7.38 billion. The compound annual revenue growth rate since 2005 is an impressive 6.5 percent, and since the onset of the recession in 2007, the rate is a striking 5.5 percent.[2]

Revenue growth, together with effective cost controls, has led to a substantial appreciation in franchise values. In 2009 the Chicago Cubs sold for a record $845 million. The Texas Rangers sold in a bankruptcy auction in August 2010 for $593 million. In November 2011 the Houston Astros were purchased for $611 million, and in April 2012 the Los Angeles Dodgers sold for $2.15 billion. The Dodgers and affiliated assets had been previously purchased in 2004 for $430 million; thus, the team's value grew a phenomenal fivefold over eight years. The San Diego Padres, bought by John Moores in 1994 for $75 million, were sold in August 2012 for $800 million. Whether or not the current owners of the Dodgers or Padres overpaid, these recent franchise sales are indicative of strong valuations in what is increasingly perceived to be a robust industry—even as the macroeconomy languishes with slow growth and high unemployment.

Ownership Turnover

Given the 2008 financial collapse in the U.S. economy, it is little wonder that several MLB owners found themselves buried in financial difficulty. Erstwhile Texas Rangers owner Tom Hicks was forced to declare bankruptcy and auction off his team. New York Mets owner Fred Wilpon was caught in the crosshairs of the Bernie Madoff scandal. He was confronted with a costly legal challenge from the Madoff victims' trustee Irving Picard, a downturn in team performance, massive debt service on the bonds for the team's new $800 million stadium, among other financial misfortunes. Commissioner Selig lent Wilpon $25 million from MLB funds and stood by Wilpon despite appreciable push back. Wilpon eventually settled with Picard on favorable terms and raised capital by selling minority shares in the team. Wilpon and the Mets appear to have emerged from their crisis.

The largest ownership crisis came, of course, with Frank and Jamie McCourt, owners of the Dodgers from 2004 through April 2012. The Dodgers had experienced effective and stable ownership for over fifty years under Walter and Peter O'Malley until the team was sold to Ruppert Murdoch's FOX in 1998 for $311 million. The network reportedly averaged yearly losses on the team of close to $40 million but accomplished its goal—preventing Disney from creating a new RSN in Southern California. Mission accomplished, FOX turned to sell the team, but for several years the only buyers wanted FOX's two Los Angeles RSNs along with the team. The RSNs were the profit centers, and FOX was unwilling to sell them.

Finally, along came Frank McCourt, a maverick Boston real estate developer who had unsuccessfully tried to buy the Red Sox in 2002. McCourt was willing to buy the Dodgers without the RSNs and also to sign a new long-term contract through 2013 with FOX's RSN Prime Ticket. He borrowed most of the $430 million that he paid for the team, and fans, rightfully, were concerned that McCourt was cash poor. With the help of the Dodgers, however, McCourt wouldn't remain cash poor for long.

In October 2009 Frank and Jamie McCourt announced that they would be seeking a divorce. A week later Frank fired Jamie as team CEO, and he soon locked the doors to her office. The divorce proceedings became a public soap opera, as Dodgers operating documents were made public and Frank and Jamie hurled accusations at each other.

Frank McCourt seems to have run the team rather like his personal ATM. According to reports from the court documents and the media, Frank drew an annual salary in the $5–6 million range. McCourt Consulting Company was paid $3.6 million a year by the Dodgers. Jamie was paid $2 million as CEO. Two of their sons, one with a job at Goldman and the other a student at Stanford, were on the Dodgers' payroll to the tune of $600,000. Neither Jamie nor Frank were able to explain in court what their sons did for the team. Frank divided the team into sixteen separate entities and used the revenue flow from each as collateral for bank loans. For instance, in 2005 Frank set up Dodger Ticket LLC with rights to sell all game tickets and took out a $390 million loan off it. According to a report from Commissioner Selig's office, over five years McCourt took out $180 million from the team in payments and disbursements and paid no taxes. These funds were used by the McCourts to finance an obscenely opulent lifestyle, including the ownership of nine homes (with two in Brentwood, two in Malibu, one in Los Cabos, one in Montana, one on Cape Cod, one in Boston, and one in Vail), $10,000 a week for a hair stylist, and $800,000 a year for a personal security staff and driver. The McCourts also hired a psychic living in Boston to watch Dodgers games on television and channel energy to the team.

Selig finally put his foot down in 2011, vetoing a proposed television deal between FOX and the Dodgers. McCourt was cash short, with a reported debt of over $700 million and a looming divorce settlement payment to Jamie of $130 million. He was forced to sell the team, and baseball's sad, sordid episode with Frank McCourt came to an end in April 2012. Many believe, however, that justice wasn't served. McCourt was rewarded for his misdeeds when he sold the franchise for an eye-popping $2.15 billion.

Through all the ownership embarrassments and travails, MLB came out fine. The baseball industry also learned that it must be more careful with its new owner vetting procedures in the future.

Challenges Ahead

While inter-ownership disputes have been brought under control during Selig's commissionership, no one should believe that they have disappeared or will disappear in the future. There are still some pesky ones confronting baseball.

When the San Francisco Giants were looking for a new home in the city during the 1980s and losing one referendum for public funding after another, the then owner of the team, Bob Lurie, was exploring the option of moving the team to San Jose. At the time, Santa Clara County was part of the MLB territory of the Oakland A's. To pursue San Jose, Lurie needed the permission of the then A's owner, Walter Haas. Magnanimously, Haas granted permission, and Santa Clara became Giants territory. When the Giants' new owner, Peter Magowan, decided to build a new stadium for the Giants in China Basin on the Bay and fund it privately, he did so with the understanding that Santa Clara was part of his territory. Of course, in the intervening years, San Jose experienced the electronics and Internet boom and came to be known as Silicon Valley, one of the wealthiest areas in the country.

Fast-forward to the present. The A's are limping at the coliseum in Oakland. The market is small and the stadium is old and underequipped. By today's standards, the A's need a new stadium; after trying various alternatives, the team's current owner, Lewis Wolff, has his eyes set on Santa Clara County. The only problem is that the Giants refuse to cede the territory back to the A's and are aggressively threatening to sue if MLB allows the A's to relocate.

What to do? Internecine warfare is ugly and expensive, and it potentially airs dirty laundry. Selig has been trying to broker a compromise for a few years. There is a strong argument that it is in baseball's best interests to have the A's in a new stadium in a rich market, rather than an antiquated stadium in a poor market. It would seem that an indemnity payment to the Giants should be workable, but thus far a settlement has been elusive. Selig values owner peace (or, at least, the appearance of peace) and wants to keep the lid on the enmity.

Meanwhile, another struggle threatens to surface on the opposite coast. When Bob DuPuy brokered a deal with Baltimore Orioles owner Peter Angelos back in March 2006, Angelos was concerned that the Expos moving to Washington DC would impinge on his designated television territory and wanted adequate compensation. The deal with DuPuy provided that a new RSN would be created

(MASN) and that Angelos would initially own 90 percent of it. This share would diminish to 67 percent over thirty years, with the balance being held by the owners of the Washington Nationals. Major League Baseball paid Angelos $75 million for the Nationals' eventual 33 percent ownership of MASN. Finally, the deal provided that MASN would pay the Nationals a yearly rights fee, to be determined by a third party and based upon the methodology utilized by MLB's Revenue Sharing Definitions Committee (RSDC) in reviewing media related-party transactions. In 2011 this fee was $29 million, plus the Nationals received an additional $6 million of profit distribution based on their share in MASN.

The problem is the Nationals believe that because (a) the team is rising to new competitive heights with several star players, (b) the local rights fee market is soaring for baseball teams, and (c) the greater DC television market is the ninth largest in the country, their rights fee should increase to some $120 million in 2013. Angelos argues that the proper fee should be around $35 million in 2013, rising to $46 million in 2017. The resolution of this disagreement has been delegated to the RSDC under the original agreement, with the commissioner waiting in the wings. The litigation flag has been waved by both sides. The commissioner's office has set a resolution date a few times, and each time the deadline has been extended.

The Tampa Bay Rays play at Tropicana Field (the Trop) in St. Petersburg, Florida. Tampa-St. Pete is a midsize market, with below-average income and below-average corporate penetration. The Trop is a domed stadium with poor sightlines and few amenities. Most consider it the worst facility in Major League Baseball (though some may say that it receives tough competition for this honor from the Oakland Coliseum). It lies away from downtown St. Pete and roughly ten miles across an extended causeway from downtown Tampa, where the concentration of the area population and businesses reside. Over the past several years, the team has performed at top competitive levels, but it is saddled year after year with the lowest or near lowest attendance in MLB, as well as a diminutive local television contract. The team owners have devised various stadium alternatives in the area with innovative financing plans, but they have been resisted by the St. Pete government, which has asserted that it intends to hold the team to its lease, which goes through 2027 at the Trop. Here too is an untenable situation that must be resolved. And here too Selig has avoided heavy-handedness, hoping for the interested parties to reach a rational compromise. Rays owner Stu Sternberg has thus far been exemplary in his patience and in the absence of threats to move the team. But, it seems, something will have to give.

Television, as we have seen, has been a bright spot for the baseball industry in recent years. Major League Baseball is about to sign a new national contract that promises to show a significant increase in rights fees. But the future of baseball's television revenue remains uncertain for various reasons. The current explosion in the value of local television contracts has many hallmarks of a conventional bubble. Institutional uncertainty causing RSNs and video distributors to buy the programming source, competition among existing and new video distributors lifting rights fees, and the impact of the DVR's increasing widespread use are all conjunctural forces behind the revenue growth. Their impact will fade. As it does, other forces, such as the geometric multiplication of video programming options and the fragmentation of audiences, will assert themselves.

Further, baseball will face the troubling issue of the unfavorable demographics of its fans. Baseball's fan base has always been older than that of basketball and football. The data in the following table, representing the average for all MLB teams, suggest that, if anything, MLB's television audience is getting slightly older. The good news is that local television markets continue to grow and that the minority component of baseball's viewing audience is increasing.[3] Nonetheless, if MLB does not reverse the aging distribution of its television audience, ratings will continue to slide over time and rights fees are likely to follow.

MLB's Television Viewership Demographics, 1990–2009

	TV Homes	White	Black	Hispanic	Median Age	Over 65
Average 1990s	2,177,078	74.7%	13.0%	11.4%	34.8	11.5%
Average 2000–2004	2,318,323	71.5%	12.8%	14.6%	36.0	11.6%
Average 2005–2009	2,487,318	69.6%	14.0%	16.2%	36.7	11.8%

The other ramification from the explosion in local TV revenue is that teams whose television contracts are expiring between 2010 and 2014 are likely to experience anywhere from a doubling to a quintupling of their rights fees. This will amount to extra tens of millions of dollars—in some cases nearly $100 million—annually. Other teams whose long-term contracts will not expire until after 2014 (sometimes long after that) will see basically flat revenue. Inequality across teams will break out along new lines, creating new tensions and new issues for competitive balance.

Relatedly, the emergence of an institutionalized secondary ticket market and the decision to study the functioning of the IMRA (baseball's Internet marketing rights agreement from 2000) raise touchy questions about the centralization of decision-making in baseball, as well as the distribution of revenue.

All these issues and more will be on the table in the months and years ahead. None are easily resolved. One fascinating and vitally important question is who will be leading baseball as the industry works through these challenges.

Bud Selig assumed leadership of the game back in 1992. He was the ultimate inside candidate. He had been a team owner and had been actively involved in the game's governance since 1970. Prior commissioners came from outside the game and had neither the understanding nor the relationships to enable them to move the game forward.

A sports league commissioner is called upon to lead a motley and contentious group of some thirty hypercompetitive team owners (or partnerships). For baseball—or any sport—to survive or progress it needs to move beyond daily troubleshooting and to develop a strategy for industry growth. Prior to 1992, getting all the owners on the same page to fashion such a strategy had been practically an impossibility. Bud Selig, however, evolved a management method that combined guile, sticks and carrots, heavy-handedness, hand-holding, and ego massaging to suppress open dissent long enough to develop a strategy for growth and change. The success of this method required experience, intelligence, an uncanny ability to communicate, indefatigable energy, effective relationships with virtually all of the owners, and a deep knowledge and love of the game. Bud Selig, for all of his shortcomings, embodied these requisite qualities.

Baseball's owners have recognized this, and that is why they have continually rehired him each time his existing contract expired. Selig has held the game together and he has moved it forward. The owners fear what will happen in his absence. But his absence is about to come. Selig has announced that he will step down when his current term ends after the 2014 season. Of course, Selig has been saying this since his initial interim appointment as acting commissioner in 1992, and he has said so again each time an existing contract is about to expire.

What makes this time different? When the 2014 season ends, Bud Selig will be eighty years and three months old. He has endowed a chair at his alma mater, the University of Wisconsin–Madison, in history. He would like to occupy the chair, teach, and write his memoirs. I suspect that he would also like to be around when he is inducted into Cooperstown. When he discusses leaving the commissioner's office, Selig's tone and his conviction are different now than ever before. Around baseball, owners, CEOs, and GMs talk about Selig's departure with resignation.

Baseball must face the challenge of succession. It will not be easy to find a new leader. If the analysis in this book is correct, the next commissioner cannot be an outsider. Yet, finding an insider will not be easy either. Insiders tend to be associated with parochial interests, and insiders are more likely to have made enemies. Nonetheless, there are some insiders who have worked across interest groups, who have extensive experience, and who are broadly respected. Replacing Bud Selig, while daunting, is not impossible. Baseball's greatest challenges will lie elsewhere.

NOTES

Chapter 1. Introduction: Running a League

1. This quote and other information about Selig's melanoma comes from Tom Boswell, "Steroids? Politics? Selig Discovers Perspective," *Washington Post*, December 25, 2004, p. D1, and from the author's interviews with Bud Selig.

2. As Bud Selig and Don Fehr discovered in 2005, dealing with Congress is not always a cakewalk. Not only were they hauled before congressional committees multiple times around MLB's antidoping policies, but in June 2005 representative Tom Davis, Republican of Virginia, threatened to take away baseball's antitrust exemption if it allowed the ownership group with George Soros to buy the Washington Nationals. Davis criticized Soros for making $5 million in contributions to defeat George Bush in 2004. Soros, of course, is primarily known for being one of the most successful investors and generous philanthropists in recent times. At the All-Star Game press conference on July 12, 2005, Selig appropriately stated that Soros's involvement will have "no effect on how on we select the ownership in Washington. This is a baseball decision. It is not a political decision, nor should politics interfere with any decision we're making." Ron Blum, "Selig Says Davis Remark Has No Effect," Associated Press, July 12, 2005.

3. Not surprisingly, open leagues have their own set of problems. For a full discussion of these issues, see Stefan Szymanski and Andrew Zimbalist, *National Pastime: How Americans Play Baseball and the Rest of the World Plays Soccer*. Washington, D.C.: Brookings, 2005.

4. For a fuller discussion of related party transactions, see Andrew Zimbalist, *May the Best Team Win: Baseball Economics and Public Policy*. Washington, D.C.: Brookings, 2004.

5. Owners also can use their team assets as collateral to obtain more favorable terms on personal loans. Some leagues have rules about the percentage of team assets that can be thusly collateralized.

6. See Zimbalist, *May the Best Team Win*, pp. 72–74.

7. Of course, just because a league is a monopoly, it does not guarantee a profit. Monopolists must have sufficient demand for their output and be well managed to be profitable.

8. Two years earlier, the Supreme Court held that the exemption did not apply to the sport of boxing in *U.S. v. International Boxing Club*, 348 U.S. 236 (1955). Boxing, however, is not a team sport and therefore did not face many of the labor market and competitive balance issues that justified, according to some, an antitrust exemption for team sports. The Court's 1957 *Radovich* decision correctly reflected inter alia the broader conception of interstate commerce prevalent since the late 1930s.

9. U.S. Senate Committee on the Judiciary, Subcommittee on Antitrust and Monopoly, *Organized Professional Team Sports*, 85th Cong., 2nd sess., July 9, 15–18, 22–24, 28–31, 1958. (Washington, D.C.: USGPO, 1958, p. 423.)

10. Of course, MLB adduced other arguments as well to support its claim to an antitrust exemption. For a discussion of these, see Zimbalist, *May the Best Team Win*, ch. 2.

Chapter 2. The History of the Commissioner's Role

1. Lee Allen, *100 Years of Baseball*. New York: Bartholomew House, 1950, pp. 24, 28.

2. Quoted in Daniel Ginsburg, *The Fix Is In: A History of Baseball Gambling and Game Fixing Scandals*. Jefferson, N.C.: McFarland, 1995, p. 17.

3. See, for example, Joe Durso's *Baseball and the American Dream*. St. Louis: Sporting News Press, 1986, pp. 16–18; and Ted Vincent's *Mudville's Revenge: The Rise and Fall of American Sport*. New York: Seaview Books, 1981, p. 102.

4. Vincent, *Mudville's Revenge*, p. 107.

5. Allen, *100 Years of Baseball*, p. 27.

6. Ginsburg, *The Fix Is In*, p. 35.

7. A nice discussion of Hulbert's actions in 1875 is provided by John Rosenburg, *They Gave Us Baseball: The 12 Extraordinary Men Who Shaped the Game*. Harrisburg, Pa.: Stackpole Books, 1989.

8. It should give some solace to people who see no compelling reason for Pete Rose to be excluded from the Hall of Fame to know that William Hulbert was not elected to the hall until 1995. In contrast, Morgan Bulkeley, who served for only nine months as the NL's first president and accomplished nothing in that period, was inducted in 1939 when the hall opened. (Bulkeley was actually elected by the Veterans' Committee in 1937, but, as with all members who were elected during 1936–1938, his induction awaited the physical opening of the Cooperstown facility in 1939.) Hulbert succeeded Bulkeley as the NL president, a position he retained until his death at age fifty in 1882. Bulkeley was simply Hulbert's vehicle to buy acceptance of his plan for the NL from the Eastern club backers.

9. William Akin, "William A. Hulbert," in Robert Tiemann and Mark Rucker, eds., *Nineteenth Century Stars*. Kansas City, Kans.: Society for American Baseball Research, 1989. Robert Barney and Frank Dallier, "William A. Hulbert, Civic Pride and the Birth of the National League," in *Nine: A Journal of Baseball History and Social Policy Perspectives* 2, no. 1 (Fall 1973).

10. Quoted in Barney and Dallier, "William A. Hulbert," p. 42.

11. Quoted in Peter Levine, *A. G. Spalding and the Rise of Baseball*. New York: Oxford University Press, 1985, p. 22.

12. Because the launch of the NL was preceded by an article in the *Chicago Tribune* in October 1875 criticizing the association and citing the need for a new league with certain characteristics, some have claimed that Hulbert got his ideas from the article's author, Lewis Meacham. More recent scholarship, however, has followed the interpretation of Harold Seymour (*Baseball: The Early Years*. New York: Oxford Uni-

versity Press, 1960, pp. 76–78) that Meacham's article most likely came from Hulbert's head.

13. Ibid., pp. 24, 134.

14. Alas, although Hulbert's intransigent disciplining of these players sent a strong message and improved the game's image, it failed to root out player and umpire corruption. After a brief hiatus, scandals reappeared. For details, see Ginsburg, op. cit.

15. Cited in Seymour, *Baseball: The Early Years*, p. 90.

16. These challenges and arrangements are described in detail in Szymanski and Zimbalist, *National Pastime* (see ch. 1, n. 3).

17. The precise clause (Article I, Section 4) in the 1896 Agreement read as follows: "In the performance of its duties the Board shall have power to impose fines or penalties upon associations, clubs, club officers, players, managers, scorers and umpires, and to suspend any such organization or person . . . if it or he shall have been guilty of conduct detrimental to the general welfare of the game or in violation of the letter or spirit of the National Agreement."

18. Robert F. Burk, *Never Just a Game: Players, Owners, and American Baseball to 1920*. Chapel Hill: University of North Carolina Press, 1994, p. 166.

19. Andrew Zimbalist, *Baseball and Billions*. New York: Basic Books, 1994, p. 9.

20. Competition from the FL also facilitated nonsalary gains for the players. The fraternity presented the AL and the NL owners with a list of seventeen demands in January 1914. Several were met, including that the owners agreed to pay for players' uniforms (except shoes) and travel expenses to spring training; the owners agreed to provide written notification and explanation of suspensions or releases and promised nondiscrimination against fraternity members; and the owners agreed to provide all players with written contracts. Though modest concessions, they were important steps toward recognizing that players had some legal rights.

21. Harold Seymour, *Baseball: The Golden Age*. New York: Oxford University Press, 1971, pp. 205–07.

22. Burk, *Never Just a Game*, p. 203.

23. David Voigt, *American Baseball*, vol. 2. University Park: Pennsylvania State University Press, 1983, p. 117.

24. Cited in Burk, *Never Just a Game*, p. 208.

25. Zimbalist, *Baseball and Billions*, p. 9.

26. The new NL president, John Heydler, however, was able to secure $2,500 for the Braves in exchange for Perry staying with the Athletics. Burk, *Never Just a Game*, p. 226.

27. The citations from this case are from Paul Weiler and Gary Roberts, *Sports and the Law: Text, Cases, Problems*. St. Paul, Minn.: West Group, 1998, pp. 8–9.

Chapter 3. The First Commissioner: Kenesaw Mountain Landis

1. It was not uncommon for baseball's top players to earn between $10,000 and $20,000 during the 1910s. In 1910, Christy Mathewson earned $10,000 and Nap Lajoie $12,000. Player-manager Honus Wagner was paid $18,000 that same year. Ty Cobb earned $20,000 as early as 1915. Babe Ruth, however, did not earn his first $20,000 contract until 1920 with the Yankees.

2. Asinoff's account may be apocryphal. Cicotte's contract in the archives of the National Baseball Hall of Fame library does not indicate that any such clause was memorialized in the contract. There, of course, may have been a subsequent arrangement, oral or written, that is the basis for Asinoff's claim.

3. Quoted in David Pietrusza, *Judge and Jury: The Life and Times of Judge Kenesaw Mountain Landis*. South Bend, Ind.: Diamond Communications, Inc., 1998, p. 172.

4. Ibid., p. 170.

5. Ibid.

6. Quoted in Jerome Holtzman, *The Commissioners: Baseball's Midlife Crisis*. New York: Total Sports, 1998, pp. 26–28.

7. Quoted in Pietrusza, *Judge and Jury*, p. 174.

8. This discord goes back to baseball's earliest days. One striking, pre-Landis indication of animosity among the owners was provided by the famous player, entrepreneur, and owner Albert G. Spalding. When he was an owner of the Chicago NL club and on the verge of being elected league president, Spalding wrote, "The trouble now was not with gamblers or with players, but with club officials, generally termed magnates, and it will be readily understood how difficult a matter it was to deal with them . . . [because of their] personal cussedness and disregard for the future welfare of the game. . . . With these men it was simply a mercenary question of dollars and cents. Everything must yield to the one consideration of inordinate greed." Szymanski and Zimbalist, *National Pastime*, pp. 301–02 (see ch. 1, n. 3).

9. Pietrusza, *Judge and Jury*, p. 11.

10. Ibid., p. 134.

11. Ibid., p. 140.

12. Ibid., p. 145.

13. Ibid., p. 149.

14. Although the Supreme Court actually called for a new trial, in 1922 the government dropped all charges against the Socialists.

15. Quoted in Holtzman, *The Commissioners*, p. 18.

16. Although in his biography of Landis, J. G. Taylor Spink states that Landis was only a social drinker. Spink also notes that Landis smoked heavily, right to the end. J. G. Taylor Spink, *Judge Landis and 25 Years of Baseball*. St. Louis: *Sporting News*, 1974, p. 241. In his memoirs, Kuhn produces a different image of Landis. Comparing Landis and his successor Happy Chandler, Kuhn writes, "Happy is as warm-spirited as Landis was crusty; as homespun as Landis was profane; as much a teetotaler as Landis was a drinker; as much a Democrat as Landis was a Republican; as voluble as Landis was terse; as kindly as Landis was pugnacious." Bowie Kuhn, *Hardball: The Education of a Baseball Commissioner*. Lincoln: University of Nebraska Press, 1987, p. 25.

17. Quoted in Holtzman, *The Commissioners*, p. 16.

18. Ibid., pp. 19–20.

19. Leonard Koppett, *Koppett's Concise History of Major League Baseball*. Philadelphia: Temple University Press, 1998, p. 161. Koppett's "concise" history is 521 pages in length.

20. Quoted in Pietrusza, *Judge and Jury*, p. 202.

21. Ibid., p. 206.

22. For a good discussion of Rickey's methods and his struggles with Landis, see, for one, Andrew O'Toole, *Branch Rickey in Pittsburgh: Baseball's Trailblazing General Manager for the Pirates, 1950–1955* (Jefferson, N.C.: McFarland, 2000).

23. Quoted in Paul Weiler and Gary Roberts, *Sports and the Law: Text, Cases, Problems*. St. Paul, Minn.: West Group, 1998, p. 11.

24. Landis did, however, take an occasional step that curbed a team's minor league excesses. In 1938, for instance, he made seventy-three prospects in the Cards' system free agents. In 1939, he freed ninety players in the Tigers' system. In these

instances, he was taking action against an individual owner to the benefit of baseball's remaining fifteen owners.

25. U.S. Congress. House. House Committee on the Judiciary. *Celler Hearings.* Washington, D.C.: USGPO, 1951, p. 260.

26. See, for one, Szymanski and Zimbalist, *National Pastime*, ch. 7 (see ch. 1, n. 3).

27. Koppett, *Koppett's Concise History*, p. 222. It is unclear, however, whether these clubs were serious about signing a black player.

Chapter 4. The Undistinguished Middle I: From Chandler to Eckert

1. This provision was subsequently changed to a three-quarters vote in each league. It was changed again under Commissioner Ueberroth, so that the commissioner still needed a three-quarters vote to be initially elected but only a simple majority within each league to be reappointed. With the centralization of league administration within the commissioner's office in 2000, the three-quarters and simple majority thresholds came to apply to the two leagues combined.

2. Although, as we shall see, the commissioner's salary was raised back up to $65,000 in 1951 when Ford Frick assumed the post. Happy Chandler, however, could not have been too disappointed—his $50,000 salary was five times what he was earning as a U.S. senator.

3. This structure was modified again in November 1946 when a new Major League Agreement was passed.

4. Happy Chandler with Vance Trimble, *Heroes, Plain Folks and Skunks: The Life and Times of Happy Chandler.* Chicago: Bonus Books, 1989, p. 7.

5. Lee Lowenfish, *The Imperfect Diamond.* New York: Da Capo Press, 1991, p. 125.

6. Chandler and Trimble, *Heroes, Plain Folks and Skunks*, p. 187.

7. Rickey, however, did not announce the signing publicly until October 23, after the 1945 World Series.

8. Lowenfish provides some vivid anecdotes about the cruel impact Chandler's policy had on the lives of individual players. See *The Imperfect Diamond*, chs. 8–10.

9. Cited in Water Champion, "Baseball's Third Strike: Labor Law and the National Pastime," *Pennsylvania Law Journal@Reporter* 4, no. 20, May 25, 1981, p. 2.

10. Quoted in Holtzman, *The Commissioners*, p. 53 (see ch. 3, n. 6).

11. Ibid.

12. Ibid., p. 65.

13. Ibid., p. 64.

14. See, for one, the discussion of this report in Robert F. Burk, *Much More Than a Game: Players, Owners & American Baseball since 1921.* Chapel Hill: University of North Carolina Press, 2001, pp. 97–98.

15. To be sure, there is some disagreement about the timing and the exact nature of this vote. Chandler, for instance, in his autobiography (*Heroes, Plain Folks and Skunks*, p. 226) states that the vote took place in early January 1947 at an owners' meeting at the Waldorf in New York City and that the vote was explicitly on Rickey's proposal to bring Robinson up to the majors. Various owners have disputed this account, and historians generally adhere to the story told in the text.

One baseball person who tells a different version is Buzzie Bavasi, the long-time general manager for the Brooklyn and Los Angeles Dodgers (1951–1967), the president of the San Diego Padres (1968–1977), and the executive vice president and the general manager of the California Angels (1977–1984). In a 2005 interview, Bavasi states, "Happy Chandler had nothing whatsoever to do with it. Happy Chandler liked to say that the vote was 15–1 against bringing Jackie to the major leagues. Hogwash. At the meeting Horace [Stoneham] said he would vote for the move because his club was within a mile of Harlem. Mr. Wrigley said he would vote yes because 35% of his business throughout the world came from the black people. Bill Veeck said to the Dodgers, hurry up and bring him up because I have an African-American that might be better than Jackie. Meaning Larry Doby. John Galbreath said it was a club matter not a league matter. No vote was ever taken." www.businessofbaseball.com/bavasi_interview .htm (accessed November 12, 2004).

16. Chandler *Heroes, Plain Folks and Skunks*, pp. 227–29.

17. Ford Frick, *Games, Asterisks and People: Memoirs of a Lucky Fan*. New York: Crown, 1973, p. 95.

18. Burk, *Much More Than a Game*, p. 110.

19. Chandler, *Heroes, Plain Folks and Skunks*, p. 189.

20. *Celler Hearings*, pp. 345, 302, 261, and 257 (see ch. 3, n. 25).

21. This memorandum is reproduced in full in ibid., pp. 1271–75.

22. Quoted in Holtzman, *The Commissioners*, p. 87 (see ch. 3, n. 6).

23. Ibid., p. 88.

24. Ibid., p. 104.

25. Ibid., p. 95.

26. Koppett, *Koppett's Concise History*, p. 229 (see ch. 3, n. 19).

27. *Celler Hearings*, p. 27.

28. In 1957, Commissioner Bell testified at new congressional hearings, suggesting a league ticket policy that would be music to ears of American sports fans: "I believe that any adult should pay one dollar and a half for a reserved seat, plus tax, and a dollar for an unreserved seat. I believe all kids, where you have room . . . should be let in for nothing." U.S. House of Representatives, *Hearings*, June–August 1957, p. 2533. Converted for inflation, $1.50 in 1957 would be approximately $10.25 in 2005—still not a bad deal for today's fans. Interesting treatments of Bell's productive years as NFL commissioner can be found in David Harris, *The League*. New York: Bantam Books, 1986; and in Michael MacCambridge, *America's Game*. New York: Random House, 2004.

29. Bill Veeck, *Veeck—as in Wreck*. Chicago: University of Chicago Press, 1959, p. 367.

30. Senate Committee on the Judiciary, Subcommittee on Antitrust and Monopoly. *Organized Professional Team Sports*, 85th Cong., 2nd sess., July 9, 1958. (Washington, D.C.: USGPO, 1958, pp. 165 and 171.)

31. Statistics cited in MacCambridge, *America's Game*, p. xv.

32. The report "Analysis of the State of Baseball" was written in August 1955. It is part of the personal files of former American League president Joe Cronin and was provided to me by Cronin's grandson, Chris Hayward.

33. Quoted in John Helyar, *Lords of the Realm*. New York: Villard Books, 1994, p. 77. Also quoted in an Associated Press story appearing in the *New York Times*, "Leaders Warned by Commissioner," November 6, 1964, p. 43.

34. Quoted in Holtzman, *The Commissioners*, p. 85 (see ch. 3, n. 6).

35. Senate Committee on the Judiciary, Subcommittee on Antitrust and Monopoly. *Organized Professional Team Sports*, 85th Cong., 1st sess., June–August, 1957. (Washington, D.C.: USGPO, 1957, p. 166.)

36. Quoted in Russell Schneider, "The Judge Would Have Been Proud of Frick," *Sporting News*, November 21, 1964, p. 5.

37. Veeck, *Veeck—as in Wreck*, p. 246.

38. James Miller, *The Baseball Business: Pursuing Pennants and Profits in Baltimore*. Chapel Hill: University of North Carolina Press, 1990, p. 59.

39. Hank Greenberg (with Ira Berkow), *Hank Greenberg: The Story of My Life*. New York: Times Books, 1989, p. 215.

40. Dean Chadwin, *Those Damn Yankees: The Secret Life of America's Greatest Franchise*. New York: Verso, 1999, pp. 85–88.

41. The actual wording of this clause was changed after Frick's commissionership, from preventing "conduct detrimental to baseball" to preventing conduct not in baseball's "best interests." The latter is more inclusive since it enables the commissioner to act in matters that might have a relatively neutral impact on baseball's development.

42. Edgar Munzel, "Game Requires Dynamic Boss," *Sporting News*, November 21, 1964, pp. 5–7.

43. E-mail communication from Clark Griffith, February 21, 2005.

44. Quoted in Holtzman, *The Commissioners*, p. 122.

45. Ibid., p. 123.

Chapter 5. The Undistinguished Middle II: From Kuhn to Vincent

1. Kuhn, *Hardball*, p. 15 (see ch. 3, n. 16).

2. Ibid., p. 14.

3. Ibid.

4. Ibid., p. 33.

5. Quoted in Holtzman, *The Commissioners*, p. 135 (see ch. 3, n. 6).

6. Quoted in Steve Gietschier, "Bowie Kuhn: Toward a Reassessment," *Nine* 7, no. 2 (1999): 91.

7. Burk, *Much More Than a Game*, p. 161 (see ch. 4, n. 14).

8. Koppett, *Koppett's Concise History*, p. 331 (see ch. 3, n. 19).

9. Kuhn, *Hardball*, p. 93.

10. See Andrew Zimbalist, *May the Best Team Win: Baseball Economics and Public Policy*. Washington, D.C.: Brookings Institution Press, 2004, ch. 2.

11. Kuhn, *Hardball*, p. 87.

12. Marvin Miller, *A Whole Different Ball Game: The Sport and Business of Baseball*. New York: Birch Lane Press, 1991, p. 91. Miller did not pull any punches in going after Kuhn. Kuhn had given Miller similar treatment in his book *Hardball*, published four years earlier. Miller describes *Hardball* as error-riddled and provides substantial evidence for this claim (p. 85 and passim).

13. Quoted in Holtzman, *The Commissioners*, pp. 170–71.

14. Weiler and Roberts, *Sports and the Law*, p. 20 (see ch. 3, n. 23).

15. Kuhn, *Hardball*, p. 127.

16. Ibid., p. 206.

17. Koppett, *Koppett's Concise History*, p. 333.

18. Kuhn, *Hardball*, p. 374.

19. Ibid., p. 429.

20. Ibid., p. 429. Several have questioned the accuracy of Kuhn's account of various incidents in his autobiography. This contradiction seems to support the skeptics.

21. Kuhn, *Hardball*, p. 447.

22. See, for one, Murray Chass, "Kuhn's Descent from Commissioner to Legal Outcast," *New York Times*, May 12, 1991.

23. Jane Leavy, "Ueberroth," *Washington Post*, April 15, 1984, p. F1.

24. Ibid.

25. Ibid.

26. Quoted in Shirley Povich, "Help Wanted: Magnates Seek Disposable Leader," *Washington Post*, October 1, 1983, p. D3.

27. Quoted in Helyar, *Lords of the Realm*, p. 331 (see ch. 4, n. 33).

28. Ibid., p. 321.

29. Quoted in Helyar, *Lords of the Realm*, p. 334.

30. The three collusion cases and the arbitration proceedings are described in greater detail in Zimbalist, *Baseball and Billions*, ch. 1 (see ch. 2, n. 19).

31. Quoted in Helyar, *Lords of the Realm*, p. 341. Helyar also reports that Ueberroth rewarded Phillies president Bill Giles for his good behavior by requiring the new buyers of the team to give Giles an extra 10 percent of team stock (p. 353).

32. Life at Yale had grown difficult for Giamatti. Giamatti had taken a hardline stand against the unions and came under sustained criticism from many faculty, alumnae, and staff.

33. A. Bartlett Giamatti, *Take Time for Paradise: Americans and Their Games*. New York: Summit Books, 1989, pp. 42–44.

34. Ibid., pp. 13, 15, 38, and 83.

35. What Giamatti's letter actually stated was that he was convinced of the veracity of Paul Janszen's testimony. Janszen was an associate of Rose's who went to *Sports Illustrated* to sell the story that Rose was betting on baseball games. Fay Vincent, *The Last Commissioner: A Baseball Valentine*. New York: Simon & Schuster, 2002, ch. 4.

36. As Giamatti discovered, baseball's rules provided that any player put on the ineligible list had the right to apply for reinstatement after one year. Hence, the earlier suggestion that Rose would be on such a list for ten or seven years before he could apply for reinstatement was an explicit violation of MLB's own rules.

37. Koppett, *Koppett's Concise History*, p. 408.

38. Quoted in Helyar, *Lords of the Realm*, p. 406.

39. Ibid., p. 410.

40. Quoted in Holtzman, *The Commissioners*, p. 259.

41. Ibid.

42. The accident is described by Vincent in his book *The Last Commissioner*, pp. 54–55. It was elaborated upon in an interview with the author on October 8, 2004. The interview and subsequent e-mail communications with Vincent also inform the discussion in the text.

43. Greenberg's trajectory in baseball is a story in itself. During the 1980s, Greenberg was Arn Tellum's partner and a successful Los Angeles–based player agent. After Vincent resigned, Greenberg was marginalized in MLB's governance. He gave his ninety-day notice in January 1993 and left the commissioner's office in April. Greenberg then went on to start his Classic Sports Network in 1994, which he sold to ESPN in 1997 and which is now ESPN Classic. Since January 2002, Greenberg has worked at the investment banking house of Allen & Company, where he has been involved in several of baseball's most important deals, including the purchase by Fred Wilpon of Nelson Doubleday's 50 percent share of the Mets, the creation of the Chicago RSN involving the Cubs and the White Sox, the sale of the Brewers from the Selig family to Mark Attanasio in early 2005, the setting up of the N.Y. Mets' new RSN with Time Warner and Comcast, and the resolution of the MASN/Orioles/Nationals deal. That is, after being marginalized in 1992/1993, Greenberg is once again central to baseball's governance. One is left to wonder what would have happened to baseball had Greenberg been kept on by MLB and promoted to commissioner after the resignation of Vincent. The owners surely did not want Greenberg's conciliatory pos-

ture around when they were trying to install a salary cap back in 1994, but had they kept him, it seems likely that the 1994–1995 strike could have been avoided. Today, although Greenberg has nothing to do with baseball's labor negotiations, it is clear that he is highly valued by Selig and the owners for his knowledge of the industry.

44. The expansion teams would also be deprived of national television revenues for one year.

45. Quoted in Weiler and Roberts, *Sports and the Law*, pp. 28–29.

46. These figures are the 2004 tallies as of March 2004. They are still subject to MLB's auditing review and may be adjusted.

47. Quoted in Helyar, *Lords of the Realm*, p. 513.

Chapter 6. Bud Selig: A Lifetime in Preparation

1. Tom Friend, "Milwaukee Players Are Still in Selig Fan Club," *New York Times*, April 10, 1995.

2. Quoted in Tom Haudricourt, "Selig Rode Up Front on the Roller Coaster," *Milwaukee Journal-Sentinel*, September 23, 2000.

3. Transcript of trial, *State of Wisconsin v. Milwaukee Braves, Inc., et al.*, U.S. District Court for the Eastern District of Wisconsin, 1965, p. 1468.

4. Perini bought the Boston Braves in 1945 for $311,508. He sold the Milwaukee Braves in November 1962 for $6.218 million. In the interim, the team generated more than $7 million in accumulated pre-tax profits, according to documents from *State of Wisconsin v. Milwaukee Braves, Inc., et al.*, U.S. District Court for the Eastern District of Wisconsin, 1965.

5. Bud Selig made a more convincing argument in his presentation to the NL owners in Miami Beach. Selig used an analysis from the Braves' ticket office about the geographical distribution of ticket purchasers and concluded that it was unlikely that the Twins had diminished the Braves' fan base by more than 5 percent.

6. Memo from Ralph Andreano, October 5, 2004.

7. Deposition of Commissioner Ford Frick, October 7, 1965, pp. 25, 48, 50, 67–68.

8. More precisely, on April 13, 1966, Judge Elmer Roller found that the defendants had violated the state's antitrust laws and awarded the plaintiff a judgment of $5,000 against each NL team. The court also restrained and enjoined the Braves from playing in any city other than Milwaukee, then stayed the order pending submission of a written plan for expansion of the NL to permit major league baseball to be played in Milwaukee in 1967. The Braves and the other NL teams appealed Roller's decision to the Wisconsin Supreme Court, where the judgment was reversed. The Supreme Court majority was divided in its reasoning. Some judges believed that the NL was protected by MLB's judicially conferred antitrust exemption, while others believed that enforcement of the state's antitrust laws in this matter would unconstitutionally burden interstate commerce. In December 1966, the State of Wisconsin petitioned unsuccessfully for a writ of certiorari to take the case to the U.S. Supreme Court but was denied. The state then petitioned for a rehearing of the State Supreme Court's order, but that was denied as well, and the case was ended.

9. Senate Committee on the Judiciary, *The Application of Federal Antitrust Laws to Major League Baseball*, 107th Cong., 2nd sess., February 13, 2002. (Washington, D.C.: GPO, 2002, p. 10.)

10. "Selig Hints at Trial: Political Climate Hurt Franchise Bid," *Washington Post*, March 10, 1966, p. E5.

11. Quoted in Haudricourt, "Selig Rode Up Front."

12. Ibid.

13. Steve Fainaru, "The Expos and Bud Selig," *Washington Post*, June 27, 2004, p. A1.

14. Quoted in ibid.

15. Quoted from *Sports Illustrated,* in Nicholas Thompson, "Bud Selig: A Baseball Hero. Really," *Slate Magazine* (May 5, 2005).

16. Fitzgerald came from a wealthy family and was the CEO of the old Cutler Hammer company. Ed and Bud would use Fitzgerald's plane to fly to meetings. Fitzgerald apparently wanted Selig to serve as team president with no pay. The other board members overruled Fitzgerald, and Selig initially was given $40,000 a year. Bruce Murphy, "Storm Warnings," *Milwaukee Magazine*, April 1996.

17. Interview with Bud Selig, February 1, 2005, Milwaukee.

18. Murphy, "Storm Warnings."

19. Helyar, *Lords of the Realm*, p. 475 (see ch. 4, n. 33).

20. Mike Bauman, "Buddy Just Won't Let Us Quit," mlb.com, January 29, 2005, reprinted in *Sports Business News: The Daily Dose*, January 30, 2005.

21. "Selig Protests," *Washington Post*, July 29, 1974, p. D2.

22. Thomas Boswell, "The Zero Hour Ticks Away for Baseball, Kuhn," *Washington Post*, August 15, 1982, p. E1.

23. See, for one, Murray Chass, "Baseball Union Says Rule Curbs Salaries," *New York Times*, February 6, 1983, p. S6.

24. The amortization period for all intangible assets was fixed at fifteen years. Nonetheless, the value of the tax shelter was increased by roughly between 30 and 50 percent, depending on the discount rate one uses.

25. Murray Chass, "Selig Is Directed to His Backyard," *New York Times*, September 6, 1983, p. B19.

26. Murray Chass, "Baseball Owners Lean toward Lockout," *New York Times*, September 11, 1992, p. B11.

Chapter 7. Baseball's Acting Commissioner, 1992–1998

1. Interview with Bud Selig, February 1, 2005, Milwaukee, Wisconsin.

2. Ira Berkow, "Welcome to the Major Leagues, Bud Selig," *New York Times*, September 27, 1992, p. S1.

3. Murray Chass, "Newly Empowered Owners Rescind Order to Realign," *New York Times*, September 25, 1992, p. B9.

4. Claire Smith, "Coming Eventually: A New Commissioner," *New York Times*, December 12, 1992, p. 34.

5. Senate Committee on the Judiciary, Subcommittee on Antitrust, Monopolies and Business Rights, *Baseball's Antitrust Immunity*, 102nd Cong., 2nd sess., 1992. (Washington, D.C.: USGPO, 1993, p. 2.)

6. Quoted in Kenneth Jennings, *Balls and Strikes: The Money Game in Professional Baseball.* New York: Praeger, 1990, p. 77.

7. Zimbalist, *Baseball and Billions*, p. 38 (see ch. 2, n. 19).

8. Murray Chass, "Owners Link Salaries and Revenue Sharing," *New York Times*, February 18, 1993, p. B17.

9. John Ellis (Seattle), Drayton McLane (Houston), Mike Illitch (Detroit), Peter Magowan (San Francisco), Wayne Huizenga (Florida), and Jerry McMorris (Colorado).

10. Zimbalist, *Baseball and Billions*, p. 218.

11. This is the recollection of Paul Beeston, who was the president of the Toronto Blue Jays—at the time, the highest-revenue team in baseball. Interview with Beeston,

February 25, 2005. Interestingly, neither the Cubs nor the Braves joined the high-revenue caucus at Kohler, each fearing that if they did it might further aggravate the low-revenue clubs and lead them to demand a greater share of the Cubs' and the Braves' superstation revenues. According to Bud Selig, the first time the owners broke into caucuses was at owners' meetings in 1991. Apparently, it wasn't pleasant that time around either. Interview with Selig, February 1, 2005.

12. Interview with Selig, February 1, 2005.

13. Murray Chass, "Owners Looking Hard at Revenue Sharing," *New York Times*, August 12, 1993, p. B16.

14. Interview with Selig, February 1, 2005.

15. Murray Chass, "Six to Eight Are on List for New Commissioner," *New York Times*, September 8, 1993, p. B17.

16. Murray Chass, "One Year Later," *New York Times*, September 5, 1993, p. S9.

17. Murray Chass, "A Title Is Diminished but the Salary Soars," *New York Times*, February 15, 1994, p. B7. Legislative Audit Bureau, State of Wisconsin. *The Milwaukee Brewers Baseball Club Finances.* May 2004, p. 18. According to the W2 statements filed with the IRS, Bud Selig's compensation from the Brewers was $542,622 in 1994; $452,693 in 1995; $457,683 in 1996; $450,705 in 1997; and $316,926 in 1998. (Selig was elected as permanent commissioner on July 8, 1998, and assumed the role on August 1, so the latter sum essentially represents seven months of pay.) In 1998, his daughter Wendy Selig earned $223,332 from the Brewers and her husband, Laurel Prieb, earned $133,306. These compensation figures exclude 401K payments and other benefits. They include travel reimbursements.

18. Murray Chass, "Selig Swears His Job Isn't What Most Think It Is," *New York Times*, February 23, 1997, p. S1; and Murray Chass, "Selig's Job Title Could Change because of Brewers' Problems," *New York Times*, September 3, 1995. Murray Chass, "Selig Set to Drop 'Acting' from Commissioner," *New York Times*, June 18, 1998, p. A1.

19. Murray Chass, "Take Away the 'Acting' Label: Selig Is Baseball's Commissioner," *New York Times*, July 9, 1998, p. C1. Chass also reports that in his first year as permanent commissioner, Selig was paid at least $3 million.

20. Murray Chass, "Selig Still Doesn't Want to Be Commissioner," *New York Times*, October 23, 1993.

21. Each major league team has twenty-five players on the active roster and another fifteen on major league contracts who are either in the minor leagues or on the disabled list.

22. Murray Chass, "Snow Blows, Fog Arrives, Revenue Meetings Swirl," *New York Times*, January 7, 1994, p. B13.

23. Murray Chass, "Threat of a Veto Hangs Over Meetings," *New York Times*, January 16, 1994, p. S8; Murray Chass, "Owners Adopt Revenue Plan, but It's Tied to Salary Cap," *New York Times*, January 19, 2004, p. B11; and Murray Chass, "A Decision: No New Commissioner," *New York Times*, January 20, 1994, p. B15.

24. Ibid.

25. Selig also elaborated on this view in an op-ed piece: "Baseball's 'Best Interests' Phrasing Best Viewed Narrowly," *New York Times*, March 6, 1994, p. A1.

26. The owners and the players actually had a negotiating session in Tampa, Florida, in March 1994, and a few intervening sessions, but the main issues were not on the table and little was accomplished.

27. Interview with Dick Ravitch, November 21, 2004.

28. Murray Chass, "The First Sign of What's to Come," *New York Times*, January 18, 1995, p. B10.

29. Curiously, when asked about the meeting, Selig told the press that he did not believe the commissioner should be involved in labor matters. This comment seemed to contradict the clarification in the 1994 restructuring, and Selig corrected himself two weeks later, stating that he would be happy to be involved. See Murray Chass, "Owners Chose Their Course," *New York Times,* February 12, 1995; and Murray Chass, "Day 200," *New York Times,* February 28, 1995.

30. Levine had served as Steinbrenner's outside attorney during the early 1990s. When he left the PRC in May 1997, he became New York City's deputy commissioner under Giuliani. He has served as president of the Yankees since January 2000.

31. Stadium expenses include operating and capital costs. Capital outlays can either be depreciated over ten years, or the payments on the principal of the associated debt can be deducted over the life of the bond.

32. This system replaced the gate sharing (20 percent in the AL and around 4 percent in the NL) and the minimal cable revenue sharing in the AL that previously existed.

33. As baroque as these formulas may seem, the text here actually is a simplification of the system. One can only wonder how many hours of bargaining it took to decide that the tax rate would drop from 35 percent in 1998 to 34 percent in 1999.

34. Doug Pappas, "Will Selig Be Commissioner in 2007?" *Baseball Prospectus* (April 23, 2003).

35. Murray Chass, "Owners on a Path to Realign Leagues," *New York Times,* January 17, 1997, p. B9.

36. Interview with Marvin Goldklang, May 11, 2005.

37. *Miami Baseball Club v. Bud Selig,* U.S. District Court, Southern District of New York, February 1997. Murray Chass, "Selig Swears His Job Isn't What Most Think It Is," p. S1.

38. See David Boies, *Courting Justice.* New York: Hyperion, 2004, ch. 2.

39. Len Coleman was hired by Fay Vincent in 1991 as director of market development, and Coleman hired Kathy Francis as his director of marketing. But Coleman's job centered on opening up relations with the African American media and community, and Francis's work was primarily a community relations position. Coleman was instrumental in involving baseball in the RBI program (Reviving Baseball in the Inner Cities) that had been launched independently in Los Angeles in 1989. Coleman also initiated weekly half-hour programs on the Black Entertainment Network and Telemundo. The programs had a male and a female co-host and featured an interview with a retired minority star, a news story focusing on a person or an issue, a playing tip, and baseball news. The programs began in 1992 and ended with the strike in 1994. They were never revived. While Coleman was director of market development, however, MLB still had no marketing budget and the AL and the NL had no marketing operations. The first committed marketing budget came in 1996 when $10.5 million was allocated. When Coleman was named as NL president in 1994, he took the RBI program with him to the NL office, and his position was not replaced. Of course, isolated marketing efforts were made earlier by the MLB Promotions Corp., by Rick White at MLB Properties, and by Ueberroth and others. E-mail from baseball's COO Bob DuPuy, June 6, 2005; interview with Len Coleman, June 14, 2005; and, various e-mails from Fay Vincent.

40. Richard Sandomir, "Seligging Americans Their Own Pastime," *New York Times,* June 12, 1996.

41. Quoted in Murray Chass, "Take Away the 'Acting' Label," p. C1.

42. One senior club executive commented, "I think the whole thing was orchestrated. He was telling a small group of people from day one he wanted it but told

everyone else he didn't. Then came the draft and he said he would accept it." Quoted in Chass, "Selig Set to Drop 'Acting' from Commissioner," p. A1.

Chapter 8. Baseball's Permanent Commissioner, 1998–

1. Tom Haudricourt, "Selig Elected Commissioner in Unanimous Vote," *Milwaukee Journal-Sentinel*, July 9, 1998.

2. In early 2005, the three members on the owners' revenue-sharing committee were Dick Freeman of San Diego, Chuck Armstrong of Seattle, and Paul Dolan of Cleveland.

3. Strictly speaking, there was also a diminutive amount of local cable revenue sharing in the American League until 1996.

4. The specific terminology used to describe the distribution systems was *split pool* and *straight pool*. The 1996 agreement used a split pool system, wherein 25 percent of the collected funds are distributed only to the bottom half of teams. The Blue Ribbon Panel recommended the use of the straight pool, wherein collected funds are distributed equally to all teams. The latter hits hardest on the top quarter of teams, relatively advantages the middle two quarters, and provides a smaller benefit to the bottom quarter of teams. Because the middle two quartiles benefit from the straight pool and the straight pool hits the top clubs hardest (notably, the Yankees), it was the more popular system among the owners. Since the Blue Ribbon group included twelve owners, this preference was reflected in its recommendations.

5. This version of the events was corroborated by both Steve Fehr and Paul Beeston, who were involved in the discussions.

6. Another possible explanation is that the owners were simply trying to get the PA to tip its hand in the initial phase of bargaining. This explanation is based on the notion that the owners' hand had already been revealed in the Blue Ribbon report. (If so, this was another reason for Selig to have appointed a bilateral panel to study the game's economics.) However, discussions with participants on the owners' side suggest that there was too much disunity for any such manipulative scheme to have been possible. Rob Manfred, who was part of the owners' negotiating team with Beeston, had a different explanation. He told me that Beeston was misinformed if he believed that the owners were on the verge of an agreement with the players. Manfred said that the negotiations with the players at that time focused entirely around the new revenue-sharing system and did not address the luxury tax. According to Manfred, the owners simply believed that the Beeston negotiations were taking one step forward, not concluding an agreement. While Manfred's explanation is certainly possible, since both Beeston (representing the commissioner) and Don Fehr (representing the players) agree that they were on the doorstep of an agreement, I have gone with that interpretation in the text.

7. It will be recalled that the commissioner was made the permanent chair of the Player Relations Committee in the 1994 Major League Agreement (referred to as the Major League Constitution since 2000).

8. The reason why the union found these demands to be unacceptable is analyzed in detail in Zimbalist, *May the Best Team Win*, pp. 95–100 (see ch. 5, n. 10).

9. This discussion is obviously simplified and, among other things, assumes no risk.

10. Other financial factors, of course, enter into this decision. On the one hand, Beltran will be able to make much more money in endorsement deals in New York

than in Kansas City, so at the same salary he may choose New York. On the other hand, state and city income taxes and the cost of living are considerably higher in New York than in Kansas City. Naturally, nonfinancial factors will also enter into his decision.

11. The standard deviation of payrolls also steadily increased over this stretch.

12. Meanwhile, the Angels, in the country's second-largest media market, received $1.9 million.

13. The Dodgers, in the second-largest media market, paid only $9.5 million in 2003. The Red Sox and the Dodgers figures for 2003 are preliminary. The final 2003 figures are subject to modification by the owners' revenue-sharing committee. The Sox 2003 figure, based on a new assessment of team revenue from NESN, was raised several million dollars in June 2005. The Red Sox then appealed the decision to the commissioner.

14. Each team has a certain television territory that baseball calls its home market. No other team can sell rights to its games in another team's television market (except, of course, in the case of markets with two teams, such as New York). Baseball's television territories often deviate substantially from the size of a team's local media market. For instance, the Boston Red Sox play in the country's sixth largest media market but have baseball's twentieth largest television territory.

15. The 17.5 percent rate for first-time offenders rises to 22 percent in 2004 and 2005. First-time offenders in 2006 pay no luxury tax.

16. Fifteen times for teams with a new stadium.

17. Quoted in Steve Fainaru, "Expos for Sale: Team Becomes Pawn of Selig," *Washington Post*, June 28, 2004, p. A1.

18. Quoted in the written testimony of Florida attorney general Bob Butterworth, Senate Judiciary Committee, February 13, 2002.

19. Quoted in Steve Fainaru, "Expos for Sale," p. A1.

20. The $30 million represents the present value of a sales tax rebate of $2 million per year over thirty years.

21. As I write in mid-May 2005, it seems that a preliminary local deal has been struck for a new stadium in Minneapolis for the Twins. The increase of .15 percent in the Hennepin County Sales tax contemplated in the deal awaits approval from the state legislature. One interesting feature of the deal is that any sale in the first ten years after stadium construction began would benefit a newly created public ballpark authority that would build and own the stadium. The authority would receive 18 percent of the gross sales price if Pohlad sells the team in the year construction begins; the share going to the authority then declines by 1.8 percentage points annually.

Selig made his first appeal on behalf of Carl Pohlad, his longtime crony and the Twins owner, before the Minnesota state legislature in April 1997. He warned that "if there isn't anything on the horizon to change the economics, baseball will allow that club to move. We'll have no alternative." Paul Demko, "The Deal That Wouldn't Die," *City Pages*, May 11, 2005. Of course, for many cities on this list, the threat was only that the team would move or would not come. It wasn't necessary to also threaten contraction.

22. House Committee on the Judiciary, Subcommittee on Economic and Commercial Law, *Baseball's Antitrust Exemption*, 103rd Cong., 2nd sess., 1994. (Washington, D.C.: USGPO, 1994, pp. 57–58.)

23. Quoted in Steve Fainaru, "The Expos and Bud Selig," p. A1 (see ch. 6, n. 13).

24. Selig repeated this pledge when he testified before the U.S. Senate Judiciary Committee in December 1992: "We are going to build a new stadium in Milwaukee

that, frankly, the Brewers are very hopeful to build. We have worked out a relationship with the public where they have committed to take care of the infrastructure costs and the Brewers are going to build the stadium. That is unique. . . ." Senate Committee on the Judiciary, Subcommittee on Antitrust, Monopolies and Business Rights, *Baseball's Antitrust Immunity*, 102nd Cong., 2nd sess., December 10, 1992. (Washington, D.C., USGPO, 1993, p. 101.)

25. Murphy, "Storm Warnings" (see ch. 6, n. 16).

26. Fainaru, "The Expos and Bud Selig," p. A1.

27. Ibid.

28. This is from the Brewers' financial analysis provided to prospective investors in July 2003.

29. Quoted in the *Milwaukee Journal-Sentinel*, November 13, 2003. Secretary Thompson stated in a radio interview on January 21, 2004, that he considers the decision to reduce the team's 2004 payroll to around $30 million "a breach of faith with taxpayers." He went on to say, "They promised me, they promised the legislature, that they were going to field a very competitive team if we built the stadium. And we did that. We relied upon those promises and . . . they didn't come through." *Milwaukee Journal-Sentinel*, January 22, 2004.

30. Zimbalist, *May the Best Team Win*, p. 165.

31. Cited in the *Milwaukee Journal-Sentinel*, November 16, 2003.

32. Cited in the *Sports Business Daily*, December 15, 2003.

33. Quoted in Jack Curry, "Brewers Announce the Team Is for Sale," *New York Times*, January 17, 2004, p. B15.

34. Quoted in Steve Fainaru, "The Expos and Bud Selig," p. A1.

35. Ibid.

36. There was also a bid from a group headed by the New York lawyer Miles Prentice. But Prentice's bid had too many holes, starting with the adequacy of his financing.

37. Quoted in Steve Fainaru, "Expos for Sale," p. A1.

38. The tweaking, in essence, gave D.C. the right to seek private financing to assume some of the construction burden. In all likelihood, this means that D.C. will concede development rights in the area of the ballpark to companies at below market value. These companies, in turn, will contribute part of the public commitment to building the new stadium. Another change provided that cost overrun insurance would be purchased, with the premium split between D.C. and MLB.

39. Interview with Bud Selig, February 1, 2005, in Milwaukee, Wisconsin.

40. Though, as I write in May 2005, MLB is considering allowing the nine groups who are bidding to buy the Nationals to decide whether they want to buy the team without buying a share of MASN.

41. This problem can be potentially circumvented if the team is sold without MASN.

42. The formal creation of MLB's "marketing department" did not occur until 1999, although a systematic and budgeted marketing effort was initiated in 1996. Marketing has been expanded and made more sophisticated each year. In 2003, for instance, based upon marketing research, MLB launched its "I Live for This" campaign that highlights the avidity and the passion of its fans and players. In 2004, MLB began its "eventizing" strategy whereby the entire season is marked by a series of branded events, e.g., "Eight Teams, One Champion," "Mother's Day" (tied to striking out breast cancer), "Father's Day" (tied to prostate cancer), "The Commissioner's Initiative for Kids" (raising more than $1 million for childhood cancer research), and "Rally Monday," which marks the day prior to postseason play.

43. MLBAM is a separate company owned by the thirty clubs. It has an eight-person board of directors that includes Bob DuPuy, baseball's COO, and seven owners. MLBAM's CEO is Bob Bowman.

44. This was the so-called IMRA, or the Internet Media Rights Agreement among the thirty MLB clubs.

45. This represented a threefold increase over the annual rights fee in the previous MLB TV deal in Japan. In 2003, there were 272 MLB games televised in Japan, with an average of 1.5 million viewers. These numbers have been rising appreciably every year.

46. Nippon Professional Baseball initially objected because the World Baseball Classic would disrupt its spring training and because it wanted a larger share of the proceeds.

47. All-Star Game ratings have drifted steadily downward since the early 1990s. They were 17.4 in 1991, 15.7 in 1994, 13.3 in 1998, and 11.0 in 2001.

48. To be sure, there is also some imbalance in the determination of a league's wild card winner, since there is an imbalanced schedule across divisions within a league.

49. Other critics complain that the mystery of the postseason is diminished when interleague teams match up during the year. Some also extend this argument to the All-Star Game.

50. See, for instance, Michael Butler, "Interleague Play and Baseball Attendance," *Journal of Sports Economics* 3, no. 4 (November 2002): 320–334. Butler finds that only one-third of the increased attendance at interleague games was from the interleague characteristic per se. In 1999, 44 percent of interleague play was in weekend series, and a disproportionate share of the interleague series were played in June and July.

51. The number of Little League participants peaked worldwide in 1997 at 2.59 million. By 2003, this number had fallen 10.5 percent to 2.32 million. The Sporting Goods Manufacturers Association reports that baseball participation declined 4.6 percent between 2001 and 2004; fast pitch softball has declined 15.3 percent; and slow pitch softball has declined 18.7 percent.

52. MLB's practice is to report attendance according to the number of tickets purchased, rather than the number of people actually at the game (i.e., people passing through the turnstiles). In the case of the Initiative for Kids, those few teams that do not have an inventory of unsold tickets, such as the Red Sox, do not participate in the ticket giveaway program.

53. This issue is discussed in more detail in Szymanski and Zimbalist, *National Pastime*, ch. 8 (see ch. 1, n. 3).

54. In his new, and somewhat sloppy, book, *Juicing the Game*, Howard Bryant erroneously lays much of the blame for baseball's steroids problem on Selig. Howard Bryant, *Juicing the Game*, New York: Viking, 2005.

55. Arthur Allyn, the former owner of the Chicago White Sox, also expressed strong views on this subject in November 1964:

> The new commissioner will be selected not as a representative of the owners, but as a representative of the public. . . . It was generally agreed that no politicians and no person connected with baseball would be considered. . . . It cannot be someone in baseball, because no matter who he is and no matter how unimpeachable his character, there are some ties and associations from which he cannot divorce himself. And even if as commissioner he made every decision fairly and without prejudice, nobody would believe it if it happened to involve a club or a league office in which he previously had a position.

Quoted in Edgar Munzel, "Game Requires Dynamic Boss," *Sporting News*, November 21, 1964, pp. 5–7.

56. Interview with Bud Selig, February 1, 2005, in Milwaukee, Wisconsin.

57. Quoted in Murphy, "Storm Warnings" (see ch. 6, n. 16).

58. Selig also allowed another loan from Pohlad's financial institution to Jerry McMorris, the former co-owner of the Colorado Rockies.

59. Selig did this study when he was trying to persuade the Braves that the Milwaukee market was good enough for the team. At the time, Bartholomay claimed the impact was larger, but Selig had looked more systematically at the evidence.

60. *Basic Agreement between the 30 Major League Clubs and Major League Baseball Players Association*, effective September 30, 1992, p. 106.

61. One anonymous medium-market club owner told the *Illinois Daily Herald* in late July 2002,

> You think this is funny but this is how Bud operates. He tells 30 owners 30 different things and then slaps a gag order on us and threatens us with a million-dollar fine so that the players don't find out we all hate what's going on. We're supposed to be unified? That's laughable. Lift the gag order again, and you'll see how unified. Now, on top of everything else in Montreal, the [former Expos] minority owners have filed racketeering charges against Bud and [Marlins Managing General Partner] Jeff [Loria], and if the books of every team are exposed during that legal fight, you can say goodbye to Bud and any deal with the players. This is more dangerous than you can imagine. Bud is playing with fire here and we're all getting burned. I'm convinced Bud got his contract extension by threatening 10 of us, making promises to the other 10 and loaning money to the last 10. This thing is on the track headed for a disaster, and Bud is right there in the front of the train conducting the whole operation.

This was quoted in *Sports Business Daily*, July 25, 2002, p. 11.

Chapter 9. Governing Baseball: Assessing the Past and Anticipating the Future

1. The drafting of scores of major leaguers to fight in World War II, of course, proved to be another disruption, but it did not represent an economic problem as such.

2. *Radovich v. National Football League*, 352 U.S. 445 (1957). Two years earlier, the Supreme Court held that the exemption did not apply to the sport of boxing in *U.S. v. International Boxing Club*, 348 U.S. 236 (1955).

3. "Analysis of the State of Baseball" (see ch. 4, n. 32).

4. Quoted in Schneider, "The Judge Would Have Been Proud of Frick" (see ch. 4, n. 36).

5. Interview with Bud Selig, February 1, 2005, in Milwaukee, Wisconsin.

6. Quoted in Helyar, *Lords of the Realm*, p. 468 (see ch. 4, n. 33).

7. Strictly speaking, Miller was followed by Ken Moffett, who served as the union's executive director for ten months with Don Fehr as his general counsel. Little happened under Moffett, who was a mismatch in the union from day one, and Don Fehr was in the saddle before the next round of collective bargaining began. Marvin Miller was also still actively involved as a consultant during this period.

8. Arguably, from a broader perspective, the case could be made that Steve Greenberg, the deputy commissioner under Vincent, would have made an excellent choice at the time. However, from the owners' perspective, Greenberg was too soft on labor, as Vincent had been.

9. Baseball could revert to the same defense for its restrictive practices that the other leagues used; namely, that they help to preserve competitive balance and geographical stability, both of which are necessary for a healthy sports league. By preserving a healthy league, it is enhancing competition in the broader sports industry, and hence, by the rule of reason, their behavior passes antitrust standards. In addition, whenever Congress has talked about legislatively lifting baseball's exemption, it almost always has exempted the minor leagues.

10. Quoted in Steve Fainaru, "Angelos, Selig Last Men Standing in D.C.'s Way," *Washington Post*, June 29, 2004, p. A1.

11. Although not one of the more important divisions among owners, anti-Semitism has reared its ugly head at times. Former Dodgers owner Peter O'Malley is said to have complained, "The Jews are taking over baseball," and John McMullen, the former owner of the Astros, is said to have resonated to such remarks. When Fay Vincent put forward Steve Greenberg's name to serve as his deputy commissioner, Fred Wilpon, who is Jewish, warned Fay that such an appointment may cause difficulty because of anti-Semitism among some owners. Vincent, never accused of being weak-kneed when it comes to minority rights, made the appointment anyway. Vincent also actively promoted the hiring of blacks, including Len Coleman, Jamie Lee Solomon, and Bill White, into top executive positions within baseball and succeeded in getting the Negro League alumni covered by MLB's health plan. Fay Vincent, interview, June 4, 2005.

12. For an elaboration of this point, see Andrew Zimbalist, "Labor Relations in Major League Baseball," *Journal of Sports Economics* (Winter 2004).

13. Depending on the outcome of disputes currently before the owners' revenue-sharing committee, the Yankees' and the Red Sox' tax bills could go even higher than this.

14. MLBAM and the Internet are weakening the ability of TBS and WGN to reap this advantage.

15. I am not arguing here that the revenue-sharing committee will necessarily assign too high a number for the market-based rights fee, due the Red Sox from NESN, the Yankees from YES, the Orioles from MASN, and so on. Rather, I am suggesting that if the committee's objectivity is questioned, it will be more difficult to have the clubs accept its rulings as legitimate, which, in turn, will undermine the stability of the revenue-sharing system and make baseball's governance more problematic. The potential conflict around the assignment of an arms' length transaction value to teams' rights fees and the issue of the quantity of capital put at risk to set up or purchase an RSN can be happily avoided by adopting a sharing system based on forecasted, rather than actual, revenue, wherein forecasted revenue is a function of each team's market characteristics, rather than of its performance.

Epilogue

1. In real terms (2007 prices), ticket revenue in 2011 would be $6.44 billion. That is, there would still be a positive growth of $348 million since 2007.

2. These rates are in nominal terms. Corrected for inflation, they are 4.5 percent and 3.5 percent respectively. Major League Baseball's nominal industry-wide revenue in 2011 was $6.93 billion.

3. Of further concern for MLB is that (a) overall team TV ratings have drifted downward and (b) youth surveys of baseball's popularity reveal a declining trend. For instance, the number of children who named baseball as their favorite sport fell from 15.85 million in 2000 to 14.59 million in 2010, a drop of 8.1 percent. Sports Business Journal, *Sports Business Resource Guide and Fact Book, 2012*, p. D-100.

INDEX